BERLITZ®

·B·L·U·E·P·R·I·N·T·

SPAIN

Editor
AMANDA HOPKINS

Photography
CLAUDE HUBER

Layout and Design
DORIS HALDEMANN

Design Leisure Routes
DOMINIQUE MICHELLOD

Cartography
HALLWAG AG, Bern

In-depth information on several main cities and regions of Spain is available in pocket-size format in the Berlitz Travel Guide series.

Although we make every effort to ensure the accuracy of all the information in this book, changes occur incessantly. We cannot therefore take responsibility for facts, addresses and circumstances in general that are constantly subject to alteration.

2nd Printing; 1990/1991 Edition

Cover picture: Casares, Andalusia.
Photo KEN WELSH

Additional photography: Pages 28, 217, 219, 227, 228, 240, 243, KEN WELSH; pp. 60, 69, 116, DANY GIGNOUX; pp. 71, 72 (below), 161 (below) ANDRÉ HELD; pp. 117 (both), 160, 161 (top), 213 A.G.E. PHOTOSTOCK; pp. 214, 220–221 DANIEL VITTET.

Acknowledgements
We would like to extend our thanks to the Spanish National Tourist Offices in Geneva and Zurich for their cooperation and information. We are also very grateful to Carmen Andrés de Francoli, Alan Mee, and to the staff of tourist offices throughout Spain for their assistance in the preparation of this book.

2

BERLITZ®

·B·L·U·E·P·R·I·N·T·

SPAIN

By KEN BERNSTEIN

and the Staff of Berlitz Guides

FRANCE

La Coruña
Santander
Santiago
de Compostela
Oviedo
Bilbao
San Sebastián
Pontevedra
León
Pamplona
ANDORRA
Burgos
Zaragoza
Gerona
Valladolid
Barcelona
Tarragona
Salamanca
Segovia
MADRID
Cuenca
Menorca
Toledo
Majorca
Cáceres
Valencia
Mérida
Ibiza
Formentera
Alicante
Córdoba
Seville
PORTUGAL
Granada
Jerez
Málaga
Almería
Cádiz
Gibraltar

ATLANTIC
OCEAN

MEDITERRANEAN SEA

MOROCCO

La Palma
Lanzarote
Fuerteventura
Gomera
Tenerife
El Hierro
Gran Canaria

ALGERIA

N

0   50   100 km

0   50   100 miles

4

Contents

MAPS: Madrid 64–5, Toledo 75, Salamanca 88, San Sebastián 121, Barcelona 149, Valencia 165, Málaga 181, Seville 196, Granada 197.

All towns shown on the Road Atlas have a map reference next to their heading.

Prosperous, Up to Date, Handsome and Free

As evening approaches, most of Europe takes a seat. Back home, Britons and Germans gather around their dinner tables, while the café-prone French linger over apéritifs. But not in Spain, where every town and village is abuzz, as if something big is afoot. What's really afoot is the population. The *paseo*, the evening promenade, is an exercise in sociability. Re-enacted daily, the compressed excitement—all but tangible—will absorb you. It's impossible not to join in.

From the Atlantic to the Mediterranean, millions of Spaniards swarm into the streets at sunset for a ritual that even cars and television haven't changed. Well-dressed citizens stroll through parks, plazas, and streets specially barred to traffic, exchanging handshakes, nods or conversation with friends and neighbours. Perambulated babies, dressed to the nines, are extravagantly admired. Window-shoppers eye the luxurious displays. Feigning indifference, teenagers slyly manoeuvre towards the evening's rendezvous. The constitutional, generously interspersed with snacks, stirs the appetite for dinner, which may begin any time after about 10 p.m. As the slogan used to say, Spain is different.

Cut off from the rest of the world by mountains and seas, the country was bound to differ. But with the almost mystically crucial year of 1992 in sight, the land of flamenco and fiestas is looking ever more European. Today's Spain is democratic, prosperous, handsome... and as modern as credit cards and towaway zones.

1992 is the 500th anniversary of two memorable triumphs of the great Ferdinand and Isabella. In 1492 the "Catholic Monarchs" sponsored the transatlantic saga of Christopher Columbus, and, at home, presided over the final push in the long struggle to expel the occupying Moors. In 1992 Spain becomes fully integrated into the European Community, and takes the yearlong honours as Europe's cultural capital. Two colossal international events round out a year to remember: the summer Olympics in Barcelona and the world fair in Seville.

The black of grandmother's mantilla sets the tone for a trendy member of the new generation of independent Spanish women.

Down with Fuddy-duddies!

In historical terms it's less than the blink of an eye since the end of dictatorship and isolation. But Spain has changed radically. The old fogeys have given way to young, energetic government and economic leaders. And newspaper cartoonists and TV comics now poke fun at them. The workday has changed: in much of the country, economic pressures have forced out the gracious tradition of the siesta. Also, for better or worse, the chaperones who guarded the morals of young ladies are but a memory. (Those young ladies are becoming taller and more independent all the time; some even join the Civil Guard.) Hamburgers, pizzas and indescribable junk food have won a beachhead in Spain, but the connoisseur of fine dining can still find cuisine that's worth a detour. The good news is that, in spite of its dizzyingly fast Europeanization, Spain remains different.

Spain is the world's most popular tourist destination. Some 50 million foreign travellers, substantially more numerous than the native population, arrive every year. This may disconcert people who hate crowds. Don't despair: the tourist throng is well contained along the beaten path, essentially a very long, narrow strip of highly desirable beachfront. The rest of the country, almost anywhere inland, greets the hardy explorer with small-town curiosity and traditional courtesy. Anywhere in Spain, the visitor has every chance of sharing in the abundant sun, fun and excitement.

The country is so diverse that the ancient Romans assigned it a plural name: Hispaniae, "the Spains". The internal differences, which began with the landscape and the tribes who settled there, persist. Geographically "the Spains" are as varied as snowy mountains and sun-baked sand-dunes, orange groves and rice fields. In the average year the green north-west receives six times as much rainfall as the parched plain of La Mancha. From region to region the land, the

crops, the houses and the people are as unalike as Scotland and Sicily. Unfortunately for national cohesion, the centrifugal forces can reach tense levels in areas where language and culture diverge from the Spanish mainstream. In fact, the very concept of Spanishness has become controversial.

A Case of Peninsularity

Bigger than Italy, smaller than France, Spain is about three-quarters the size of Texas but no less proud. (After all, in

In the heart of Quixote country, in breezy La Mancha, evocative windmills still adorn the horizon. Nowadays, incomparably more efficient designs—propellers mounted on tall, slim towers—convert wind power into electricity on some gale-prone Spanish coasts.

its Golden Age, Spain ruled Texas—and Florida and Mexico, too.) Most of its national boundaries consist of coastline, about 1,100 km. (700 miles) along the Mediterranean Sea, and, less touristically, almost 1,000 km. (over 600 miles) along the Atlantic Ocean and Bay of Biscay. In the north-east, the Pyrenees wall off Spain from France and the duty-free ministate of Andorra. The only other contiguous country, Portugal, clings along most of the Iberian peninsula's west coast.

Tourists broiling shoulder to shoulder on Spain's *costas* are often unaware that this is Europe's second most mountainous country, after Switzerland. (The skiing season here goes on into May.) Madrid is Europe's highest capital, even if its altitude at 640 m. (2,100 ft.) is unlikely to flutter the heart or strain the lungs. Elsewhere in Spain the summits soar well over 3,000 m. (beyond 11,000 ft.). For the record, though, the country's highest mountain, at 3,718 m. (12,198 ft.), is an offshore volcanic peak, a snowcapped mirage on the lush island of Tenerife.

Madrid, a compromise capital, a sort of 16th-century Brasilia, was built in the middle of Spain's central plateau, which is almost encircled by mountains. The plateau's climate is officially described as "continental". In practice that boils down to oven-hot summers and icy winters. Spain offers a choice of two other climates: "temperate marine" (meaning mild but often wet) in the north and north-west, and "Mediterranean" (the tourist's dream) on the east and south coasts.

In other European countries the rivers have an economic as well as a scenic importance; it's hard to imagine Germany without the Rhine or Italy with no Po. But only one of Spain's waterways is notably navigable. The Guadalquivir links Seville to the sea 100 km. (60 miles) away, hardly an Amazonian challenge. Other rivers may look as serious as they are beautiful, but they can dwindle to a trickle at certain times of the year. When you cross a bridge in Spain, you never know whether the advertised torrent below is going to be wet or dry.

Portrait of a Spaniard

Jutting like a mailed fist south-westwards into the Atlantic from the rest of Europe, Spain almost touches North Africa. In turn, North Africa has touched Spain in profound, visible ways. The Moors ruled the country for centuries. They left behind their forts and fountains, crafts and music, and their genes. But they were only one of many influences on the face and character of Spain.

The Spanish family tree is a tangle of intertwining cultures, as civilizing as the Greek and Roman, as tough as the Visigothic, as exotic as the Arab and Jewish. In addition, Celts settled in the north, as you might guess from the sight today of local bagpipers with red beards. Where the industrious Basques came from is

*S*olid citizens of Cáceres, in Estremadura, share the honour of bearing the revered image of the Virgin of the Mountain on the annual procession up into the hills. The statue, elaborately dressed for each occasion, is thought to have been carved around the time of Columbus.

harder to determine, hidden as they are behind an inscrutable language, but they beat the Romans to Spain. Another independent-minded group are the Catalans, who once had an empire of their own, and still strongly prefer speaking Catalan to Spanish. With all these variants to choose from, the stereotype of a Spaniard has gone by default to the Andalusian cliché—those dark flashing eyes, clacking castanets and stamping heels. The image is Spanish, all right, but only one piece of the whole, variegated jigsaw.

Whether the eyes are black or blue or green, some traits do seem representative of the Spaniards. Consider generosity. Anyone who has been swept up into the embrace of a Spanish family is an expert on the subject. (And you'll notice how generosity spells prosperity for the beggars on the street or at the doors of churches.)

Just because they cheer the events in the bullring doesn't mean Spaniards are cruel to animals. See the pampered dogs being promenaded in the *paseo*. And the pigeons in the plaza at the Pilar church in Zaragoza may be the best fed in the world: bags of pigeon-snacks sell like hot cakes to the sentimental visitors.

Superstition flickers in the subconscious of the millions of Spaniards who regularly play the several competing lotteries; they spend a fortune after gravely consulting omens, lucky numbers and the success record of the particular ticket vendor. The winning numerals are so avidly awaited that they are posted nightly on the television news.

Spanish dignity is apparent in the unwavering gaze of the peasant along the road, to say nothing of the straight-backed posture and meticulous attire of the man or woman in the city. There's a narrow line, of course, between dignity and arrogance.

As the traffic jam in any Spanish city shows, organization and cooperation are *not* national strong points. Spaniards tend not to be team players. Like all the great thinkers and explorers, they prefer going it alone. (That great thinker and explorer, Don Quixote, went *almost* alone, advised by Sancho Panza but not a committee.)

Perhaps one sure generalization is that Spaniards are unpredictable. Church-going has declined to a minority activity, yet the religious festivals continue as Spanishly all-consuming as ever. Spaniards are accomplished drinkers, with pub-crawling virtually a daily rite, yet they almost never get drunk. (Snack-grazing as they go is a reliable defence against intoxication; so is pride.) Jekyll and Hyde in the underworld: when the packed metro train arrives in the station, hand-kissing politeness yields to the law of the jungle. Above ground, rush-hour drivers show similar ferocity. The birth-rate is down, divorce (legalized as recently as 1981) is booming, pre- and extra-marital hanky-panky common-place; but the sense of the inviolable family seems eternal. See the possessive way Spaniards spoil their babies, wrapping them in old-fashioned love. (The objects of so much indulgence soon become Europe's noisiest tots, but nobody ever claimed silence was a Spanish virtue.)

Beyond the Crowded *Costas*

Mass tourism, much disparaged by sophisticates and environmentalists, seethes along the east and south coasts and the holiday islands. As happy as the sun-blessed millions may be, anchored to packed beaches backed by high-rise hotels and apartment blocks, they are skimping on some supreme cultural and natural wonders. It's as if tourists visiting the United States never ventured farther north than Florida, as though visitors to the U.K. stopped at Brighton.

Even the beaches, though, reflect the intriguing diversity of "the Spains": the hidden coves of the Costa Brava are a world away from the endless sweep of sand on the neighbouring Costa Dorada. And most of the tourist enclaves adjoin towns or villages with more to commend them than just restaurants and souvenir shops. Within walking distance of the most contrived tourist colony, you can probably discover a historic church or buildings of architectural interest or an offbeat museum worth writing home about.

Some of the coastal cities, gateways to sprawling tourist complexes, deserve particular attention. The capital of the north-eastern *costas*, Barcelona, a vital and very European city, offers everything from medieval monuments to the "sandcastle cathedral" by the brilliant Catalan architect, Antoni Gaudí. Palma, the metropolis of the tourist-inundated island of Majorca, is crowned by one of Spain's most impressive Gothic cathedrals and an ancient Moorish palace.

Inland, the distractions are as serious or light-hearted as you please. Madrid is strong on museums, from the paramount Prado to quirky specialist institutions. At the other end of the scale, the capital's nightlife goes on later and louder than almost anywhere in the world.

Collecting cathedrals? Try Toledo, Seville, Burgos and León for four of the world's most beautiful.

Relics of the Moorish era? Visit the awesome mosque-cathedral in Córdoba, Granada's Alhambra palace, and fortresses, bridges and gateways all over the country.

Castles in Spain? Ten thousand were built, and although there's not exactly one on every hilltop, you can hardly miss them. Among the greatest: Segovia, Toledo, Peñafiel and Belmonte. You can also *sleep* in a castle, or perhaps an ancient monastery—part of a network of government-sponsored hotels.

Wide-open spaces? Horizons don't come any wider than on Spain's central plateau. Or go up a few notches and climb a mountain in Andalusia or Cantabria.

As Spain's highway network improves, you can pack in more scenery and more towns per day. Or boycott the motorways and savour the old-fashioned byroads.

Ulterior Motives

A constant threat to a successful holiday is self-inflicted cultural overkill. Even the most earnest collector of Romanesque churches or museums of decorative arts can't go at it full tilt, day after day. Scenery, too, can be overwhelming when it's as green as the Asturian mountains or as blindingly white as the hill towns in Andalusia.

The prescribed respite is a drastic change of pace. Spain is well supplied with distractions as relaxing as sports or as exhausting as shopping.

The sporting life clearly thrives along the coasts, with everything from sailing to scuba diving. On dry land there's golf galore, tennis, horse riding, and—for spectating—the world's fastest ball game, *jai alai*.

As for the shopping, when it comes to appeasing the hordes of souvenir-hunting tourists, Spain can be as tasteless as any other country. But at their best, Spain's artisans meet the standards of the most demanding buyers. Fashion designers equal those of Paris and Milan. And everybody loves the animated air of discovery at a Spanish flea market.

Festivals and fêtes are everywhere, just about all year round. They are as solemnly theatrical as Holy Week, as riotous as Carnival or Pamplona's running of the bulls, or as unpredictable and uninhibited as the saint's day of any town or village you happen upon.

Anyone keen on food and drink soon becomes enthusiastic about the broad scope of possibilities. You don't have to be an expert or a snob to appreciate Spanish wines, as unpretentious as a carafe of the house red, or as sublime as La Rioja's best. Starting with the seafood and spreading in all delicious directions, the regional delights of the Spanish kitchen captivate visiting gourmets. For dieters, though, it's a disaster.

All you can do is stave off dinner until as late as possible—say, 10 o'clock, after the evening promenade. The way the Spaniards do.

HISTORY

Spanish Saga: From Outsiders to Model Modern Europeans

Half a million years ago, palaeozoologists tell us, lions roamed the Iberian peninsula. The local cavemen hunted the lions, and vice versa; to discourage visits by large, hungry, man-eating cats, it was considered a good idea to keep the home fires burning.

In many regions of Spain, modern fossil diggers have turned up bonanzas of bones of Neanderthal-like people, along with the remains of the big beasts that shared the land with them. Many of the animals were even bigger than lions; specifically rhinoceros, hippopotamus, even elephant.

How did the big game and the hunters arrive in Spain? Evidently they walked. In the beginning, it's believed, Europe and Africa were linked by a land bridge between Gibraltar and Morocco.

During the Ice Age, the lions, rhinos, hippos and elephants wisely headed back to sunny Africa. The first Spaniards put on their bearskin coats, turned up the fire and stayed put, and the fauna now consisted mostly of deer, bison and wild horses.

Guarding entry to Burgos, the Arch of St. Mary includes statues of Charles V and the mighty El Cid, the 11th-century warrior interred in Burgos Cathedral.

These are among the northerly animals pictured on the walls and ceilings of certain caves in Spain (best known are those of Altamira, in Cantabria). Prehistoric artists who could convey the concepts of mass and motion left us a vivid notion of the hunter's life and thoughts. Their talent dates back at least 15,000 years. By the standards of any age it could be called genius.

No great advances were reported during the Neolithic period, except for the development of agriculture and pottery-making. In the rock paintings of the new age, simple human figures accompany the images of animals. The women, we deduce, wore skirts.

Life had changed profoundly by the start of the Bronze Age, not only in the tools at hand but the crops raised and the design of houses and villages. Settlements arose on hilltops, the better to deal with danger. Centuries later this strategic plan evolved into a network of castles in Spain.

During the Bronze Age, Celtic immigrants populated northern and central Spain, while the south and east were inhabited by various Iberian tribes. The Celts were illiterate and rather uncouth, whereas the Iberians had their own written language, sophisticated industry and

*S*till in working order after nearly 2,000 years,
an elegant Roman aqueduct straddles the centre of Segovia.
All that has changed over the centuries is the figure in the niche over
the tallest arch: in a 16th-century afterthought, the original statue
of Hercules was replaced by a Christian image.

contribution to the betterment of humankind was the invention of a two-edged warrior's sword. It was to become standard equipment in the Roman army.

Meanwhile, the Phoenicians, sailing from bases in North Africa, founded colonies in southern Spain. The first was called Gadir (now Cádiz). With advanced technology and keen trading instincts, they parlayed Spanish fish and salt into a big fish-curing export industry.

Carthage, itself a Phoenician colony at the outset, established an empire of its own, which spread to Spain. Carthaginian power extended as far north as Barcelona (named, it's believed, after General Hamilcar Barca, father of the legendary Hannibal). The dour, ruthless Carthaginians stressed profit instead of political power or cultural interests; they exploited Spain's silver and lead mines and drafted able-bodied young Spaniards into their army.

In the 3rd century B.C., the Carthaginians under Hannibal were defeated by the Romans in the Second Punic War, leaving the way open for Rome to take control of the Iberian peninsula. But that still left the plucky Celtiberians.

Spain Under the Caesars

All over the country the stamp of ancient Rome remains: walls and roadways, villas, monuments and vineyards... and three living languages descended from Latin: Spanish (or Castilian as it is correctly called), Catalan and Galician. Roman law is still the basis of the Spanish legal system. Spain gave birth to Roman emperors as memorable as Trajan and Hadrian and writers such as Seneca and Martial, still quoted today.

The Celtiberians didn't yield to the civilizing Roman war machine without a fight. In fact it took nearly 200 years for Rome to complete the conquest of Iberia. The founder of the Roman Empire, Augustus Caesar, personally commanded the seven Roman legions deployed for the last battle, which closed the book on the Cantabrian War in 19 B.C.

admirable art. The supreme work of Iberian art, a stone sculpture of a gorgeous goddess now called the Lady of Elche, reigns as the star attraction at Madrid's Archaeological Museum. Some experts find elements of classical Greek style in this statue; the Greeks were among the first foreign influences on the peninsula.

As time went by, the Celts and Iberians interacted where their territories overlapped, and soon the peninsula had a Celtiberian culture. The Celtiberians gained fame as soldiers; their principal

The Romans at first divided the peninsula into two Hispaniae—Ulterior and Citerior ("farther" and "nearer"). When this region was carved up into three provinces, the capital cities were established in what are now Tarragona, Córdoba and Mérida. Soon the symbols of Roman civilization—graceful bridges and aqueducts, vast arenas and baths—could be found all over Spain. The impact on society was no less obvious. By the turn of the millennium, most of the local languages were muted; to get ahead in the world you had to speak Latin.

Early in the multifaith Roman period the new religion called Christianity came to Spain. The word may have been carried by St. Paul himself. The pioneering Christian communities suffered persecution. By the time the 4th-century Emperor Constantine was himself converted, the golden age of the empire was about to yield to the Dark Ages.

Overstretched and increasingly corrupt, Rome watched its far-flung enterprise disintegrate. Germanic tribes, some with a deserved reputation for barbarism, hastened into the vacuum. The Vandals (the name and behaviour live on today), had little to contribute to Spanish culture, but the Visigoths brought their intricate arts and built opulent churches.

Religion was a sore point in the career of an embattled 6th-century Visigothic king called Leovigild. He ruled, on the whole effectively, from Toledo. While fighting off all manner of foes, he tried to convert his subjects to Arianism, a religious faction deemed heretical by the Christians. He was better at war than missionary work; he failed to convince his own son, who became a Catholic.

FACTS AND FIGURES

Geography:	Spain extends over most of the Iberian peninsula on the south-western tip of Europe, with a land mass of 504,788 sq. km. (194,898 sq. miles). It is bounded by three seas, the Bay of Biscay, the Atlantic Ocean and the Mediterranean, and shares borders with France and Portugal. The two main groups of Spanish islands are the Balearics in the Mediterranean and the Canaries in the Atlantic. Spain also has possessions in Africa, namely Ceuta and Melilla. Highest point: Pico del Teide (Tenerife), 3,718 m. (12,198 ft.)
Population:	38,400,000 inhabitants.
Languages:	Castilian (Spanish) is spoken everywhere, as a first or second tongue. Official regional languages are Catalan, Basque and Galician.
Capital:	Madrid (3.2 million inhabitants)
Major cities:	Barcelona (1,751,000), Valencia (745,000), Seville (668,000), Zaragoza (595,000), Málaga (538,000), Bilbao (397,000), Las Palmas de Gran Canaria (366,000).
Government:	A constitutional monarchy with King Juan Carlos I as head of state. A prime minister presides over the *cortes*, composed of the Congress of Deputies and the Senate or upper chamber. Spain has 17 autonomous communities with legislative assemblies. The 8,022 municipalities are run by elected councils.
Religion:	Predominantly Catholic (no longer the state religion), 250,000 Protestants, small Jewish and Muslim communities.

An eccentric feature of the Visigothic regime was the royal succession. The monarchy was elective rather than hereditary, prompting a spate of palace intrigues and assassinations to hijack the crown. These and other problems were often blamed on the handiest scapegoat: the Jews. They had fared well in Spain under the Romans and the early Visigoths, but starting in the 7th century they began to feel the heat. Much later, when the Spanish Inquisition hit its stride, the persecution quotient was cranked up to full steam.

D-Day for the Moors

In A.D. 711 a mighty expeditionary force of Arab-led Berber troops from North Africa sailed across the Strait of Gibraltar and poured ashore into Spain. The expertly planned invasion was led by General Tariq ibn Ziyad. The name "Gibraltar" is a corruption of *Gibel-Tariq*—Tariq's Rock.

The takeover spread nearly as fast as the invaders could march along those good, straight Roman roads, for the Visigoths put up only fitful resistance. Within a few years, the Moors or *moros* (as North African Muslims are usually called in Spanish history) advanced all the way to the Pyrenees. Bypassing pockets of Christian resistance, the aggressors continued the drive into France. There the relentless Islamic tide was finally turned by the Frankish leader Charles Martel at the Battle of Poitiers, in 732, to the relief of the rest of Europe.

The secret of the Moors' initial success was not only their religious zeal. They also cashed in on the military disorganization of the Visigoths, who became casualties of their own internal strife. Nor did the home front help the defenders. For many ordinary citizens the new regime, offering lower taxes and a chance of freedom for serfs, looked like a change for the better. And the harried Spanish Jews tended to welcome the Moors as liberators, for the occupation decreed tolerance of other faiths. Conversion to

Islam was strongly encouraged, though, and throngs of Christians chose to embrace the younger religion.

Reminders of the Muslim era may be found today in most of Spain, and not only in the obvious fields of music and dance. South-coast towns like Algeciras, Almuñécar and Tarifa have Arabic names. "Andalusia" comes from *al-Andalus*, meaning "the land of the west". (And Spaniards often use the wistful exclamation *¡ojalá!*, meaning "may God grant", derived from *in sha' allah*, or "if Allah wills it".)

More tangible relics, now among Spain's greatest tourist attractions, are the exquisite Moorish mosques and palaces, designed by engineers and architects whose skills were unknown elsewhere in Europe. And the art of the medieval Moorish craftsmen is perpetuated in today's best shopping bets—Spanish ceramics, tooled leather, and silver work.

Thanks to irrigation techniques imported from North Africa, crops like rice, cotton and sugar were planted, and orchards of oranges, peaches and pomegranates soon blossomed. Other Moorish innovations made possible the manufacture of paper and glass.

The Moors established their capital in Córdoba, which from the 8th to 11th centuries ranked as one of the great cities of the world, famed for its culture and erudition as well as its palaces and gardens. The emirs and caliphs surrounded themselves with poets and philosophers, doctors and geographers, mathematicians and abstract artists. Life in the Spanish cities of the Moors, by all accounts, was at least as refined as anywhere in Europe.

Meanwhile, at the Front...

The Moorish juggernaut that trundled north from Gibraltar in 711 met no serious resistance. It was eleven years before the fragmented defenders of Christian Spain won their first battle. Visigothic nobles exiled to the northern territory of Asturias joined with the local mountain folk to fight back. The winning general, a legend-endowed hero named Pelayo, is credited with striking the first blow for the *Reconquista* or Reconquest. Further Christian victories would be a long time in coming, but the Battle of Covadonga (the village is now a shrine) gave heart to a costly struggle that was to simmer for centuries.

In the middle of the 8th century the Christians of Asturias under King Alfonso I took advantage of a rebellion by Berber troops and occupied the neighbouring region of Galicia. This is where a peasant (led, the legend says, by a star in the sky) was to discover the tomb of the apostle St. James. Santiago de Compostela became the religious focus for all Spanish Christians and a favourite for pilgrims from many countries—the world's first and most indefatigable international tourists.

More breathing space from Moorish pressure was won in what became Catalonia. The devout, dynamic Charlemagne captured Barcelona, which gained independence in 878 under a local hero called Wilfred the Hairy. In the area between Catalonia and Asturias, Christian kingdoms expanded southwards. The region soon had so many castles that it was called Castile.

For hundreds of years the Reconquest seesawed according to the state of political alliances, military talent and morale. Early in the 10th century the Asturian capital was confidently transferred about 120 km. (75 miles) south from Oviedo to León—a big symbolic step deep into what had hitherto been "infidel" territory. But the Muslims were far from finished, and León fell to the megalomaniac ruler of Córdoba, al-Mansur. So did Barcelona and Burgos. In a severe blow to Christian hopes, al-Mansur sacked sacred Santiago de Compostela.

On the way back from his 50th battle al-Mansur died. The Christian forces moved to regain lost ground and self-assurance. Taking advantage of Moorish civil wars, they turned the tables in 1010 and with medieval gusto plundered Córdoba.

For the *Reconquista,* the big breakthrough of the 11th century was the capture of the beautiful, rich city of Toledo from the Moors. King Alfonso VI of Castile and León, who presided over this great victory, had himself crowned "Emperor of Toledo".

The fall of Toledo, an intellectual hothouse of Muslim Spain, sent out shock waves to the Moorish rulers elsewhere in the peninsula. They called for help from North Africa, from the Almoravids, a confederation of Berber tribes based in Marrakech. These puritanical Muslim zealots, known for their military prowess, succeeded in pushing back the

Signalling the way to Mecca, the thousand-year-old mihrab of Córdoba's great mosque stands among the world's finest Muslim art.

El Cid—and Still the Champion

Spain's national folk hero was born Rodrigo Díaz de Vivar, near Burgos, around 1040. He is remembered as *El Cid*, from the Arabic for "the Lord", with the additional title *el Campeador*—"the Champion". His exploits in peace and, mostly, war are recounted in the national epic, *El cantar de mío Cid* (the Song of the Cid), a very long poem about knighthood in flower. (A play and a film were to follow.) While the poem is an indelible part of the Spanish consciousness, the actual facts are hard to come by.

El Cid was an extraordinarily successful soldier of fortune who apparently never lost a battle. He was flexible about his loyalties, working for both Christian and Moorish sponsors. This seems not to have affected his popularity, since he tended to oppose tyrants of either persuasion. His most famous victory was the siege of Muslim-controlled Valencia, which ended in 1094 with El Cid ruling the city. But even that great moment has an unsatisfying postlude: the Moors soon retook Valencia and held it for more than a century. A cynic might say, *Cid transit gloria mundi.*

Reconquest, which by now was the longest of the medieval crusades.

Followers of another Berber sect with a similar-looking name, the fundamentalist Almohads, then intervened, dividing the Muslim front. The ensuing civil war among the Moors spelled doom for the Almohad empire. By the early 13th century the Christian forces had regained most of Spain all the way down to Andalusia. Then Ferdinand III of Castile and León retook two prizes, Córdoba and (after a terrible siege) Seville. Muslim refugees flooded into Granada, the last stronghold, where they lingered for another 2½ centuries amid intellectual and artistic splendour. As for Ferdinand III, his good works won him elevation to sainthood; call him San Fernando.

A Singular Nation

Until the 15th century "the Spains" had always stayed resolutely plural. There were sporadic moves toward unity—a royal marriage between Catalonia and Aragon, for example, and nuptials linking Navarre and Castile. But in most cases something divisive happened before the alliance could be solidified.

The greatest royal marriage, presumably made in heaven, brought together the shrewd King Ferdinand of Aragon and the fervently religious and patriotic Queen Isabella of Castile. Under the Catholic Monarchs (as Pope Alexander VI entitled them) a single Spain was created, comprising most of the nation we now know. However, the components of the united kingdom retained their individuality and institutions, and in the long term even this superficial integration failed to endure.

Aiming to unite Spain, Ferdinand and Isabella made history in other ways. To purge the nation of spiritual ills, the Inquisition, a marathon of interrogation and torture, was inaugurated in 1478. Isabella's confessor, the tireless Tomás de Torquemada, presided over the purge of converts to Christianity: *conversos* (Jews) and *moriscos* (Muslims). Several thousand of the suspects, judged heretical or at least insincere, went up in flames. (Later the Inquisition turned its attention to Protestants.)

In the eventful year of 1492 the influential Torquemada convinced Ferdinand and Isabella to expel all the surviving unconverted Jews. Perhaps 200,000 Jews, including some of the country's best educated and most productive people, were sent packing to North Africa and various refuges in Europe. Left behind were the *conversos*, who were to make great contributions to the evolution of Spanish civilization.

The struggle against the Moors was always a unifying force, and the final push evoked harmonious cheers of thanksgiving from Spaniards, and from all of Christendom. In 1492, when the Reconquest captured the last Muslim redoubt, Granada, Ferdinand and Isabella took it personally... literally. They ceremoniously accepted the keys to the Alhambra, the city's wondrous palace. It was all very chivalrous, except that the religious freedom guaranteed to the Muslims was soon revoked and mass conversions were decreed.

The crowning achievement of 1492 was the voyage of the *Niña*, the *Pinta* and the *Santa María* to what Columbus thought was the Indies. Sponsored by Ferdinand and Isabella, the lucky navigator from Genoa brought back news of a New World, which was promptly annexed to the Spanish realm. Even at its earliest stage, the American project proved a useful stimulus for homefront morale.

And one more achievement of Ferdinand and Isabella. In the royal marriage mart, the Catholic Monarchs sent two daughters to bigger and better international alliances. Princess Catherine of Aragon was married to the imposing Henry VIII of England; Princess Juana was wed to Philip the Fair, the good-looking son of Austria's Emperor Maximilian. These however turned out to be less than perfect matches: Henry divorced Catherine, precipitating the English Reformation. And Juana the Mad was deemed too potty to handle the job of Queen of Spain.

Kings with a Hapsburg Accent

Ferdinand and Isabella personified Spanishness, but their grandson, Charles I, born in Flanders in 1500, could barely compose a sentence in Spanish. A Hapsburg, he assumed the throne in 1516, packed his retinue with Burgundian and Flemish nobles and occupied himself with affairs of state far from Spain. All the while Spanish gold from the New World paid the empire's bills.

Soon after his arrival in Spain, the lantern-jawed young man inherited the title of Holy Roman Emperor, and the number of Charles V. This weighty crown necessarily kept him busy away from the royal residences of Toledo, Segovia, Valladolid and Madrid. While the monarch was off on one of his business trips, his increasingly dissatisfied Spanish subjects resorted to violent protest. The revolt of the *comuneros*, or townsmen, was put down and the leaders executed, but the king got the message. He cut some taxes and began to pay more attention to his Spanish constituency.

Among the emperor's distractions was a seemingly endless series of wars he waged—using mostly Spanish troops—against France, against the Ottoman Empire, and against Germany's new religious sect, the Lutherans. He failed in the last siege, which is how German Protestants won their right to religious freedom.

In 1556, Charles abdicated in favour of his only son, Philip II, which seemed to be good news for Spain. The new king had grown up in Spain, and he gave many a top European job to Castilians. Philip proclaimed Madrid his capital, converting an unimpressive town of less than 15,000 into the powerhouse of the greatest empire of the age.

On the war front Philip was exhilarated by a rousing Christian victory in the Mediterranean in 1571: a combined Spanish, Venetian and papal fleet tore up the Turkish navy in the Battle of Lepanto. The news inspired overconfidence in the emperor, who decided to take on Protestant England, for religious, political and personal reasons. The mission of the vaunted Spanish Armada ended in disaster; England ruled the waves and Spain was left to lick its wounds.

Ten years after the Armada fiasco, Philip died in devout seclusion in El Escorial, the superb palace and monastery he had built in the hills north-west of Madrid. In spite of his failures, Spain was still the master of Europe's greatest empire, extending from the Americas (North, Central and South) to the Philippines (named, in all modesty, after himself). But the Golden Age passed swiftly in a rush of reckless spending.

Philip III, who succeeded his father, turned in a lacklustre performance on the throne. His most memorable achievement was expelling the remaining *moriscos*. Hundreds of thousands were thrown

Doom of the Invincible Armada

Everything went wrong for the Spanish Armada. The commander died before the fleet sailed; his replacement, the wealthy Duke of Medina Sidonia, barely knew port from starboard. He was to face English aces like Sir Francis Drake and Sir John Hawkins.

Almost as soon as the Armada left Lisbon it ran into destructive gales and was forced to return for two months of repairs. But even at their best, the 130 clumsy, inadequately armed ships were outnumbered by the more manoeuverable British fleet.

In the first battle, the Spanish realized that their ships would soon run out of ammunition; but the English, close to home, could easily resupply.

A planned invasion of England with soldiers based in the Netherlands—the whole point of the exercise—had to be called off. Then the British transformed expendable ships into torches and aimed them at the heart of the Spanish fleet, causing panic, irreparable confusion and severe damage.

Due to a combination of bad luck, ill winds and British naval superiority, the Armada sacrificed thousands of sailors and about half its ships in pursuit of failure. The English not only whipped Philip II, they lost not a single ship of their own.

out, depriving Spain of some of its hardest-working farmers.

Religious motives also influenced Spain's participation in the Thirty Years' War, pitting Catholic against Protestant Europe. Philip III and his son and heir, Philip IV (another loser), were the figureheads during this struggle, as fruitless as it was lengthy.

The last and least handsome of the Spanish Hapsburgs, Charles II, was barely old enough to go to kindergarten when his kingly father died. He grew up to be as futile as his ancestor, leaving the worries of the empire to others. Having failed to produce an heir, he willed the crown instead to the grandson of France's Louis XIV. Thus in 1700 the Duke of Anjou claimed the title of Philip V of Spain, provoking a nasty aftertaste later known as the War of the Spanish Succession.

The last century of the Hapsburg era shows a gradual, then rapid decline. The empire lost possessions in the Low Countries, Portugal, and pockets of France and Italy. Emigration, war after war, farm troubles and epidemics contributed to a severe drop in the population. But in counterpoint to all the political and military failures, the 17th century was a time of glory in Spanish art: the age of Velázquez, Zurbarán, Murillo and Ribera. Ironically, most of them couldn't have made a living without the patronage of the otherwise uninspired royal court.

Bourbons on the Throne

The War of the Spanish Succession (1701–14) pitted Britain and Austria against France's claim to a Bourbon Spain. Catalonia took the opportunity to try to elude Madrid's control, only to be slapped down when Philip V won the war. Punishment for joining the wrong side included a ban on official use of the Catalan language. (The Spanish Civil War of 1936-39 provided striking historical parallels.)

The war cost Spain much of its dwindling empire—Belgium, Luxembourg, Milan, Sicily and Sardinia. And Britain won the strategic prize of the Rock of Gibraltar. But all was not lost: by the end of the war, the unification of Spain was almost achieved. Only Navarre and the Basque country escaped direct rule from Madrid.

The most successful Spanish king of the 18th century, Charles III, recruited capable administrators and invigorated the economy. He paved and lit the streets of Madrid and built what became the Prado museum. Under his reign Spain acquired from France the Louisiana Territory—a nice compensation for earlier losses in Europe. However, the expansionist fling lasted only until 1800, when Louisiana was returned to France, which sold it to the United States three years later.

Events in France itself unbalanced the regime of Charles IV, a barely competent king at the best of times. His 20-year reign, destined to be peppered by the ricochets of the French Revolution, ended in all-round disaster: abdication, arrest and war. Napoleon invaded Spain and invested his older, taller and more agreeable brother, Joseph, as King José I. The imposition of an interloper roused Spain to an uprising which developed into the Peninsular War (Spaniards call it the War of Independence). This went on murderously but inconclusively for six years. Finally, with the help of the Duke of Wellington, the Spanish expelled the occupying forces. Incidentally, the dethroned José I spent 17 years in exile in an unconventional and mildly unglamorous sanctuary, New Jersey.

Another loser of the war was the Spanish empire. Taking advantage of the strife and confusion in Europe, Spain's richest Western Hemisphere colonies revolted and won their independence.

Ferdinand VII, having been deposed by Napoleon, was reinstated in 1814. His subjects had nicknamed him "Ferdinand the Desired", so they were disillusioned when he tore up the constitution and ruled as an absolute monarch. Political infighting, power struggles and repression followed.

Ferdinand died in 1833 at the end of what was called the Ominous Decade. Worse was to come: a succession of wars of succession. The Carlist Wars rumbled on, spanning a period of half a century, interrupted by occasional breathing spaces and the proclamation of a short-lived republic. The Carlists—named after Don Carlos, who claimed the throne at the expense of his niece—scored many victories but lost in the end to King Alfonso XII, a Sandhurst-educated Bourbon.

Although he survived a couple of assassination attempts, Alfonso's reign was destined to be brief: he died of tuberculosis at the age of 28. His legacy to Spain was unaccustomed peace and prosperity and a system of limited parliamentary rule.

Some months after he died, Queen María Cristina produced his posthumous son and heir. The lad was called Alfonso XIII (an inauspicious number, as it turned out). The queen, who ran the palace until her son came of age, took a heavy defeat in 1898. The Spanish-American War cost Spain the last remnants of its empire: Cuba, Puerto Rico and the Philippines. The military debacle understandably jolted the nation's morale, but it inspired the creative renaissance of a generation of Spanish intellectuals.

Spain escaped the rigours of World War I, observing the carnage from the perspective of the camp of the neutrals. But a subsequent war in Morocco proved a disaster for Spanish troops.

Having watched the failures of revolving-door constitutional governments, Alfonso XIII backed the dictatorship of General Miguel Primo de Rivera. The hard line lost him friends, and in municipal elections in 1931 the anti-royalist forces won a landslide. The king got the message. Although he declined to abdicate, he agreed to go into exile... from which the last Alfonso never returned.

The Spanish Civil War

Life under the new Republic continued turbulent. Bitter ideological conflicts divided parties and factions; the church was also involved. The 1933 parliamentary elections brought a swing to the right. But in 1936 a Popular Front of left-wing parties won by a squeak and formed a radical government. Conservatives feared that a Marxist revolution was at hand. The shaky bridge of political compromise collapsed.

With anarchy in the wind, a large section of the army rose in revolt against the Republican government. The leader of the insurrection was a one-time war hero, General Francisco Franco. As supreme commander of the Nationalist forces he was promoted to *generalísimo*.

Support for the uprising came from monarchists and conservatives, as well as the right-wing Falange organization and the Roman Catholic Church; on the other side, liberals, socialists, communists and anarchists cast their lot with the government. The Civil War became one of the great causes of the 20th century; many Europeans saw it as a crucial confrontation between democracy and dictatorship, or, from the other side, as a choice between law and order or chaos and social revolution. Help for both sides came from abroad, with Germany and Italy in Franco's team and Russia and the volunteers of the International Brigades fighting alongside the Republicans.

Cruel slow-motion battles (and horrific atrocities perpetrated by both sides) kept the blood flowing for three years and cost many thousands of lives. The sober, wily Franco emerged as *caudillo* (leader) of a shattered postwar Spain. Many Republicans went into exile; others simply disappeared.

After the war the hardship continued. But Franco managed to slip out of Hitler's embrace and keep Spain from combat in World War II. Spain was admitted to the United Nations in 1955, opening the gates to an unprecedented tourist invasion, with profound effects on both the economy and the national mentality.

A New Spain Enters Europe

Even while Franco lay protractedly on his deathbed, in 1975, Spain was taking the first steps towards liberalization. The pace picked up two days after his death when, in accordance with the *caudillo*'s wishes, the monarchy was restored in the person of King Juan Carlos. The young grandson of the Bourbon Alfonso XIII surprised his handlers and the world and became Spain's helmsman on the road to democracy. Juan Carlos's most heroic moment arrived in 1981 when he thwarted a military coup.

Fundamental changes in the political landscape came thick and fast in the late 1970s and the '80s. The Falange was wound down and the communists regained legality. The church was disestablished. Divorce was legalized. Autonomy in varying degrees was granted to areas

Franco had deprived of their identities, most notably Catalonia and the Basque country. (But Basque separatist extremists, still dissatisfied, continue their campaign of violence.)

Spain joined NATO and, four years later, the European Economic Community. On the domestic scene, troubles like inflation, unemployment, crime and pollution precluded any overconfidence. But a free, democratic Spain could note with satisfaction that the long separation from Europe's mainstream was ended.

Spaniards can never forget the centuries of the Reconquest, when the Christian forces slowly but relentlessly expelled the Muslims. The town of Alcoy celebrates its liberation in an annual "Moors-and-Christians" festival, which runs for three days. Tourists flock to see battles re-enacted in melodramatic costumes. The Moors look like losers.

HISTORICAL LANDMARKS

*G*alloping to victory: Ferdinand and Isabella in stained glass.

Prehistory	500,000 B.C.	Hunters may have inhabited Iberia.
	15,000 B.C.	Altamira cavemen paint realistic scenes.
	3,000 B.C.	Bronze age traders establish villages.
Colonists	1,000 B.C.	Celts settle in north, Phoenicians colonize southern Iberia.
	3rd century B.C.	Carthaginians conquer Spain; Punic Wars ensue.
Roman Spain	1st century B.C.	Romans complete conquest of Spain, imposing Latin language and culture.
	1st century A.D.	Christianity reaches Spain (legend says St. Paul himself brought the word).
	4th century	Empire declining, Dark Ages loom.

Middle Ages	6th century	Conquering Visigoths make Toledo their capital.
	711	Arab-led Berber troops invade Andalusia, soon control most of Spain.
	722	At Covadonga (Asturias), Christian forces win their first victory against Moors.
	758	Córdoba becomes capital of Moorish Spain, ushering in city's golden age.
	1085	Tide is turning: Reconquest of Toledo.
United Spain	1469	Ferdinand, Prince of Aragon weds Isabella of Castile.
	1478	"Catholic Monarchs" unleash Inquisition.
	1479	Ferdinand becomes King of Aragon; Christian Spain united.
	1492	Final triumph of Reconquest: capture of Granada. Ferdinand and Isabella expel the Jews. Columbus reaches America.
The Hapsburgs	1516	Charles I inherits throne and riches from Indies, becomes Holy Roman Emperor.
	1556–98	Philip II rules; Madrid his capital.
	1588	Britain routs Spanish Armada.
	1618–48	Thirty Years' War, Spain the big loser; meanwhile, Spanish art's age of glory.
Bourbon Spain	1701–14	War of Spanish Succession; Spain loses territories; Philip V wins crown.
	1759–1788	Under Charles III economy revives.
	1804	Napoleon invades; "War of Independence".
	1805	Battle of Trafalgar: Britannia rules waves.
	1814	Ferdinand VII regains throne, rules as absolute monarch.
19th Century	1833–76	Carlist Wars: costly, long-running chaos.
	1835	Religious orders suppressed.
	1873	First Spanish Republic proclaimed.
	1875	Monarchy restored under Alfonso XII.
	1898	Spanish-American War: end of empire.
20th Century	1914–18	Spain stays neutral in World War I; domestic unrest.
	1921	Revolt in Morocco; heavy losses for Spanish troops.
	1923	Alfonso XIII backs law-and-order dictatorship of General Primo de Rivera.
	1931	Anti-royalist landslide in local elections; king chooses exile.
War and Beyond	1936	Left-wing Popular Front wins election, forms radical government; chaos in the wind. Army revolts; Franco leads invasion of Andalusia. Civil War, with foreign intervention on both sides.
	1939	Republicans defeated, Franco rules.
	1955	Spain admitted to United Nations.
	1975	Franco dies, Bourbon Juan Carlos crowned. Rebirth of democracy, leading to integration into Europe.

Slicing Up Spain

Western Europe's second-biggest country is just too much of a good thing: you can't begin to do justice to Spain in one visit. This means some fundamental decisions: will the accent be on beachcombing or history? Mountain or plain? Cathedrals and museums or shopping and wine tasting? Actually, the choices don't have to be so stark; light relief is usually near enough to the serious sights. And with modern communications, the distances often prove less burdensome than you'd expect. It's just a matter of planning.

To arrange this book for easy use, we've sliced up Spain, sometimes arbitrarily, into nine regions. These extend, in most cases, beyond conventional borders, as we lump together contiguous provinces and administrative regions. Our groupings have no political significance; they're merely for organizational convenience. If you can't find a place you're looking for, check our comprehensive index at the back of the book.

We begin with the nation's capital and biggest city, Madrid, including the day-trip attractions in its hinterland. After exploring this geographical and touristic bull's-eye, we cover the remainder of Central Spain—a huge area encompassing approximately the regions of Castile and León. Thereafter we go clockwise around the peninsula, starting with the North-West (coinciding with Galicia). Then come the North (Asturias, Cantabria, the Basque Country and beyond); the North-East (the Pyrenees, Navarre, northern Aragon and Catalonia); the East (mostly Valencia and Murcia); the South (Andalusia); and, rounding out mainland Spain, what we are calling the West (essentially Estremadura). The final chapter turns to insular matters: Spain's popular holiday islands of the Atlantic and Mediterranean. (As on the mainland, there's much more to the Canaries and the Balearics than decorates the tourist posters.)

This Berlitz Blueprint guide is not intended to be encyclopaedic. But it does cover most of the places a visitor from abroad is likely to find interesting... enough, indeed, for several long, leisurely holidays. Among the sights *omitted* are some towns of purely (sometimes

At the sign of the scallop shell, a symbol of the apostle St. James the Great, a pilgrim reaches his goal in Santiago de Compostela.

impurely) industrial importance and a few isolated spots of value that are just too hard to reach to justify the trip.

If time permits, try to combine two or three of our nine regions to get a sense of the plurality of "the Spains". This is a country where the scenery and architecture—even the language—may change drastically around the next bend in the road. So a neighbouring province is almost bound to be a revelation. And it's usually an easy jaunt from the sea to the mountains; even the trip from the Mediterranean to the Atlantic is manageable.

Should you start in Madrid? In centrifugal Spain that's a controversial question. In rival Barcelona they might tell you not to bother going to the capital at all. But most of the long-haul flights land in Madrid, and the Castilian plateau around it is rich in history, scenery and sheer Spanishness.

If you decide to start in Barcelona, a city proud of an even longer pedigree than Madrid's, you can easily alternate between history and the beach life; two of Spain's best known *costas* are right at hand. Then bury the hatchet and hop over to Madrid to see the incomparable Prado.

Another inviting base, most apt for visitors arriving via France, is San Sebastián, a beautiful launching pad for excursions to the Basque Country and "Green Spain" along the Bay of Biscay. If possible, let the momentum take you all the way to Galicia, with its fjord-like *rías* and medieval monuments.

At the southern end of the peninsula, some beach time on the Costa del Sol might be the perfect complement to a tour of Andalusia's Moorish monuments. Investing a few more days, you can discover Estremadura, birthplace of the *conquistadores*.

Another way to plan a trip: follow your own interests or hobbies wherever they lead. Spain appeals to mountain climbers and windsurfers, antique collectors and hydrotherapy buffs. You can follow the peregrinations of Don Quixote, or the pilgrims on the road to Santiago de Compostela (the Way of St. James). We offer a generous sample of ideas, starting on page 39.

When to go? The climate statistics (see page 264) seem to speak for themselves, but "untypical" days or weeks do happen, even in normally sunny Spain. While summer is a fine time to be on a beach or in the sierra, you'll melt in Madrid. Winter may be chillier than you'd imagine almost anywhere in mainland Spain except close to sea level in the "deep south". To avoid the crowds in most regions, best bets are springtime (but not Easter) and autumn. If you hope to experience one of the great festival fixtures, such as the Málaga fair or the running of the bulls in Pamplona, you'll have to plan your lodgings and logistics very far in advance.

Getting Around

For on-the-spot, up-to-date advice on how to go from A to B, or to check what's going on in the area, drop in on the local tourist office. The experienced, multilingual staff may not have all the answers, but they know how to get them. A tourist office (look for the big "i" symbol) offers free brochures and maps, lists of hotels and special events, and expert advice.

The Berlitz Info section at the back of this book gives detailed practical guidance on the technicalities of travel to and through Spain, but here are some general thoughts to help you plan ahead.

Spain is big enough to make internal air travel a practical proposition. An hourly shuttle service links Madrid and Barcelona, and of course the islands are best reached by air. Other intercity flights may also appeal to travellers in a hurry. It's nearly 1,000 gruelling kilometres (some 600 miles) by road from Málaga to Bilbao but 80 minutes by scheduled flight. Note that Madrid is the hub for most domestic flights, so you may have to stop or change planes there.

Train travel within the country has its

pluses: the scenery, meeting ordinary Spanish families, avoiding the stress of driving. But the minuses include the slow local trains and the inflexibility imposed by the timetables. The national railway system, RENFE, serves almost all the main towns and many an interesting whistle stop, but there are some notable blank spots, for instance the Costa del Sol. By investing in a Tourist Card, Eurail, Inter-Rail or Rail Europ pass, visitors from abroad can sign up for unlimited rail travel at a significant saving. And another idea for train enthusiasts: check out RENFE's special excursion trains, such as the *Express Al-Andalus*, a luxurious five-day tour of historic southern cities.

Supplementing the train service are the intercity coaches, run by private companies. Information on schedules and fares can be obtained from tourist information offices or from any of the main bus stations.

If money is not the most important factor, renting a car provides travel at its most unconstrained. There is no substitute for abandoning the main route and following a secondary road towards a castle or colourful village on the horizon... at least until the road runs out. For long trips, the network of toll motorways (expressways) is useful but expensive. The rest of the road system ranges from first class to bumpy and difficult. A map is but a tentative travel planner, for road repairs—often many miles at a time—can steamroller your time estimates.

Except for ignoring the speed limits whenever it seems feasible, Spanish drivers generally are capable and courteous behind the wheel. Road-hogging truckers are usually helpful on mountain roads, signalling when it's safe to overtake them.

Many small towns control through traffic with lights which automatically turn red just ahead of you if you're speeding; others use radar and police patrols. In big cities driving and parking are apt to fray tempers. Taxis are plenti-

ful. And in Madrid, Barcelona and Valencia the metro (underground or subway) system is the most efficient way to get around.

At the end of a long day's travel and sightseeing it's a relief to know that comfortable accommodation awaits. Thus it's wise to have a confirmed reservation for your arrival in Spain, and to phone ahead as you go. Local tourist information offices have hotel lists and advice; a travel agency or your first hotel may be able to help with onward reservations.

With a tourist industry as highly developed as Spain's, you're right to expect an excellent choice of accommodation, from old-fashioned (or posh, modern) five-star luxury down to honest economy. Even if your budget directs you to the simplest *pensión* (boarding house), try to put aside some pesetas for a night at a *parador*, one of a chain of government-run inns found in offbeat locations. They often occupy castles or other historic buildings, but they cost no more than ordinary hotels of the same calibre. Barring last-minute cancellations, *paradores* have to be booked well in advance. Everybody, alas, has heard how good they are!

Finding Your Way

autopista	motorway
avenida	avenue
ayuntamiento	town hall
barrio	quarter
calle	street
carretera	road
castillo	castle
ciudad vieja	old town
correos	post office
estación	station
iglesia	church
jardín	garden
mercado	market
murallas	city walls
oficina de turismo	tourist office
paseo	boulevard
playa	beach
plaza	square
plaza de toros	bull ring
puerto	harbour
río	river

*A*t *Puerto Banús, on the Costa del Sol, it's only
a few steps from the car to the boat. One of Spain's classiest marinas,
it harbours some yachts so pompous that they fly flags of convenience.
After years of phenomenal growth in mass tourism,
at great cost to the environment, Spain is emphasizing up-market
holidays to sustain revenues.*

ON THE SHORT LIST

*You can't possibly see all Spain's highlights,
but it would be a shame to miss any
of the essentials if you're within striking distance.
Our choice of the top sights,
although inevitably arbitrary and subjective,
may help you decide where to go.*

Madrid *(3 days)*
Plaza Mayor: the perfect town square
Gran Vía: Madrid's main street
Descalzas Reales: art in a convent
The Prado: masses of Old Masters
Royal Palace: imperious and spectacular
Archaeology Museum: ancient art

Toledo *(1 day)*
Cathedral: unforgettable grandeur
Alcázar: war-scarred fort
Synagogue of St. Mary the White

Nearby Madrid *(3 days)*
El Escorial: Philip II's palace
Valle de los Caídos: war memorial
Segovia: aqueduct, Alcázar, cathedral
La Granja: palace and formal gardens

Salamanca *(1 day)*
Plaza Mayor: centre of life
Cathedrals, old and "new"
University, founded 1218

Valladolid *(1 day)*
National Museum of Sculpture
Cathedral: 16th-century strength
Cervantes House: the author's study

Burgos *(1 day)*
Arco de Santa María: city wall
Cathedral: grandeur and intimacy
Las Huelgas convent: like a fort

Galicia *(3 days)*
La Coruña: ancient port, fine houses
Pilgrims' Santiago de Compostela
West Coast: fjord-like *rías*

Green Spain *(3 days)*
Santander: port and resort
Santillana del Mar: medieval perfection
Picos de Europa: from peaks to valleys
Covadonga: cradle of the Reconquest

Basque Country *(3 days)*
San Sebastián: magnificent beaches
Basque Coast: cliffs and creeks
Vitoria: cathedrals and medieval core

Navarre *(2 days)*
Estella: churches and charm
Pamplona: cathedral, Baroque city hall
Leyre Monastery: inspiring setting

Northern Aragon *(3 days)*
Zaragoza: two cathedrals and a castle
Huesca: stately cathedral
Ordesa Park: waterfalls and wildlife

Inland Cataluña *(3 days)*
Gerona: often-besieged city
Montserrat: mountain pilgrimage
Poblet: royal monastery
Lérida: Moorish memories

Coastal Cataluña *(4–6 days)*
Costa Brava: cliffs, ports, resorts
Barcelona: history, art and dynamism
Tarragona: Romans and Catalans

East Coast *(3–5 days)*
Peñíscola: castle on a rock
Valencia: spirited orange capital
Alicante: Mediterranean bustle
Elche: a date with an infinity of palms

Coastal Andalusia *(2–4 days)*
Málaga: a taste of the real Spain
Marbella: celebrity resort
Gibraltar: bobbies and warm beer
Cádiz: ever since the Phoenicians

Inland Andalusia *(6–10 days)*
Ronda: cliff-top drama
Jerez de la Frontera: wines and horses
Seville: Moors and Christians
Córdoba: cathedral in a mosque
Granada: romance of Moorish Spain

Estremadura *(4–5 days)*
Mérida: Roman splendour
Guadalupe: smiles for the pilgrims
Trujillo: home of the Conquistadores
Cáceres: feast of medieval architecture

Going Places with Something Special in Mind

Discovering a country, it's not how much ground you cover but what you get out of it. To supplement or supplant the standard itineraries, consider pursuing your own special interests—a historical angle close to your heart, a favourite artist, or a hobby. The personal twists are infinite, from religious pilgrimages to sporting opportunities, but here, scattered around Spain, are some themes and variations to consider.

Castles

In the age of chivalry and derring-do, castles were as much a part of the Spanish countryside as today's high-tension pylons. Some medieval strongholds have tumbled into disrepair, as rock-strewn hilltops prove, but the survivors are an impressive lot. A cross-section of outstanding baileys and keeps:

1 SEGOVIA
The fairytale silhouette dates from a 19th-century restoration, but Segovia's Alcázar had been making history since the 13th century.

2 COCA (Segovia)
Moorish masons built this massive, all-brick classic of Mudéjar architecture.

3 PEÑAFIEL (Valladolid)
Long and thin and powerful, this ridge-top redoubt was begun in the early 14th century.

4 MEDINA DEL CAMPO (Valladolid)
La Mota Castle, powerful and austere, was one of the residences of Ferdinand and Isabella; the queen died here.

A Mudéjar classic, Coca Castle haughtily oversees the town founded by the ancient Iberians.

5 BUEN AMOR CASTLE (Salamanca)
The intriguingly named 13th-century fortress, once a command post of Ferdinand and Isabella, later became a palace, indeed a pleasure palace.

6 BELMONTE (Cuenca)
This compelling 15th-century fortress was restored, though not necessarily for the better, in the 19th century.

Discovering Columbus

Outward Bound
The great navigator made waves in many parts of Spain, inland as well as by the sea. Columbus-watchers can find milestones and landmarks from coast to coast; they are listed here in approximate chronological order.

1 LA RÁBIDA
Columbus endures a long wait in Franciscan monastery for the royal go-ahead. The prior gives vital support to "world is round" theory.

2 CÓRDOBA
Still awaiting a decision from Ferdinand and Isabella, the widower Columbus fathers second son, Ferdinand.

3 SANTA FÉ
April, 1492: Near recently reconquered Granada, Catholic Monarchs finally approve the Columbus expedition.

4 PONTEVEDRA
Local shipyard is said to have built flagship **Santa María.**

5 PALOS DE LA FRONTERA
August 3, 1492: With many local men in his crew, Columbus sets forth for the "Indies" from this town. (But Palos is no longer a port.)

6 CANARY ISLANDS
Brave little fleet stops at several points for supplies and repairs before tackling unknown ocean.

Triumphal Returns
7 PALOS
March 14, 1493: Columbus returns to Spain.

8 BARCELONA
King and Queen receive Columbus (and "sample" Indians) in Plaça del Rei. (See full-size replica of **Santa María** moored in Barcelona port, overlooked by Columbus statue.)

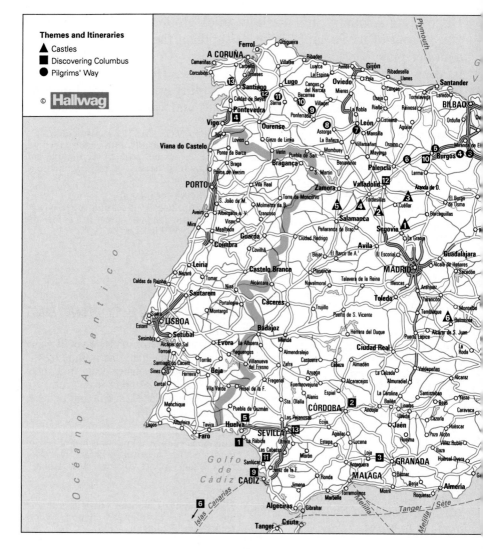

Themes and Itineraries
▲ Castles
■ Discovering Columbus
● Pilgrims' Way

© Hallwag

40

9 CÁDIZ
Sept. 5, 1493: From this fine harbour Columbus departs on second voyage to America with 17 ships and 1,500 men. (Cádiz is also port of departure for fourth expedition, 1502.)

10 BURGOS
Ferdinand and Isabella welcome him back from second trip in Burgos town house called la Casa del Cordón.

11 SANLÚCAR DE BARRAMEDA
May 30, 1498: A third Columbus venture launched, on southward course.

12 VALLADOLID
Columbus lives his last years in what is now **Casa Museo de Colón**. Dies May 21, 1506.

13 SEVILLE
Pompous 19th-century Columbus mausoleum in Seville Cathedral. Columbus books and marginal notes in Archives of the Indies.

Pilgrims' Way

In early medieval times, Santiago de Compostela ranked with Rome or Jerusalem as an inspirational destination for pilgrims. Hundreds of thousands of the faithful used to do it every year, traditionally starting in France, crossing the Pyrenees and walking all across Spain to the Galician shrine of St. James. There were two main routes and several tributaries. Here are some notable stops on one of the most heavily travelled southerly routes; you don't have to walk it.

1 PUENTE LA REINA
Old walled town, Church of the Crucifix with medieval pilgrims' hospice.

2 ESTELLA
Romanesque churches and monasteries line pilgrim road (**"la Rúa"**).

3 NÁJERA
Ancient capital of Navarre; cliffside Santa María monastery.

4 SANTO DOMINGO DE LA CALZADA
Ramparted town. St. Dominic built a bridge here to ease travel travails of 11th-century pilgrims.

5 BURGOS
Magnificent cathedral, founded in early 13th century; nearby royal convent and monastery.

6 FRÓMISTA
11th-century Romanesque church, once linked to Benedictine monastery.

7 LEÓN
Modern city on important ancient site; Gothic cathedral glowing with stained glass.

8 ASTORGA
Museum of the Ways to Santiago occupies remarkable pseudo-medieval palace by Gaudí.

9 PONFERRADA
Iron mining town with views from Templars' Castle ruins.

10 CEBREIRO
Thatched village of Celtic origin; ancient church with holy relics.

11 PORTOMARÍN
Church of Knights of St. John dismantled and re-erected on present site.

12 VILAR DE DONAS
Frescoed church with tombs of knights fallen in battles with Moors.

13 SANTIAGO DE COMPOSTELA
End of the line: cathedral's Baroque façade and Romanesque door, pilgrim hospital founded by Ferdinand and Isabella, now an up-market hotel.

Pillars of Hercules

Marking the end of the known world, the Rock of Gibraltar and Ceuta, on the North African coast, were named by the ancients the Pillars of Hercules. History and prehistory left many traces here, where the Mediterranean and Atlantic meet.

1 CAPE TRAFALGAR
Site of great naval battle between Britain's Nelson and French Villeneuve in 1805.

2 PUNTA PALOMA
Northern terminal of proposed fixed link (bridge or tunnel) between Spain and Morocco.

3 TARIFA
Guzman the Good's 13th-century castle. Belvedere above town for best views across Strait of Gibraltar.

4 ALGECIRAS
Busy port with ferries for North Africa, and Arab-style market.

5 GIBRALTAR
European Pillar of Hercules, British territory. Landing point of Moorish invasion in A.D. 711.

6 CEUTA
North African Pillar of Hercules. Spanish enclave, duty-free port.

Artists

After you've seen the Prado, you can zero in on a favourite painter, tracking down his birthplace, his studio, or a specialized museum. In chronological order:

EL GRECO
In Toledo, the Casa de El Greco is claimed to have been the house where he lived. It's furnished with authentic 16th-century pieces. Also on show are several of his paintings.

GOYA
The birthplace, the village of Fuendetodos (Zaragoza), is far off the tourist track. The humble house is sparsely furnished; upstairs, reproductions of his works are displayed. The **Museo del Grabado de Goya**, Goya Engravings Museum, with 160 prints by the artist, is nearby.

SOROLLA
The Valencian impressionist Joaquín Sorolla (1863-1923) did much of his work in Madrid. His house at Paseo del General Martínez Campos 37 contains some 300 of his paintings.

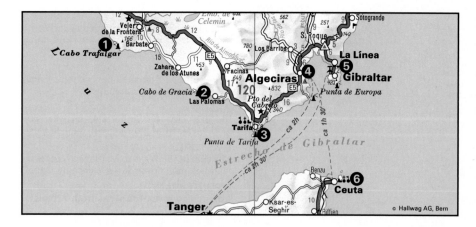

PICASSO

During the nine formative years he spent in Barcelona, Picasso lived rather more modestly than the conjunction of 13th-century palaces they've assigned his museum in Carrer de Montcada. An important collection of jottings and finished works from all his phases.

DALÍ

In Figueres, near the Costa Brava, Salvador Dalí converted a stately old theatre into a startling setting for his bizarre but brilliant whims. However, his house, overlooking the sea at Portlligat, is not open to the public.

For Children

Spaniards are famously affectionate toward children—anybody's children. They never seem to run out of ways of diverting their own youngsters, and neither will you. After the beaches have begun to pall, there are castles to explore, and palace gardens. On the lighter side, many amusements are accessible from cities and resorts. A random sampling:

MADRID

Casa de Campo park has thousands of acres of woodland interspersed with attractions like a swimming pool, sailing lake, funfair and zoo.

BARCELONA

Tibidabo's amusement park, with a roller coaster and other rides, is a favourite family destination, especially on Sundays. Near the port, Barcelona's zoo is a first-rate modern establishment.

SAFARI PARKS

Wildlife congregates within easy reach of beach resorts: for instance, Vergel and Elche, near the Costa Blanca; El Vendrell, Costa Dorada; and near Port Cristo, Majorca. There's also a safari park at Aldea del Fresno, near Madrid.

AQUAPARKS

Boundless variations on swimming pools, waterfalls, whirlpools, water slides. See Benidorm's Aqualand and Torremolinos's Atlantis Aquapark. (Benidorm has two amusement parks with rides and entertainment, Europa Park and Festilandia.)

JIJONA (Alicante)

Here's a sweet idea for a rainy day: factories producing Jijona's celebrated almond and honey treat, **turrón**, take visitors on tours.

Gaudí's Barcelona

The most significant of Barcelona's **art nouveau** architects of the late 19th and early 20th century, Antoni Gaudí left his visionary monuments all over town.

PALAU GÜELL

Just off the Ramblas, ironwork on façade and original rooftop chimney complex.

CASA CALVET

Unusual stairs and lift, from Gaudí's transitional, turn-of-century period.

CASA BATLLÓ

Sensuous curves on tiled apartment block in fashionable Passeig de Gràcia.

CASA MILÁ

"La Pedrera": undulating façade and fanciful "roof gardens" of chimneys and ventilators.

CASA VICENS

Early work; distinctive ironwork but incoherent style.

PARC GÜELL

Failed garden city development filled with Gaudí delights.

SAGRADA FAMILIA CHURCH

Wild and wonderful unfinished "sandcastle cathedral", still under construction.

PARC DE LA CIUTADELLA

Footnote: As a young student of architecture, Gaudí contributed to the design of the great fountain.

Parks and Gardens

The kings of Spain provided some, but not all, of the country's loveliest garden sanctuaries. Formal or unspoiled, the landscaping reaches great heights.

ARANJUEZ

The royal parks and gardens run from flower beds and clipped hedges to luxuriant forests.

LA GRANJA DE SAN ILDEFONSO

Thanks to French landscape gardeners, the province of Segovia enjoys a Versailles-style formal garden with lovely woodlands.

SEVILLE

Bordering the Guadalquivir, the Parque de María Luisa is another sample of French expertise, this time on the flat.

BLANES (Gerona)
Marimurtra, overlooking the Mediterranean, is a collection of 3,000 species of trees, shrubs and flowers.

GRANADA
The Moors left their mark on Spanish gardening, nowhere more profoundly than in the refreshing terraced gardens of the Alhambra and the Generalife.

TENERIFE
Founded in the 18th century, the Botanical Garden (officially called the Jardín de Aclimatación) is a cool green tropical forest.

Conquistadores

Nearly all the famous Conquistadores, who colonized the western hemisphere, came from the same striking, isolated province: Estremadura. The town of Trujillo alone, it's been said, conceived 20 American nations. The Conquistadores took overseas an old Estremadura tradition of intensely religious, intrepid knights. But some joined the adventure to escape poverty. A voyage to the roots of the conquerors:

1 GUADALUPE
Shrine of "Spanishness"; the conquerors dedicated their exploits to the Virgin of Guadalupe.

2 MEDELLÍN
Birthplace, in 1485, of Hernán Cortés, conqueror of Mexico.

3 TRUJILLO
Home of the Pizarro family (Peru and Ecuador) and of Francisco Orellana, explorer of the Amazon.

4 CÁCERES
Returning colonists invested their gold in mansions here.

5 MÉRIDA
Monument-strewn ancient Roman provincial capital; perhaps an inspiration for later empire builders?

6 BADAJOZ
Birthplace of Pedro de Alvarado, aide of Cortés and cruel conqueror of Guatemala.

7 JEREZ DE LOS CABALLEROS
Home of Vasco Nuñez de Balboa ("discoverer" of the Pacific) and Hernando de Soto, explorer of the Mississippi.

Nostalgia

The sentimental traveller can pursue the past in present-day Spain, where they still make swords, folding fans, illustrated glazed tiles, wrought iron grillwork, and classical saddles. To track down the best

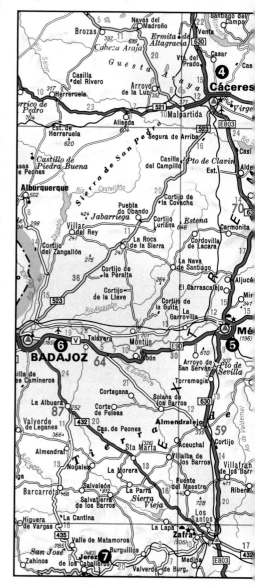

44

examples of the originals, look for the specialized museums:

MADRID

The Museo Romántico, Calle de San Mateo, 13, has furniture, art and knickknacks recalling the era of swooning señoritas and their eagle-eyed chaperones.

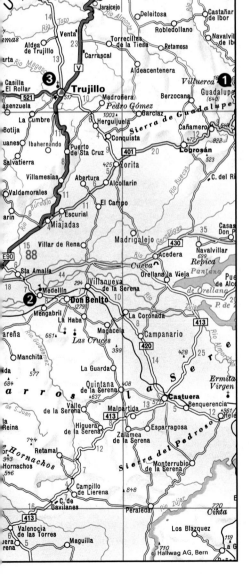

SITGES (Barcelona)

In an old mansion, the Museu Romàntic shows 19th-century furniture, clocks, and music boxes that work.

ARANJUEZ

In the Royal Palace, the Museum of Court Dress displays the costumes worn by Spain's kings and queens from the 16th to 20th century. A children's room contains royal cradles, cribs and a rocking horse.

SILS (Gerona)

The Colecció d'Automòbils de Salvador Claret is a stable of 80 antique cars in working order, going back to an 1883 single-cylinder coal-burner.

BARCELONA

Tibidabo's Museu d'Autòmats is a museum devoted to 19th-century mechanical toys and dolls.

Golf

For abundance and variety of courses and quality of instruction, golfers would be hard pressed to find a holiday destination to outdo Spain. Thanks to its climate, the Costa del Sol is the nation's golfing capital. The Madrid area and the east coast are also strongholds of the game. And in deepest winter, golfers find springtime in the Canary Islands. Of the more than 90 courses around the country, here are a few that are special.

GOLF EL PARAÍSO

Estepona (Málaga): Gary Player is credited as co-designer of this 18-hole layout.

CLUB DE CAMPO DE MÁLAGA (Málaga)

Fine old 18-hole course with its own small **parador**.

REAL GOLF DE PEDREÑA (Santander)

Severiano Ballesteros caddied here as a boy.

HERRERÍA CLUB DE GOLF

San Lorenzo del Escorial (Madrid): Alongside the majestic 16th-century Escorial palace.

CAMP DE GOLF EL SALER (Valencia)

A government-run *parador* abuts this admirable 18-hole course.

CLUB DE GOLF DE LAS PALMAS (Gran Canaria)

Spain's oldest golf club (1891), alongside an extinct volcano.

Cities Behind Walls

From the establishment of Jericho to the development of mobile artillery, walled cities enjoyed invulnerability. Marauders of all kinds, pirates or hostile armies, tended to keep their distance. Partial remains of city walls—gateways or fortifications—can still be found in many parts of Spain. But several walled cities are still impressively intact.

ÁVILA
Local publicists call Ávila "best-walled city in the world"; storybook fortifications have a circumference of about 2½ km. (a mile and a half).

CÁCERES
Ramparts surround attractive complex of weathered stone mansions and churches.

CIUDAD RODRIGO
Hilltop town with medieval wall more than two km. (over a mile) around; sentry path still walkable.

LUGO
Romans built the original city wall, often destroyed and rebuilt thereafter.

NIEBLA
Somewhat dilapidated but nonetheless formidable walls encircle old Andalusian town.

Offbeat Museums

Spain's art museums, starting with the great Prado, could keep you busy for weeks. But for a change of perspective, drop in on one of the country's more unconventional museums:

ETHNOGRAPHY
Málaga's Museo de Artes Populares, in a historic 17th-century inn, contains folk art, an old forge, bakery and print shop.

WINE
In the wine museum in Vilafranca del Penedès you can see a 2,000-year-old wine press, and glasses, bottles and jugs that quenched centuries of thirst.

BULLS
Córdoba's Museo Municipal Taurino has souvenirs of famous matadors—swords, capes, costumes, photos, posters.

UNDERTAKINGS
Barcelona's Funeral Museum (Sancho de Ávila, 2) displays two hundred or so years of fashions in hearses and mortuary relics.

CARDS
In Vitoria-Gasteiz (Álava), the Provincial Fine Arts Museum contains the definitive collection of playing cards.

MONEY
On the top floor of Madrid's Fábrica Nacional de Moneda y Timbre (the mint) is a money museum with 25,000 exhibits. You don't have to be a numismatist to catch the significance of the vibration of the great presses downstairs, manufacturing millions of pesetas.

Paradores

Demobilized castles, unemployed palaces and former monasteries are among the buildings that have taken on new life as **paradores**, government-run hotels. Begun under Alfonso XIII, the network is now so well developed that you're rarely more than a couple of hours' drive from the next parador. Not all the buildings can boast historical credentials; the modern ones usually make up for this failure with a view that's worth the visit in itself.

A few typical addresses, from coast to coast, from mid-priced to most luxurious:

SANTIAGO DE COMPOSTELA
The five-star Hotel Los Reyes Católicos was founded as the royal hospital for pilgrims in 1499. The altogether splendid building, in the shadow of the cathedral, is crammed with works of art.

*F*erdinand and Isabella established this inn for pilgrims reaching Santiago de Compostela. Now even tourists can stay here, expensively but unforgettably, in one of Spain's proudest paradores.

BENICARLÒ (Castellón)
A modern, air-conditioned, three-star hotel in a fishing village; a gardened refuge from the tourist crescendo nearby.

LEÓN
A 16th-century convent on the pilgrim way, now a 246-room hotel rated five stars plus. Behind the glorious Plateresque façade remains a church; the Chapterhouse is now an archaeological museum.

GUADALUPE (Cáceres)
Roomy, tranquil three-star comfort in what began as a medieval hospital across the street from the famous monastery. Ferdinand and Isabella slept here.

SIGÜENZA (Guadalajara)
This haughty crenellated castle was a Moorish fortress before the Reconquest, an episcopal palace after. It has 79 four-star rooms and a grand patio suitable for concerts.

GRANADA
You can't get closer to the majestic Alhambra. Soon after the Reconquest of Granada the Catholic Monarchs founded a convent within the Alhambra complex. Now it's a four-star hotel.

In the Footsteps of El Cid

Rodrigo Diaz, an 11th-century soldier of fortune, was immortalized as the knight El Cid. His exploits as a valiant free-lance warrior won a permanent place in Spanish hearts. From Castile to the Mediterranean, many a town and village along the back roads holds memories of the great man.

Beginnings

1 BURGOS
El Cid is buried in the superb cathedral here, only a few miles south of his birthplace, Vivar del Cid.

2 QUINTANILLA DE LAS VIÑAS
Predating El Cid, remains of church of Santa María de Lara has extraordinary Visigothic carvings.

3 HORTIGUELA
Alongside the River Arlanza, the ruins of a monastery begun in days of El Cid.

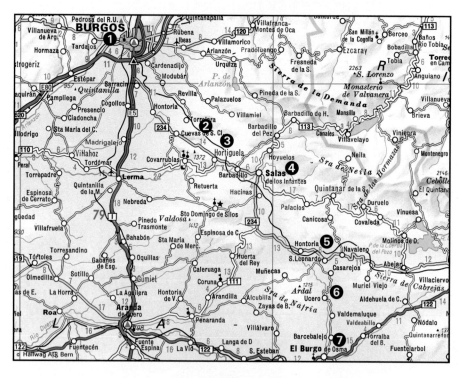

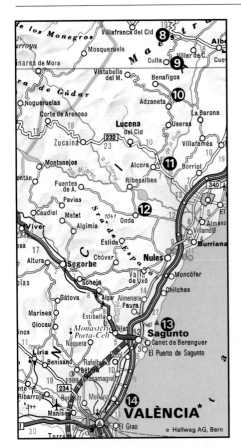

10 ADZANETA
Candle-making village; Moorish ruins.

11 ALCORA
Castle of Alcalaten overlooks this town, known for artistic ceramics production.

12 ONDA
Remains of "300-towered" Moorish castle; Romanesque-Gothic church; pottery-making centre.

13 SAGUNTO
Ancient ruins mark heroic town where Hannibal kicked off the Second Punic War.

14 VALENCIA
El Cid, who captured the city from the Moors and became Duke of Valencia, died here in 1099. Splendid medieval buildings.

Jewish Spain

In the Middle Ages Spain's Jewish community contributed considerably to the national culture. Jewish scientists, philosophers, financiers and administrators made their mark, and in certain epochs relations were good with their Christian and Moslem neighbours. After the expulsion of the Jews in 1492 little was left to commemorate the Jewish Golden Age, yet there are traces all over the country.

GALICIA
Best preserved Jewish quarter is in the untouristy town of Ribadavia. In Orense, the former **aljama** was centred on the present Rua Nova.

SEGOVIA
Old Jewish quarter is near the city ramparts; among the streets: Calle de la Judería Vieja (Street of the Old Jewish Quarter).

TUDELA
In what was Navarre's biggest medieval Jewish centre, relics of the synagogue are found in the Romanesque cloister of Tudela's cathedral.

CATALONIA
The heart of medieval Jewish life was in the narrow streets around Barcelona's Carrer del Call. In Gerona, the **Isaac el Cec** (the Blind) Centre, a restored Jewish home, shows exhibitions on Sephardic life.

MAJORCA
There are Jewish relics in Palma cathedral; the great Majorcan mapmakers of the middle ages were Jews.

4 SALAS DE LOS INFANTES
Village named after seven brothers and sisters supposedly slain by Moors.

5 SAN LEONARDO DE YAGÜE
Verdant summer resort village lost in mountainous region.

6 UCERO
Near spectacular Lobos River Canyon, ruins of a castle of the Knights Templar.

7 EL BURGO DE OSMA
In this attractive old town, see the stately Gothic cathedral, where a manuscript of El Cid saga was discovered.

To the Sea
8 VILLAFRANCA DEL CID
As village name implies, El Cid slept here. See the 16th-century parish church.

9 CULLA
Former Templar capital; fine views from ruins of Arab castle on hilltop.

49

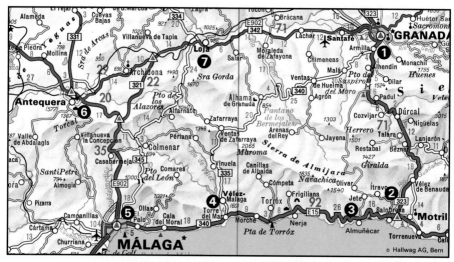

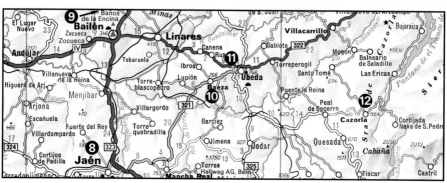

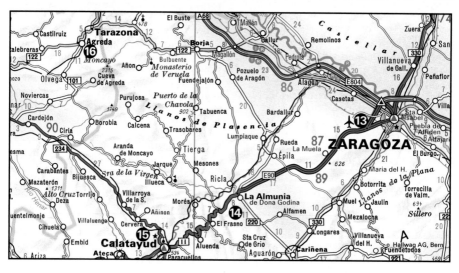

50

TOLEDO
Alfonso the Wise had many Jews in his entourage. See two beautifully decorated former synagogues, El Tránsito and Santa María la Blanca.

CÓRDOBA
In the Old Jewish quarter, northwest of the cathedral, look for a 14th-century synagogue.

SEVILLE
The old Jewish quarter is now called the Barrio de Santa Cruz; four old churches once were synagogues.

Moslem Spain

For nearly eight centuries the Moors ruled at least part of Spain. The artistic and architectural legacy is remarkably widespread. The best known, most grandiose monuments are in the south—Córdoba, Granada and Seville, for instance. Beyond those obvious destinations, interesting relics of the Moorish era can also be found in some lesser-known pockets.

From Granada to the Sea

1 GRANADA
Greatest glory of Moorish Spain deserves a week, but Alcázar, Alhambra and Generalife can be rushed in a day.

2 SALOBREÑA
Street plan and old castle remain as reminders of Arab rule.

3 ALMUÑECAR
Busy resort with Arab name and history.

4 VÉLEZ-MÁLAGA
Remains of an important Moorish castle; Santa María church replaced a mosque.

5 MÁLAGA
Alcazaba fort dates from 11th century, adjoining Gibralfaro ramparts from 14th.

6 ANTEQUERA
Fine view from ruins of fortress much fought over during Reconquest.

7 LOJA
Gateway to Alcazaba still stands; fort was key to Moors' defence of Granada.

Northern Andalusia

8 JAÉN
Once capital of a Moorish kingdom; Ali's Bath dates from 11th century.

9 BAÑOS DE LA ENCINA
Bristling 10th-century Moorish castle tops the town.

10 BAEZA
Town clock stands on Tower of the Aliatares, recalling Arab rulers.

11 UBEDA
Amidst elegant Renaissance palaces, traces of Moorish fortifications and houses.

12 CAZORLA
Moors held out in this dramatically sited mountain redoubt for eight centuries.

Around Zaragoza

13 ZARAGOZA
Once capital of a Moorish kingdom, city's main relic is elaborate Aljafería palace.

14 LA ALUMNIA DE DOÑA GODINA
Remains of Moorish fortifications visible.

15 CALATAYUD
City founded soon after Moorish invasion; 9th-century ramparts remain.

16 AGREDA
See 10th-century gateway and parts of defensive walls.

Traces of the Romans

In many parts of Spain, from the east coast to Estremadura, the legacy of the ancient Romans who colonized Iberia is visible in everlasting monuments. Some are still in use. A few of the highlights:

ALCÁNTARA
The drystone bridge over the Río Tajo just outside Alcántara (Cáceres) dates from around A.D. 100.

AMPURIAS
Roman enclave on the Costa Brava, overlooking remains of a Greek town. Wander through the old forum, ruins of shops and apartments.

CÓRDOBA
Birthplace of the Seneca family. With so many monuments from the Moorish caliphate, you could miss the Roman Bridge across the Guadalquivir.

ITÁLICA
Just outside Seville, this archaeological site contains the ruins of a huge Roman amphitheatre, a forum and some mosaics.

MÉRIDA
The old capital of Roman Lusitania is strewn with stately monuments, from an arena for 14,000 spectators to a couple of bridges. The National Museum of Roman Art is here.

SEGOVIA
Engineers, architects and sightseers marvel over Segovia's Roman aqueduct, still supplying some of the city's water.

TARRAGONA
Former capital of Rome's biggest Spanish province, Tarragona has an amphitheatre, a forum, an archaeological promenade and an important museum.

SANTIAGO DE COMPOSTELA
Behind the famous Baroque façade, a precious Romanesque doorway.

SEGOVIA
Last of the great Spanish Gothic cathedrals (begun 1525).

SEVILLE
World's third largest Gothic church, with minaret for bell tower.

TOLEDO
Gothic heart with centuries of adornments and innovations.

VALENCIA
Medieval glory beautifully supplemented by later styles.

Ten Best Cathedrals

Generations of architects, stonecutters and artists collaborated on the cathedrals of Spain. In many cases the results are superlative, for the originality of design, the unexpected combinations of style, the genius evident in the sculpture and painting. From Romanesque to neo-Gothic, from the manipulation of received ideas to wholly new departures, there's no end to the innovation. Every one of these cathedrals is quite different from every other.

BARCELONA
Catalan Gothic grace with 19th-century amendments.

BURGOS
Splendid spires top this complicated complex filled with art treasures.

LÉON
Gothic classic with uniquely vast expanse of stained glass.

MURCIA
Lovely Baroque façade on 14th-century Gothic building on ruins of mosque.

SALAMANCA
Old and new cathedrals link 12th through 18th centuries.

Royal Palaces

Among Spain's outstanding monuments are royal palaces built by storied kings, for official pomp or merely relaxation. Some of the palaces with wall-to-wall history:

ARANJUEZ
Country palace begun in 16th century surrounded by delightful parks and formal gardens.

EL ESCORIAL
Enormous Spanish Renaissance monument west of Madrid, Built by order of Philip II, who died there in 1598.

GRANADA
Charles V turned up his imperial nose at Moorish palaces all around and built a Renaissance residence in the middle of the Alcázar.

LA GRANJA DE SAN ILDEFONSO
French landscape gardeners contrived Versailles-style gardens for Philip V; they're more memorable than the palace itself.

ROYAL PALACE (Madrid)
Eighteenth-century complex in the heart of the capital, still used for official functions.

TORDESILLAS
Medieval palace converted to a convent, where Juana the Mad spent lonely years.

Generations of stonemasons, sculptors and artists in glass created the solemn statement of Toledo's cathedral, a work-in-progress since the 13th century.

White Villages of Andalusia

The whitewalled villages of mountainous southern Spain are the picturesque legacy of Moorish urban planning. A tour can be a handy escape from an overdose of the Costa del Sol.

Above the Marbella coast

1 MIJAS
Quintessential whitewashed village, now devoted to serving tourism.

2 ALHAURÍN
Historic church built on Moorish foundations.

3 MONDA
Reputed site of battle between Julius Caesar and rival Pompey the Great.

4 RONDA
Distinguished old town in amazing setting, straddling awesome ravine.

5 ATAJATE
Moorish tower atop this village, surrounded by olive groves and vineyards.

6 ALGATOCÍN
Steeply sloping white village.

7 GAUCÍN
Appealing ridgetop village with ruined castle, much contested in Reconquest.

8 JIMENA DE LA FRONTERA
Hill town with Moorish castle, Gothic and Baroque churches.

9 CASTELLAR DE LA FRONTERA
Artisans at work in medieval core of town.

10 CASARES
White village spiralling up to a rugged hilltop with sweeping views.

Beyond Cádiz

11 EL PUERTO DE SANTA MARÍA
Sherry shipping town with Moorish castle; Washington Irving lived here.

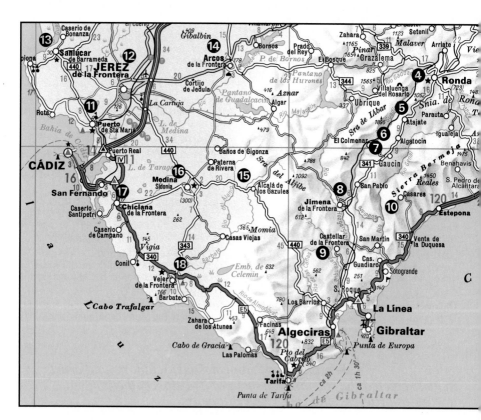

12 JEREZ DE LA FRONTERA
Birthplace of sherry and centre of horse breeding and training.

13 SANLÚCAR DE BARRAMEDA
Wine-producing fishing port, home of sherry-like Manzanilla.

14 ARCOS DE LA FRONTERA
Cliff-perched, one of region's most beautiful white villages.

15 ALCALÁ DE LOS GAZULES
On hilltop beneath Sierra del Algibe, Moorish street plan still visible.

16 MEDINA SIDONIA
Beautifully situated town with fine Gothic church built atop ruins of castle.

17 CHICLANA DE LA FRONTERA
Traditional fishing village with expansive Atlantic beaches.

18 VEJER DE LA FRONTERA
Classic white town on a lonely hilltop; 13th-century church built on remains of mosque.

© Hallwag AG, Bern

Cell for a Night

For spiritual uplift, or merely for an unusual experience, you can choose to spend a night or a week or more in a Spanish monastery. Many a historic monastery has guest accommodation. Among the highspots to contemplate:

BURGOS
Huelgas Reales Convent. Former royal palace, a convent since 12th century. Married couples or women only.

SANTO DOMINGO DE SILOS
Rebuilt in 11th century; splendid Romanesque cloister. Comfortable room and board; men only.

CATALONIA
Montserrat monastery. Spiritual heart of Catalonia. Some accommodation inside the abbey, hotels nearby for the overflow.

LA CORUÑA
Sobrado de los Monjes. Baroque church and medieval elements. Cistercians here have accommodation for men only.

ESTREMADURA
Guadalupe monastery. A two-star hotel is attached to the famous monastery, from which Conquistadores went to America.

NAVARRE
La Oliva Monastery, Carcastillo. Simple mixed accommodation is available in this 12th-century Cistersian institution.

Spas

Both the Romans and the Arabs, who gave so much to Spanish culture, were enthusiasts of thermal baths. Mineral waters for every taste and therapeutic prescription bubble forth from hundreds of springs all over the country. Dozens of these have been turned into spas. The tourist authorities issue a comprehensive map, **Guía de Balnearios**, with all the details. In provincial alphabetical order, here's a glance at the variety of places in Spain where you can "take the cure".

LA CORUÑA
Baños Viejos de Carballo, Carballo. Modern installation on site of baths first exploited by the Romans.

GERONA
Vichy Catalan, Caldas de Malavella. The well-known water is bottled here and sold all over; the spa offers everything from mud baths to inhalations.

GRANADA
Alicun de las Torres, Villanueva de las Torres. In beautiful hill country north-east of Granada, all the medicinal facilities in a relaxed atmosphere.

HUESCA
Panticosa. High in the beauty of the snowy Pyrenees near the French border, a spa dates back to the early 19th century.

LÉRIDA
Caldas de Bohí. Luxury resort atmosphere for "taking the waters", hot and cold, in grand style in the Pyrenees.

PONTEVEDRA
La Toja island. Since the turn of the century a luxury resort has exploited the curative waters of this charming little island.

ZARAGOZA
Martínez, Alhama de Aragón. Therapy and history in hot springs developed by the Romans, rediscovered by the Moors.

In Quest of Quixote

Miguel de Cervantes, who wrote the world's best-selling novel, knew well the vanishing horizons and looming windmills of moody La Mancha. He made the most of it as the background for the exploits of his immortal fictional hero, Don Quixote. Some of the villages along the way shimmer with memories. Scholars could point you to dozens of places with Quixote connections, but here are nine:

1 ARGAMASILLA DE ALBA
Cervantes began writing the book in this Ciudad Real village. A local dignitary is said to have inspired the character of the knight errant.

2 TOMELLOSO
Wine bottling town. Nearby Peñarroyo castle was setting for a Quixote adventure.

3 MOTA DEL CUERVO
Castle ruins and windmills to suggest Quixote country.

4 EL TOBOSO
Charming home town of Quixote's ideal woman, Dulcinea. "Dulcinea's house" museum.

5 CAMPO DE CRIPTANA
Some more typical windmills at which the knight may have tilted.

6 ALCÁZAR DE SAN JUAN
Old castle marks this market town; Quixote and Sancho Panza slept here.

7 CONSUEGRA
Rebuilt windmills and a castle on the local skyline.

8 PUERTO LÁPICE
Here Quixote was supposedly knighted by the local innkeeper.

9 ALCALA DE HENARES
Birthplaces (1547) of Cervantes, now an industrial city.

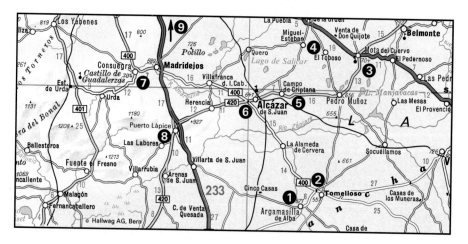

Wandering in the Pyrenees

After a few days on the beach, or in a busy city, you may be ready for some mountain scenery, fresh air and quiet. Here's one of many possible itineraries in the Pyrenees of Catalonia. You can drive around this picturesque region of peaks, gorges and waterfalls, getting out to walk when you feel energetic. It's also a winter sports area.

1 BELLVER DE CERDANYA
Quaint rocktop village overlooking Segre Valley.

2 LLES
Dramatic views from winding approach road.

3 SEU D'URGELL
Former princely city with 12th-century cathedral.

4 ANDORRA
Pop across the border into this tiny Catalan-speaking principality of duty-free shopping, isolated hamlets and posh ski resorts.

5 COLL DE NARGÓ
Near Grau de la Granta, a lake dramatically confined by cliffs.

6 BÓIXOLS
Impressive scenery around pass leading to tiny village. Caution: steep roads.

7 NOGUERA PALLARESA VALLEY
Scenic route past towering cliffs and salt beds towards more verdant mountains.

8 SORT
Turn left for Llessui Valley, lovely site for winter sports centre.

9 RIBERA DE CARDÓS
Beauty-spot resort with trout fishing.

10 ESPOT
Entrance village to Aigües Tortes national park. From here you need a four-wheel drive cross-country vehicle.

National Parks

After the traffic jams of Madrid and the teeming beaches of the **Costas** you may be ready for some wide open spaces. The escape road can lead to Spain's national parks. For instance:

PARQUE NACIONAL DOÑANA
Bordering the underexploited Costa de la Luz, this vast wildlife refuge comprises marshes, dunes and pine forests as well as beaches. Among honoured guests: more than 250 species of birds, local or in transit.

PICOS DE EUROPA
Mount Covadonga National Park, high in the Cantabrian mountains, has spectacular rugged scenery and rare flora and fauna thriving under official protection.

PARQUE NACIONAL DE ORDESA
Rubbing high shoulders with a French national park across the mountain peaks, Ordesa is called the last refuge of the Pyrenees chamois. Another superlative is the scenery, surrounding a gaping glacial canyon.

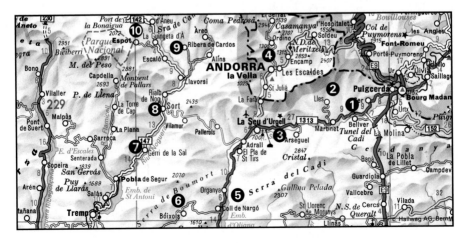

PARQUE NACIONAL DE AIGÜES TORTES Y SAN MAURICIO

In the Pyrenees of Catalonia the peaks go up to 3,000 metres (nearly 10,000 feet). The melting snow provides a wondrous scene of waterfalls, mountain lakes and fertile valleys.

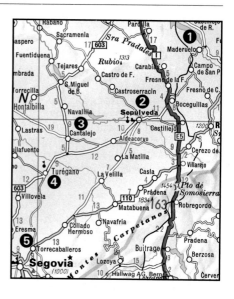

Romanesque Art

In the 11th and 12th centuries a new concept of art and architecture, now called Romanesque, swept Spain. The pinnacle of this achievement is the cathedral of Santiago de Compostela. At the other side of the country, Catalonia is especially well endowed with Romanesque churches and monasteries, and Barcelona's Museu d'Art de Catalunya is a treasurehouse. Among lesser known pockets of Romanesque culture, here are ten suggestions—five each in Aragon and Castile. A few are hard to get to via mountain roads, a sure way to avoid the crowds.

Aragon

1 JACA
11th-century cathedral inspired Road to Santiago architects and artists.

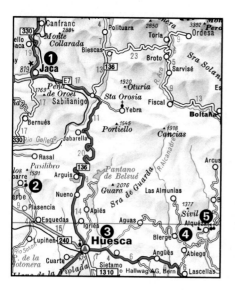

2 LOARRE
Lovely Romanesque church alongside royal castle, a mountain fortress.

3 HUESCA
Evocative stonework in cloister of old monastery of San Pedro el Viejo.

4 BIERGE
Obscure village with Romanesque church.

5 ALQUÉZAR
12th-century castle and remains of Romanesque cloister.

Castile

1 MADERUELO
Two Romanesque churches in hilltop village.

2 SEPÚLVEDA
San Salvador church, dominating hill site, is most original of town's Romanesque churches.

3 CANTALEJO
Romanesque priory north-east of here, but road is difficult.

4 TURÉGANO
Romanesque church overshadowed by one-time castle of bishops of Segovia.

5 SEGOVIA
Romanesque churches of St. Stephen, St. Martin, St. Lawrence, San Juan de los Caballeros—not to mention Roman aqueduct, medieval castle and Gothic cathedral.

Volcanoes of the Canaries

Calling all vulcanophiles! The Canary Islands, seven products of volcanic eruptions under the Atlantic, have everything from huge craters to lava beaches. Lanzarote alone is pockmarked with more than 300 volcanic cones. A few infernal highlights, from west to east:

1 EL HIERRO
El Golfo, on the northwest coast, is one large crater, half submerged.

2 LA PALMA
Caldera de Taburiente national park, possibly world's largest crater, fortunately long extinct.

3 GOMERA
Los Organos, seaside cliffs of volcano-produced basalt columns.

4 TENERIFE
Mount Teide, Canaries' snow-capped summit, dormant since 17th century; Cañadas national park, hills of stratified lava.

5 GRAN CANARIA
Bandama Crater, tamed extinct volcano now peaceful farmland.

6 LANZAROTE
Fire Mountains excursions with barbecues over volcanic fire; Los Verdes cave created by exploding lava.

Caveman's Majorca

The rocky coasts of the eastern Balearic islands are riddled with caverns, some of which were inhabited by prehistoric folk. Nowadays there are guided tours.

1 GÉNOVA GROTTO
Just southwest of Palma de Mallorca, small caves are theatrically lit.

2 CUEVAS DEL DRACH
Popular guided tour of "dragon caves" ends in **son et lumière** show at underground lake.

3 CUEVAS DE HAMS
Small caves show nature in a delicate, whimsical mood.

4 CUEVAS DE ARTÁ
Massive opening in seaside cliff-face leads to complex which inspired Jules Verne.

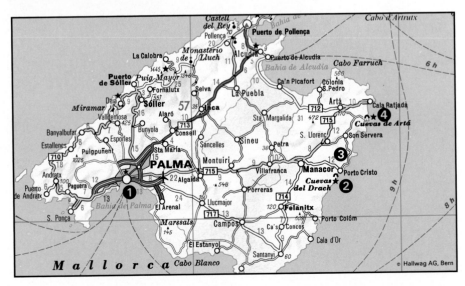

59

Capital at the Crossroads

In Europe's highest capital city it's not the altitude that takes your breath away, but the pace. As if the business of politics, government and industry weren't responsibility enough, Madrid claims the crown for culture in all its realms, from fine arts to fashion. Somehow, under all the pressure, the *joie de vivre* thrives. You have nothing to lose but your sleep.

At the geographical heart of Spain, Madrid's altitude—more than 640 m. (2,100 ft.)—and the mountain breezes generate a unique atmosphere. The city is alive with light, the sunshine filtering down through a pale sky barely dense enough to float a cloud on. Velázquez didn't invent these skies, he just painted what he saw.

When the sun goes down, Madrid comes into its own. See the *Madrileños* cramming the promenades and outdoor cafés at the hour of the *paseo*. So starts

Under a sky Velázquez might have painted, Madrid's 18th-century Royal Palace looks onto lavish gardens.
Guided tours inspect the state apartments, except when royal ceremonies take precedence.

Europe's longest evening, for the "night people" of Madrid dine very late and play even later. It's a puzzle how they manage to go to work in the morning.

Madrid's elevation from obscurity to capital power in the 16th century was conceived in political compromise. However artificial its rise, the city has grown into a natural success as a dynamic international metropolis with an instantly recognizable character of its own. You'll never have time enough to see all its facets, human, historical, religious, architectural or artistic.

At the crossroads of Spain, the centre of Madrid is "Kilometre 0" for all the radial highways. On the Castilian plateau beyond the built-up area, some of the most wondrous sights in the whole country are within day-trip distance. Give top priority to Toledo, a former capital set on a crag, with haunting memories of El Greco and with all Spain built into its houses and churches. Don't miss Segovia, a royal stronghold with a fairy tale castle and classic Roman aqueduct. Tour the ancient walled city of saints, Ávila. Closer to Madrid, see El Escorial, the monastery, college and palace that sums up Spain's Golden Age.

61

Madrid

15 D2

They've made it easy to find your way around Madrid. Outside every metro (underground/subway) station stands an oversized city map. Signs at bus stops explain where you're going and where the buses are coming from. The streets are clearly identified, often wittily with illustrated wall tiles.

The streets are washed every morning before the shrill traffic jams begin. (All the clatter and shriek makes this one of Europe's noisiest cities.) But early-morning Madrid sounds old-fashioned and neighbourly. An itinerant knife-sharpener advertises his trade on a Pan-style flute. A gypsy junk-collector walking beside his donkey-cart chants his call. A grinding, tortured roar from a café means the espresso machine is boiling milk for coffee. Europe's most sleepless people, the *Madrileños*, are loping off to work again, only six hours after another late night out.

Madrid and its people run to extremes. Perhaps it has to do with the weather, which is usually either too cold or too hot (roughly one third of the population flees Madrid every August). *Madrileños* seem to be bubbling one moment and sulking the next. They go to church, but they go to X-rated amusements, too. They may bemoan the rush of modern life, but they find time to sit over coffee for an hour in a *tertulia*, an informal conversation club, discussing literature or football... or the rush of modern life.

Since there's so much to see in this city of more than three million inhabitants you'll have to divide it geographically or chronologically (Medieval, Hapsburg, Bourbon, Romantic or Modern Madrid). But you really ought to start by savouring the oldest part of the city, on foot, in the heart of the original Madrid.

Old Madrid

Little is left of medieval Madrid except the mood. You feel it in the narrow streets that meander south from the Calle

The Luck of the Draw

From the Puerta del Sol to the farthest village of Spain, the regular lotteries are a subject of daily interest. Once a year, though, the luck of the draw brings virtually the entire nation to a halt for a couple of hours. Many billions of pesetas are at stake in the Christmas lottery, *El Gordo*—"the Fat One". Radio and TV provide endless, live coverage as angelic-looking school children draw hundreds of lucky and luckier numbers. *El Gordo* magically enriches many small investors, often people of humble background. The big killing can transform a group of drinking buddies into a clutch of millionaires. It's such a breathtaking drama that even the serious newspapers devote page after page to photos and interviews with the delirious winners. And, of course, they print the two-page official chart of every last winning number. So the small winners and the losers can study the form while waiting for next year's miracle.

Mayor (Main Street). Dimly lit shops sell religious habits, military medals, books, berets, capes and cheeses. Artisans chip away at their woodwork. A beggar-woman, holding somebody else's baby, asks for a coin. A greengrocer builds a tomato pyramid. A blind lottery-ticket salesman, tapping his white cane to attract attention, recites a poem promising instant riches.

Vendors on foot and in kiosks sell several varieties of lottery tickets around the **Puerta del Sol** (Gate of the Sun), the hub of ten converging streets. The plaza is also a hotbed of pinball palaces jangling with electronic and jackpot machines. For centuries this has been the city's nerve centre. Facing all the plaza's bustle is a statue based on Madrid's coat of arms, showing a bear standing against a *madroño* tree (an arbutus, or strawberry tree). This same bear is seen as a symbol all over Madrid—look on the doors of taxis.

The **Plaza Mayor** (Main Square), a few blocks away, is a 17th-century architectural symphony in bold but balanced tones. Broad arcades surround a vast cobbled rectangle. Plaza Mayor may be entered from all four sides through any of nine archways, but mercifully not by motor vehicles. In the past, this was the scene of pageants, bullfights, even executions; residents disposing of one of the more than 400 balconies overlooking the square used to sell tickets for such events. A statue of King Philip III occupies the place of honour but is no obstacle to events ranging from pop concerts to theatre festivals. Take a seat at one of the outdoor cafés in the square and enjoy the perfect proportions of Madrid's most elegant architectural ensemble.

Farther along Calle Mayor, the old Plaza de la Villa juxtaposes stately 16th- and 17th-century buildings of varied style. The **Casa de Cisneros**, built in the mid-16th century by a nephew of the intrepid inquisitor, Cardinal Cisneros, belongs to the fine, intricate style of architecture known as Plateresque. The style is so called because it seems as delicate as a silversmith's work (*platero* means silversmith). The **Ayuntamiento** (City Hall) represents the Hapsburg era, with the towers and slate spires characteristic of the 17th-century official buildings all around the capital.

Although there are more than 200 churches in Madrid, very few could be classified among the essential tourist attractions. The city is too young to have a great medieval cathedral. The present (provisional) cathedral in Calle de Toledo, the **Catedral de San Isidro,** needed a lot of rebuilding; it was badly damaged during the Civil War. Under its massive dome, among many relics, are the revered remains of the city's patron saint, San Isidro Labrador (St. Isidore the Husbandman).

Just down Calle de Toledo from the cathedral is the site of the **Rastro,** Madrid's phenomenal Sunday flea market.

A formidable Madrid church of the mid-18th century is the **Basílica de San Francisco el Grande,** dedicated to St. Francis of Assisi. The curved neoclassical façade somewhat curtails the effect of the church's most superlative feature. Once inside, you'll realize that the dome is out of the ordinary. Indeed, its inner diameter exceeds that of the cupolas of St. Paul's of London or Les Invalides in Paris. Imposing statues of the apostles in white Carrara marble surround the rotunda. Seven richly ornamented chapels fan out from the centre. In the chapel of San Bernardino de Siena, notice the large painting above the altar. In this lively scene by Francisco de Goya, the second figure from the right, dressed in yellow, is said to be a self-portrait.

Central Madrid

Plaza de la Cibeles would be perfect were it not for the intensity of the traffic, vehemently directed by pony-tailed policewomen. The fountain in the centre shows Cybele, a controversial Greek fertility

Sunday in Madrid

Some cities sag through sedate Sundays. Not Madrid. Try to take in the sabbatical excitement.

The Rastro. On Sunday mornings, the streets of old Madrid, beginning just south of the cathedral, are transformed into one of Europe's biggest flea markets. Tens of thousands of bargain-minded *Madrileños* join the out-of-towners in pricing clothing, antiques, pots and pans, and junk of all sorts. Care to buy a used gas mask?

Puerta de Toledo. The bait at the former central fish market is a bright collection of shops and galleries featuring antiques, art, fashion, handicrafts... and a restaurant and cafés. (Open Tuesdays to Sundays.)

The Stamp Market. Hundreds of collectors assemble in the Plaza Mayor on Sunday mornings to buy and sell stamps, coins, banknotes, cigar bands, and even used lottery tickets.

The Book Fair. Just south of the Botanical Garden, the bibliophiles throng to open-air stalls along Calle de Claudio Moyano. New and used books bought and sold: trashy novels, comics, foreign fiction and valuable old tomes.

So much for the morning. After drinks, snacks and, of course, lunch, you'll have to decide whether to watch Real Madrid play football, go to a bullfight, or follow the horses at the Zarzuela Hippodrome.

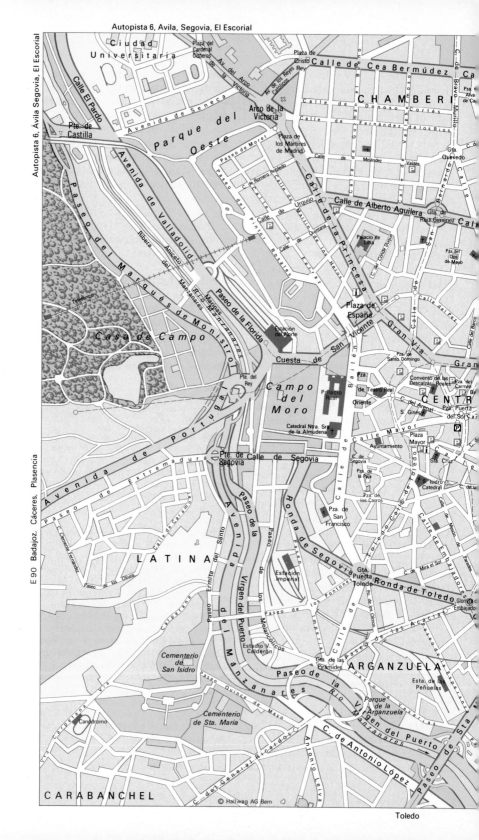

MADRID

goddess, serenely settled in a chariot pulled by two lions. The sculptural ensemble is probably the best-known fountain in all Spain.

The most unavoidable building on the plaza is the cathedral-like Palacio de Comunicaciones, sarcastically nicknamed "Our Lady of Communications". This ponderous post office was inaugurated in 1919. Across the square, the Army headquarters coyly camouflages itself behind century-old iron railings and an enviable garden dotted with statues of scantily clad nymphs.

Also facing Plaza de la Cibeles, the headquarters of the Bank of Spain combines neoclassic, Baroque and Rococo styles. It looks reassuringly solid enough to take care of the nation's money. The financial district, Madrid's "City" or "Wall Street", begins here along **Calle de Alcalá.** But Mammon doesn't occupy the whole street. Next door to the Ministry of Finance is the **Museo de la Real Academia de Bellas Artes de San Fernando:** the Museum of the Royal Academy. The academy owns a celebrated batch of Goya's paintings, including the *Burial of the Sardine,* full of action and humour, and a superb self-portrait of the artist. Rubens, Zurbarán, Velázquez and Murillo are also represented among hundreds of works on display.

The **Gran Vía,** main east–west thoroughfare and lifeline of modern Madrid, is abustle with shops, hotels, theatres, nightclubs and cafés—the street for strolling and window-gazing. Connoisseurs of traffic jams will marvel at the nightmarish stickiness of the rush hour here. Immobile drivers, at their wits' end, lean on their horns, not quite overriding the screech of the police whistles. And a special bonus: in Madrid, thanks to the siesta break, the rush hour occurs four times a day.

At **Plaza del Callao** (named after Peru's principal port), the pedestrian traffic reaches its peak. This is the centre for department stores (the two biggest glare at each other across a pedestrian mall), cinemas, cafés and bus termini. Yet only a couple of streets south of Callao's turbulence, the **Convento de las Descalzas Reales** clings to a 16th-century tranquillity. The institution was founded by Princess Joanna of Austria and subsidized by generous patrons. Cloistered nuns of the Santa Clara order stay out of sight when the public is admitted (the visiting hours are few and eccentric, so check with the tourist office before you go). The first view of the convent's splendours begins with the theatrical grand stairway. Upstairs are heavy timbered ceilings and walls covered with works of art, mostly of religious or royal significance. In one hall you can see a dozen 17th-century tapestries based on original Rubens drawings.

From Plaza del Callao, the Gran Vía continues downhill towards the **Plaza de España** through more shopping, strolling and nightlife territory. Skyscrapers of 26 and 34 storeys overlook the plaza, a sanctuary of grass, flowers, trees and fountains. A favourite sight, especially with visiting photographers, is the Cervantes monument. A stone sculpture honouring the author looms behind bronze statues of his immortal creations, Don Quixote, astride his horse, Rosinante, and Sancho Panza, on his donkey.

Calle de la Princesa, which begins at

*I*n spite of the ever-growing pressures of modern life, Spaniards can always find time for a chat, gossip or political argument.

Plaza de España, is actually an extension of the Gran Vía aimed north-west. The **Palacio de Liria**, residence of the Duchess of Alba, at Calle de la Princesa, 22, calls to mind a scaled-down Buckingham Palace. The family picture gallery includes works by Titian, El Greco, Rubens, Van Dyck, Rembrandt and Goya. The palace is closed to the public except by special arrangement.

The smart trajectory of Calle de la Princesa ends where the university district, *ciudad universitaria*, begins. The landmarks here are the Air Force headquarters (a modern copy of El Escorial) and Madrid's youngest triumphal arch (built to commemorate Franco's 1939 victory).

The Prado

All agree: Madrid's pride, the Museo del Prado, houses what is indisputably the world's greatest collection of Spanish paintings. In addition, there are hundreds of foreign masterpieces, especially of the Italian and Flemish schools. This immense treasure was collected by Spain's Hapsburg and Bourbon kings, by private patrons of the arts and by convents and monasteries around the country.

Charles III commissioned architect Juan de Villanueva to design this neoclassical building towards the end of the 18th century. It was supposed to have served as a museum of natural history, but after some eventful delays (Napoleon's invasion badly damaged the building), its mission was diverted to art.

In the 1980s, modernization projects—desperately needed air conditioning and humidity control, for instance—caused some upheaval. The practical upshot for visitors is a reordering of rooms, which inevitably outpaces the mapmakers.

A Prado annexe, the gravely colonnaded **Casón del Buen Retiro**, up the hill

*Reflected in a pool in Madrid's Plaza de España,
a bronze sculpture of Don Quixote leads Sancho Panza
to another adventure. Cervantes wrote other works, before and after,
but never so universally appealing as the novel of the knight errant.
Famous but never rich, the author died in Madrid in 1616.*

in Calle de Felipe IV, houses Picasso's monumental *Guernica*. Bulletproof glass protects this panorama of horror, provoked by the Civil War bombing of a defenceless Basque town. In small halls flanking the main event, exhibits of priceless sketches and studies show how much preparation went into what looks like Picasso's spontaneous rage.

Opposite the Prado, an elegant three-storey brick palace is being readied for the kind of art collection museum keepers might duel over. The **Palacio de Villahermosa**, a Prado annexe, is to be the home of more than 700 masterpieces owned by Baron Hans Heinrich Thyssen-Bornemisza. The German-born industrialist has agreed to transfer them from his Swiss villa under a ten-year loan arrangement. Spain hopes the loan will become permanent, but other countries have been manoeuvering to get their hands on some or all of the works, including classics by Spanish masters.

Switzerland was shocked to lose the baron's 700 best pieces. But that still leaves another 700 or so to brighten the walls of his lakeside villa at Lugano, a tourist attraction.

More Madrid

The **Royal Palace** *(Palacio Real)* is set among formal gardens on a bluff overlooking the Manzanares valley. An old Moorish fortress on this site burned down in 1734, whereupon King Philip V ordered an immense new palace in French style. His command produced this imperious residence, loaded with art and history.

On certain days, not always predictable, the palace is closed to the public to give priority to regal ceremonies and portentous events. And when it is open, visitors are forbidden, for security reasons, to wander on their own, but are escorted in groups. The basic one-hour tour takes in 50 rooms (out of 2,000).

A few highlights: the Gasparini room, Rococo at its most overwhelming; the ceremonial dining room, seating 145

guests; the throne room, with ceiling painted by Tiepolo. For an extra charge you can view the crown jewels, the museum of paintings, the royal library, pharmacy and armoury. Called the finest collection of its type in the world, the armoury is packed with authentic battle flags, trophies, shields and weapons.

On the far side of the palace, in Campo del Moro, the **Museo de Carruajes** (Carriage Museum) specializes in royal transport of all kinds, from primitive litter to ponderous motor car. The gala coach of Alfonso XIII still shows signs of damage from a 1906 assassination attempt. A stagecoach, ancient sedan chairs, sleds and saddles round out the well-organized curiosities.

More Museums

A wide-ranging, priceless private collection bequeathed to the nation fills the **Museo Lázaro Galdiano,** Calle de Serrano, 122. Ancient jewellery includes a Celtic diadem from the 2nd century B.C. And there are paintings by Bosch, El Greco, Rembrandt, Goya... even the American Gilbert Stuart. But the museum's greatest pride is a portrait of angelic beauty by Leonardo da Vinci, *The Saviour.*

Museo Sorolla, Paseo del General Martínez Campos, 37. On view are close to 300 paintings by the Valencian impressionist Joaquín Sorolla (1863–1923). The city's only museum devoted to a single painter occupies the house in which he lived and worked.

Museo de Arte Contemporáneo (Museum of Contemporary Art), Avenida de Juan de Herrera in the Ciudad Universitaria. A warm, attractive museum inside a somewhat forbidding skyscraper. Beautifully arranged displays from early 20th-century realism to post-pop art, with first-class sculpture throughout.

Panteón de Goya—Ermita de San Antonio de la Florida, Paseo de la Florida. In a rather unglamorous area between the railway yards and the river, Goya's greatest fresco covers the cupola of an

TACKLING THE PRADO

A serious student of fine art might well plan an entire Madrid itinerary around repeated visits to the Prado. But the tourist in a rush, trying to digest so many highlights, may have to settle for a hectic couple of hours. To see more old masters per mile, plan ahead. Decide what you want to see and give the remainder of the trove the merest glance. (Rest your feet, as well as your eyes, from time to time; there's no shortage of seats.)

For a hurried dash through the Prado, or an overview at the start of several visits, here are our nominations for the museum's top dozen painters (listed chronologically within their groups). To speed your rounds, we spotlight their most famous works.

Spanish

El Greco (1541–1614). *Knight with Hand on Chest*, an early portrait, realistic and alive, studies a deep-eyed, bearded *caballero* in black. It is signed, in Greek letters, "Domenikos Theotokopoulos", the artist's real name. The Prado

Surrealism at the Prado: hallucinations of Hieronymus Bosch.

is also well supplied with El Greco's mystical, passionately coloured religious paintings, such as *Adoration of the Shepherds*.

José Ribera (c. 1591-1652). Most of his life was spent in Italy, where the Valencia-born artist was known as Lo Spagnoletto. His human-interest portraits of saints, hermits and martyrs show impeccable draughtsmanship and keen lighting. A batch of his pictures of the disciples of Jesus are on view in the Prado.

Francisco de Zurbarán (1598-1664). Mysticism and realism are combined in Zurbarán's experiments in space, light and shade. He was versatile enough to excel at still life as well as mythological, religious and historical themes. The Prado owns his strained but fascinating battle picture, *The Defence of Cádiz against the English* and a rarer *Still Life* of a goblet, two vases and a pot.

Diego Velázquez (1599-1660). *Las Meninas* (The Maids of Honour), Spain's all-time favourite painting, features the family of Philip IV. It proudly has a room to itself. The artist painted himself with palette in hand at the left side of his own masterpiece. Another vast, unforgettable Velázquez canvas here is *Surrender of Breda*, a pageant with pathos. Elsewhere are his portraits of the high and the mighty along with studies of fun-loving, ordinary mortals.

Bartolomé Murillo (1617-82). In *Holy Family with a Little Bird,* Spain's most popular religious artist of his time catches revered biblical personalities off guard, almost indistinguishable from the "family next door"; even the little dog enjoys the distraction from momentous affairs. Such cozy, tender scenes as well as classical religious works with soaring angels brought Murillo international fame.

Francisco de Goya (1746-1828). Of all the Prado's paintings, none is more discussed and disputed than *The Naked Maja*, one of Spain's first nudes. The face is awkwardly superimposed on the body, suggesting that the sensuous lady's identity was thus disguised. Rumours of a scandalous affair between Goya and the Duchess of Alba are always mentioned, and usually denied. Goya's most celebrated royal portrait, *The Family of Charles IV,* is daringly frank and unflattering. On still another level, *The Executions of the 3rd of May* is one of history's most powerful protest pictures.

Dutch and Flemish

Rogier van der Weyden (c. 1400-64). His greatest painting, an altarpiece, hangs in the Prado: the powerful composition of *Descent from the Cross*, reveals brilliant draughtsmanship.

Hieronymus Bosch (c. 1450-1516). The Spanish call him "El Bosco". Here you can see three of his all-time surrealist masterpieces, including a large triptych called *The Garden of Delights*. Dangerously mixing erotic fantasies and apocalyptical nightmares, it portrays the terrors and superstitions of the medieval peasant mind. The weirdness of Bosch may hint at the hallucinations of Salvador Dalí... but the Dutch genius was 400 years ahead of his time.

Peter Paul Rubens (1577-1640). His students ran an artistic assembly line, but the prolific Rubens kept his work as original as his genius. Of the dozens of paintings by Rubens in the Prado, two show his versatility: the huge *Adoration of the Magi* is a brilliant religious extravaganza, while *The Three Graces* backs fleshy nudes with an equally lush landscape.

Italian

Raphael (1483-1520). Napoleon showed good taste when he hijacked the Prado's Raphael collection to Paris, but it was soon recovered. Centuries of investigation have failed to uncover the identity of *The Cardinal*, Raphael's explosive character study of a subject with fishy eyes, aquiline nose and cool, thin lips.

Titian (c. 1490-1576). The *Portrait of the Emperor Charles V* shows Titian's patron in armour, on horseback at the Battle of Mühlberg; it set the standard for court painters over the next century. Titian also painted religious works, but seemed to have no difficulty changing gears to the downright lascivious. *Baccanal* is about as far as an orgy can go within the bounds of a museum.

Tintoretto (1518-94). While Titian was painting kings, Tintoretto, who brought Mannerism to Venice, was aiming slightly lower on the social scale. The Prado owns, among others, his portraits of a prosecutor, a general and a senator. Look for his dramatic bible stories, originally ceiling paintings, and, on another plane, *Lady Revealing Her Bosom*.

Bonuses from Italy

On your way through the Italian rooms, keep an eye peeled for these Renaissance prodigies:

Antonello da Messina's intensely tragic *Christ Sustained by an Angel*.

Sandro Botticelli's *The Story of Nastagio degli Onesti*, a storyboard from the *Decameron*.

Fra Angelico's glowing *Annunciation*, with Adam and Eve, clothed, in supporting roles.

Goya's notorious "Naked Maja"; "Maids of Honour" by Velázquez.

18th-century chapel. An identical chapel built alongside permits the local congregation to pray in peace while tourists crane their necks next door.

Museo Arqueológico, Calle de Serrano, 13. The art of the peninsula's ancient inhabitants is on display, with miraculously preserved mosaics from 2nd-century A.D. Roman Spain and earlier Carthaginian statuettes from Ibiza. An unforgettable highlight: *La Dama de Elche* (the Lady of Elche), a stone sculpture of a noble goddess, perhaps 2,500 years old, found in Alicante province. Here, too, is an accurate reproduction of the cave paintings of Altamira, which date back some 15,000 years to the dawn of art. The underground simulation is well worth seeing, for pictures alone can't round out the three-dimensional power of these murals. The actual caves in Cantabria have been closed to tourists to protect the paintings from human heat and exhalations.

Museo de América, Avenida de los Reyes Católicos, 6 (Ciudad Universitaria). To Spaniards, "America" means Central and South America, and there are outstanding pre-Columbian statues and artefacts. Two rare Mayan manuscripts (codices) are displayed in their entirety.

Templo Egipcio de Debod. For a change of ancient pace, have a look at this 25-century-old Egyptian temple, dismantled and shipped to Madrid stone by stone. *From* the temple you have a panoramic view over Madrid.

Museo Nacional de Artes Decorativas, Calle de Montalbán, 12. The best of old Spanish glassware, woodwork, tapestry, porcelain, jewellery—all the things antique collectors dream of finding at the flea market. (But here they are genuine.)

Museo Romántico, Calle de San Mateo, 13. Spaniards seem incurably nostalgic for the age of love seats, Rococo mirrors and petticoated young princesses. The relics include some genuinely interesting works of art.

Real Fábrica de Tapices (Royal Tapestry Factory), Calle de Fuenterrabía, 2, was founded by Philip V in 1721. Goya worked here, creating the designs on which tapestries were based. They are still being copied here, along with contemporary designs.

Landmarks and Parks

Plaza de Colón (Columbus Plaza). Underground here is the city cultural centre. Above ground, a colossal abstract sculptural ensemble in the Jardines del Descubrimiento (Discovery Gardens) is inscribed with inspiring quotations about the discovery of the New World. It also gives credit to Columbus's usually unsung crewmen, all of whose names are listed here.

Paseo de la Castellana, Madrid's principal north–south avenue, runs for several miles through the heart of the city. Many of the patrician town houses in the central area have given way to banks and other commercial developments, and there are luxurious apartment blocks with landscaped balconies. Surrounded by all the traffic, the tree-shaded central strip is wide enough to provide a promenade and a lively zone of outdoor cafés.

Nuevos Ministerios (New Ministries). A bureaucrat's dream along the Castellana, this mammoth 20th-century project is reminiscent of Washington D.C. at its most monumental. Just north of the ministries is a vast urban development zone called Azca, with housing, offices, stores and gardens; it looks like an Eastern European exercise in gigantism.

Puerta de Alcalá. This super-monumental triumphal arch, surmounted by warrior angels, honours Charles III.

Parque del Retiro. Until little more than a century ago, the Retiro was a royal preserve. Now it's the easiest place for *Madrileños* to take a family outing.

Parque Casa de Campo. For a more rural Sunday in the park, another former royal preserve, forested by Philip II in 1559. Thousands of acres of woodland interspersed with attractions and amenities.

Day trips from Madrid

Toledo   23 D1

All of Spain—tradition, grandeur and art—is crammed into El Greco's adopted home town, set on a Castilian hilltop. The one-time imperial capital remains the religious centre of Spain and an incomparable treasure-house of the fine arts.

Toledo's eminence goes back to the first Christian synods and ecclesiastical councils, held here as early as the year 400. But with the Muslim invasion in 711, Christianity went underground. After Toledo's reconquest in 1085, mosques were turned into churches. Finally, in 1222, funds were appropriated for a fitting cathedral. The construction lasted two and a half centuries; the ornamentation took longer. It was worth all the trouble.

You can locate the **cathedral** of Toledo from any part of town, thanks to its Gothic tower, topped by a spire strangely ringed by spikes. But at ground level, the building is hemmed in by a clutter of back streets. No matter; its glory can be seen inside—the stained glass, wrought iron, sculpture and painting produced by platoons of geniuses.

In the centre of the five-aisled basilica, the **coro** (choir) is a marvel of woodcarving. The main altar outdoes even this. Just behind the back wall of the main chapel, the **Transparente** is the cathedral's most unforgettable innovation. It is the work of one man, Narciso Tomé —18th-century architect, sculptor and painter. He opened the ceiling and drew heavenly light into the sanctuary. While the cathedral's 750 stained-glass windows illuminate with sublime restraint, Tomé's bronze, marble and jasper ensemble of colour, shape and symbolism startles as it inspires.

The **Sala Capitular** (Chapterhouse) is a strangely oriental room with an intricate

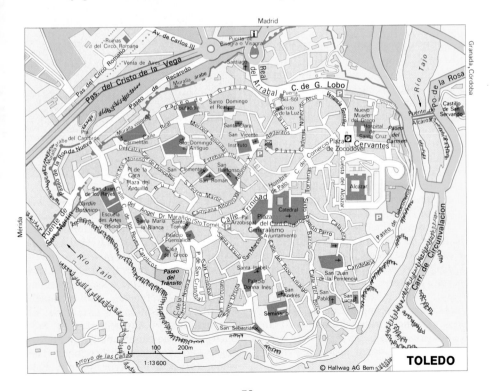

ceiling in the style called Mudéjar (the work of Muslims converted to Christianity after the Reconquest). In the **Tesoro** (Treasury), all eyes focus on the towering monstrance, composed of 5,600 parts, then gilded; precious stones add to the glitter.

The **sacristy** is a museum of art. The pictures are clearly labelled (a rarity in Spanish churches), so you won't have to keep asking, "Could this really be another genuine El Greco?" It certainly could. In all, there are 16 of them in this small collection.

The cathedral's only competitor for domination of the Toledo skyline is the **Alcázar,** a fortress destroyed and rebuilt many times since the Roman era. During the Spanish Civil War it was a stronghold of the pro-Franco forces, who held out during a 72-day siege which all but destroyed the Alcázar. The Nationalist commandant, Colonel José Moscardó Ituarte, received a telephone call from the enemy announcing that his son, held hostage, would be executed unless the fortress was surrendered. In a supremely Spanish reply, the colonel advised his son to "pray, shout 'Viva España' and die like a hero". More than a month after the son was killed, the siege was lifted.

The triangular-shaped **Plaza de Zocodover,** also rebuilt after Civil War destruction, is where the Moorish market *(zoco)* was held in the Middle Ages. It was also the scene of fiestas, tournaments and executions. Appropriately, the horseshoe arch leading from the square towards the river is called El Arco de la Sangre (Arch of Blood).

Just down the hill beyond the arch, in Calle de Cervantes, the 16th-century **Hospital de Santa Cruz** (Holy Cross Hospital) is now a museum. The main portal, of stone, is carved in the Plateresque style. Inside, great wooden ceilings add to a feeling of opulent spaciousness. Among a wide selection of El Greco's works here is his *Altarpiece of the Assumption,* painted just a year before the artist's death.

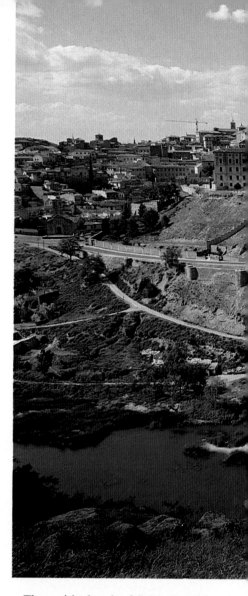

The parish church of **Santo Tomé** is a landmark because of its stately Mudéjar tower. Here they charge an admission fee to view a single picture. But what a painting! El Greco's *Burial of the Count of Orgaz* magically fuses the mundane and the spiritual. It depicts local noblemen at the count's funeral, also attended, according to tradition, by two saints. El Greco shows St. Augustine and St. Stephen lifting the count's body; up above, angels and saints crowd the clouds. The whole story is told in perfect pictorial bal-

*T*oledo's unforgettable hilltop skyline is almost
unchanged since the days when El Greco painted it. The Tagus River all
but surrounds the city. Something about the river's water is believed
to improve the quality of Toledo steel, of which swords were made
since the time of the ancient Romans.

ance and with the artist's unpredictable colours.

El Greco spent the most productive years of his prolific career in Toledo. Just down the hill from Santo Tomé, a house in which he is said to have lived has been reconstructed and linked to a museum. The **El Greco House** was originally built by Samuel Levi, a 14th-century Jewish financier and friend of King Peter I of Castile.

As devout as he was rich, Levi built a synagogue next to his home. It now bears the curious name of **La Sinagoga del Tránsito** (Synagogue of the Dormition). Muslim artists adorned the walls with filigrees intricate beyond belief, as well as inscriptions in Hebrew from the Psalms. After the expulsion of the Jews from Spain, the synagogue was converted into a church, hence the Christian tombstones in the floor. Attached to the synagogue, a **museum of Spanish Judaism** exhibits medieval scrolls and vestments.

Like the Tránsito, the **Sinagoga de Santa María la Blanca** (St. Mary the White) underwent a change of name and religion. Constructed by Muslim artisans, with 24 columns supporting horseshoe arches, it looks more like a mosque than either a synagogue or a church.

A final Toledo church, with regal connections: Ferdinand and Isabella built **San Juan de los Reyes** (St. John of the Kings) in a combination of Gothic, Renaissance and Mudéjar style. Look for a poignant souvenir on the outer wall—the

---

Living Together in Peace

In the 12th and 13th centuries Toledo was a thriving centre of Jewish life, with a matchless concentration of poets, historians and philosophers. Jews, Moors and Benedictine monks worked together in translation teams. As Europe awakened from the Dark Ages, Toledo provided a key link in the transmission of vital knowledge of Arabic science and Greek philosophy to the Western world. But the age of tolerance ended in a series of 14th-century pogroms, and in 1492 Ferdinand and Isabella expelled the survivors.

---

chains that held the Moors' Christian prisoners before their liberation. The superb double-layer cloister has elaborate stone carvings.

Ávila   15 C2

The fairy-tale stone **walls** protecting Ávila are too perfect: they make the city look like a Castilian Disneyland. But they were built in all seriousness in the last decade of the 11th century. Anyway, there's more to Ávila than the all-embracing fortifications, with 88 towers and an estimated 2,500 niches suitable for sentries or marksmen.

The **cathedral** of Ávila, built between the 12th and 16th centuries, includes Romanesque, Gothic and Renaissance elements. It nudges the city wall; the apse, in fact, is part of the wall itself. The high retable was begun by Pedro Berruguete, Spain's first great Renaissance artist, he died in 1504 before it could be finished. Behind the principal chapel is the alabaster tomb of Bishop Alonso de Madrigal, whose dark complexion won him the nickname *El Tostado* (the Toasted One). The 16th-century sepulchre portrays the bishop in full regalia, accurate right down to the embroidery on his robes. A museum of relics and art attached to the cathedral houses a silver monstrance as tall as a man.

Just outside the city walls, the **Basílica de San Vicente** is noted for an extraordinary tomb topped by a bizarre oriental-looking canopy. Knights of old used to place their hands on the 12th-century sepulchre when they took their oaths. Commemorated here are St. Vincent of Zaragoza and his two sisters, martyred in the 4th century.

Melancholy history also surrounds the royal **Monasterio de Santo Tomás,** sponsored by Ferdinand and Isabella. Their only son, Prince Don Juan, died here at the age of 19. His two tutors are buried in a small chapel near the tomb of the prince. Incidentally, this monastery was the headquarters of Torquemada, Spain's first Grand Inquisitor.

Many visitors come to Ávila in honour of the frail but tireless mystic, St. Teresa of Jesus. A much-adored reformer and personality, Teresa de Cepeda y Ahumada was born in Ávila in 1515. The convent of Santa Teresa was built on the site of her birthplace. She spent some 30 years in the convent of the Incarnación, outside the city walls, as a novice and later as prioress. The convent of San José, founded in 1562, was the first of 17 Carmelite convents that she established. She was canonized in 1622 and proclaimed a doctor of the Church in 1970. In Ávila you can see relics and manuscripts and even the habit the friendly, witty St. Teresa wore in a remarkable life of prayer, penance and poverty.

After you've seen Ávila up close, drive or take a bus across the Río Adaja to the monument called **Los Cuatro Postes** (the Four Posts). This rocky hill offers a panoramic view of the whole of medieval Avila. Especially at sunset, the invulnerable walled city looks too fabulous to be true.

El Escorial   *15 C2*

Sheer statistics don't do justice to the extravagant scale of this 16th-century royal palace complex. By official count El Escorial (containing living quarters, church, monastery, mausoleum and museum, all under one roof) has 86 stairways, more than 1,200 doors and 2,600 windows. In a distinctly Spanish version of Italian Renaissance style, it sums up the physical and spiritual superlatives of the empire's Golden Age. Hilaire Belloc called it "the supreme monument of human permanence in stone; the supreme symbol of majesty".

The overwhelming effect is eased by the adjoining, non-royal town of San Lorenzo de El Escorial. Because of the altitude at 1,055 m. (3,460 ft.), it's a popular getaway spot for *Madrileños* escaping the worst of summer, hence the generous supply of hotels, restaurants and bars.

Inside the **basilica** of El Escorial, the mood is one of devout magnificence. The immense main retable is composed of red marble, green jasper and gilded bronze. The 124 finely carved seats in the choir include a slightly roomier one for the founder, King Philip II. Of the dozens of art works collected here, none attracts more admiration than the life-sized marble crucifix by Benvenuto Cellini of Florence.

Philip II, who ordered El Escorial to be built, died here in 1598. He is buried in a family tomb tunnelled beneath the high altar of the basilica. The royal **pantheon** contains the remains of almost all Spain's kings, queens, princes and princesses over a period of four centuries. In the central hall, marble sarcophagi are stacked four high.

Above ground again, 40,000 rare books as well as manuscripts of immeasurable beauty and value are preserved in the **library.** In the **Palacio Real,** each room is more lavish than the one before. The tapestries are based on original designs by Goya and Rubens. But the most striking wall covering belongs to the **Sala de las Batallas** (hall of battles). Here, frescoes depict hundreds of soldiers, with each detail carefully painted.

The **apartments of Philip II** are modest in comforts but rich in art works. The king died here among cherished paintings, including a fantastic triptych by Hieronymus Bosch and works on religious themes by German, Flemish and Italian artists.

In addition to the fine paintings scattered through El Escorial, the **New Museums** display great works commissioned or collected by Spanish monarchs. In these stately surroundings hang pictures by Bosch, Ribera, Tintoretto, Velázquez and Veronese, and half a dozen by El Greco. It's a worthy gallery by any standards.

Valle de los Caídos   *15 C2*

A giant stone cross said to weigh 181,740 tons marks the Valley of the Fallen, a grandiose memorial to all the Civil War dead. Francisco Franco, who chose this beautiful site in a forested valley, is buried here.

The church of the Valle de los Caídos is officially termed the "largest basilica ever built in the history of mankind". It was hewn out of the side of the mountain like a railway tunnel (most of the labour provided by Franco's prisoners). You might think claustrophobia would be a problem in a tunnel without an end, but the colossal dimensions and unexpected decorations distract from any disquiet. Many statues and tapestries add to the subterranean pomp. There is plenty of room for decorations—the nave runs 262 m. (860 ft.) into the mountain.

Whatever your feelings about the architectural, artistic, religious or political implications of the Valley of the Fallen, the superlatives add up to something unique and hard to forget.

Segovia   15 C2

Before you have time to digest the glory of Segovia's natural setting, the magnificent skyline will captivate you. Then, just when this mirage of medieval Spain comes into focus, your attention is drawn to a single breathtaking monument or building. These are wonders to be savoured one at a time.

First, the site. Segovia juts out from the clean-air plateau in the heart of Old Castile. These wide-open spaces are interrupted only occasionally by a clump of trees, a lonely farmhouse, a monastery or a castle. The Sierra de Guadarrama, with two ski resorts, fills half the horizon.

Marching right through the centre of town, Segovia's **Roman aqueduct** is a work of art and a triumph of engineering. Composed of thousands of granite blocks arranged in graceful arches, sometimes two-tiered, it is nearly half a mile long and as much as 46 m. (150 ft.) high. Almost as astonishing as the engineering achievement is the fact that the aqueduct has been in constant use for 100 generations. A couple of details have been changed, but it still brings water to Segovia.

The **Alcázar**, Segovia's royal castle, was built in the most natural strategic spot. It dominates a ridge overlooking the confluence of two rivers, the Río Eresma and the Río Clamores, and has an unimpeded view of the plateau in all directions. The present storybook castle is a far cry from the simple stone fortress which took shape in the 12th century. As it grew bigger and more luxurious, it played a more significant historical role. By the 13th century, parliaments were convened here. Here in 1570, Philip II married his fourth bride, Anne of Austria. In the 16th century the Tower of Juan II became a dungeon for political prisoners. The most fanciful, photogenic parts of the castle's superstructure date from the second half of the 19th century.

The pinnacles and cupolas of the Segovia **cathedral** look as if they belong to a whole complex of churches, but, in fact, it's all a single elegant monument. Begun in 1525 (and consecrated in 1768) this is the last of the great Spanish Gothic

*S*ince its beginnings as a stark 12th-century fortress, the Alcázar, the royal castle of Segovia, has housed a heap of history: parliamentary deliberations, royal marriages, and VIPs in the dungeon. The present array of turrets dates from the late 19th century.

cathedrals. It was even taller until a lightning bolt lopped off the main tower in 1614.

Fine stained-glass windows illuminate the cathedral's majestic columns and arches. Two 18th-century organs present a strikingly flamboyant sight. Less obvious are the altarpieces in the chapels. Look for the 16th-century polychrome pietà by Juan de Juni.

On show in the museum and chapter-house is the Baroque carriage propelled through the town every Corpus Christi, with its huge 17th-century silver monstrance. Here also is the pathetic reminder of a 14th-century tragedy: the tomb of the infant Prince Pedro, son of Enrique II. He slipped from the arms of his nurse as she admired the view from an open upper window of the Alcázar. Scarcely hesitating, the nanny leaped after him to death in the moat.

Facing Segovia's most charming square is the church of **San Martín**, a 12th-century Romanesque beauty. Primitive sculptures in the square may resemble James Thurber's hippopotami, but they are really a legacy of the Celtiberians.

So much of Segovia is superlative that the 11th-century **city wall** itself is almost relegated to second-class status. The mile and a half of wall tends to be irregular but evocative, and mostly homely and lived-in. Just outside the wall and almost in the shadow of the Alcázar, the church of **Vera Cruz** dates from the early 13th century. The Knights of the Holy Sepulchre held court in its chapel surrounded by a circular nave. The Maltese Order, owner of the 12-sided church for centuries, renovated it in the 1950s. It's still moody.

La Granja de San Ildefonso   *15 D2*

Climbing the stately drive from the village of San Ildefonso to the palace of La Granja, you'll be impressed by the giant pines, the diligently tended lawns and flower beds. But all this is just a foretaste to the magnificent gardens within the gates of the estate.

San Ildefonso was founded in the mid-15th century as a modest hideaway for King Henry IV. More than 250 years later, the first Bourbon king of Spain, Philip V, had the idea of building a Versailles-style summer palace on the spot. Philip made a bit of history at La Granja when he abdicated in 1724 in favour of his son Louis. But the new king soon died and Philip resumed his rule for another 20 years.

The hillside escape from Madrid turned out more lavish than anticipated. The sumptuous Baroque rooms are all in a row, so you can look down the whole length of the palace. Several of the halls now comprise a tapestry museum containing textile masterpieces collected by the Spanish royal family. Visits are conducted in guided groups and numbers are strictly limited. As for the gardens, they feature severely clipped hedges and spectacular man-made cascades and fountains. These formalities lead on to forests of poplar, oak, elm, maple and horse chestnut trees, and all with the cooling sight of mountains in the background.

Guadalajara   *16 B2*

Not to be confused with its Mexican namesake, which is perhaps 30 times bigger, Spain's Guadalajara is a regional market town and industrial centre, founded in the days of the Iberians. It fell to the Moors early in the invasion tide and stayed under Muslim control until late in the 11th century. The name comes from the Arabic for "River among the Stones".

From the 15th to 17th centuries, the town was the seat of a powerful political and sometimes literary family, the Mendozas. They built the **Palacio del Duque del Infantado,** one of the glories of 15th-century Spain. Five centuries later, during a Civil War battle, badly aimed bombs almost obliterated the palace, but it has been rebuilt. The façade, profusely ornamented, is a brilliant introduction to the flamboyant Gothic ostentations of the two-storey patio. Here King Philip II married his third bride, Elizabeth of Valois. A provincial **museum** of fine arts has been installed on the ground floor.

Alcalá de Henares   15 D2

Only 30 km. (less than 20 miles) east of Madrid, Alcalá de Henares has seen many sons go on to better things. It was the home town of Miguel de Cervantes, who grew up here in very modest circumstances, then saw the world and wrote *Don Quixote*. This is also the birthplace of a queen and a king, Catherine of Aragon (who became the wife of England's Henry VIII) and, a few years later, the Holy Roman Emperor Ferdinand I.

Alcalá de Henares has undergone some violent ups and downs: thriving under the Romans, and again after the Reconquest, it became a battleground in the Civil War.

Near the Plaza de Cervantes, stands the **Colegio de San Ildefonso** (the old university), a harmonious three-storey structure with a fine Plateresque façade. It is the work of Rodrigo Gil de Hontañón, a star of the Spanish Renaissance. The university, founded around the turn of the 16th century, published the first polyglot Bible with texts in four ancient languages. In the 19th century it was merged with the University of Madrid.

Chinchón   15 D3

The town square of Chinchón could be a stage set. Two- and three-storey white stucco houses with wooden arcades surround an irregular, vaguely oval plaza. Watch laundry being washed in the town fountain. In season, bullfights are held right in the square, changing its Wild West image to Old Spain.

The town is celebrated as the home of various aniseed liqueurs. It also grows a much-vaunted species of garlic, sold locally in strung bouquets. Chinchón is charming proof that you only have to travel 20 km. (12 miles) from Madrid to immerse yourself in the Spain of donkeys hauling cargo through cobbled lanes.

Aranjuez   23 D1

As you cross the *Río Tajo* (the Tagus) into the centre of Aranjuez, the roomy, geometric town plan becomes apparent. The balanced main square is faced by arcaded buildings on two sides and the porticoed church of San Antonio.

But these sights take second place to the royal palaces, parks, gardens and forests. Ever since Ferdinand and Isabella, Spanish monarchs have been retreating to this oasis to escape Madrid's summer heat. Since the mid-19th century, they've enjoyed the luxury of a country palace reminiscent of Versailles.

Guided tours of the **Palacio Real** (Royal Palace) reveal a cross section of royal taste in furniture, paintings, sculpture, tapestries, clocks, pianos and bric-a-brac. Among the highlights: the Throne Room, ceremonious except for the Louis Seize chairs standing in for thrones, the Porcelain Room, dazzlingly designed with decorations created in Madrid for King Charles III in 1760 and the Smoking Room, an Arabian Nights fantasy.

Downstairs, the **Museum of Court Dress** shows reproductions and, where possible, the actual costumes worn by Spain's kings and queens from the 16th to 20th centuries.

Less than 2 km. from the Royal Palace, the **Casita del Labrador** (Farmer's Cottage) is the wildly understated name for a small palace the kings used for hunting weekends. Tours begin in the Billiard Room, filled by a behemoth billiard table beneath a formal chandelier. In the Statue Gallery a far-fetched folly of a clock incorporates simulated water jets and a large music box. The Ballroom is scarcely large enough to accommodate 200 noble swingers. The Platinum Room leads to the king's own toilet, wittily arranged as a plush throne.

Elsewhere in the Prince's Garden, you can see the "Tagus Squadron" of the royal fleet, in which kings of Spain were rowed down the river. The collection is the last word in Rococo canoes, fancy feluccas and gilt gondolas.

THE CENTRE

As Spanish as El Cid and Don Quixote

Beyond Madrid and the commutable towns around it, central Spain brims with the most typically Spanish sights: distinguished, historic towns and isolated castles and monasteries. The countryside, though often flat, offers anything but monotony. On the plateau, the infinity of the sky's the limit. But as you turn a corner, a mountain road twists ahead, and the horizon seems close enough to touch. Amid a changing scene of grain fields, grazing land, vineyards and forests, there's never a dull moment.

In this chapter we include much of the regions of Castile and León, an enormous area stretching all the way to the Portuguese border and almost to striking distance of the Bay of Biscay. Our version of the Centre also embraces La Rioja, Spain's prime wine country, and part of the ancient kingdom of Aragon. Finally, we cover the atmospheric plateau of La Mancha, Don Quixote's old stamping ground.

For organizational convenience we consider the attractions of the Centre in an arbitrary clockwise order, starting to the west of the Madrid area. This gives first place to a historic city of great dignity and beauty... and youth.

Capital idea: 16th-century sculptors provided grotesque contemplation for the Dominican nuns in a Salamanca cloister.

Salamanca   *14 B2*

What keeps this ancient city young is its university, four centuries older than Harvard and nearly as venerable as Oxford.

Students infiltrate the town, infecting everyone with their irreverence and good cheer. Exams may be a burden, but you'd never know it from their demeanour—sprawled at café tables, roistering in the taverns, and, dressed in medieval finery, strumming guitars and singing in the main square. And what a square!

The 18th-century **Plaza Mayor** (Main Square), the obvious pole of attraction for tourist and resident alike, seems to be the most perfect plaza in Spain, or anywhere on earth. But not geometrically. If you look closely, you'll discover that it is actually a slightly irregular trapezoid. Eighty-six round arches, including three that are two storeys tall, form the arcades surrounding the cobbled square. Three floors of balconied windows on all four sides add to the soothing symmetry of the design, broken only by the façades of two proud buildings, the Town Hall and the Royal Pavilion.

*The setting sun beams on the golden stone of
Salamanca's Plaza Mayor, arguably the most perfect plaza in the world.
As night falls, the population throngs to the square to take part in
a traditional Mediterranean-style promenade, even though Salamanca
is farther from the sea than any other Spanish city.*

Much of the credit for this magnificent ensemble goes to Alberto Churriguera, a member of an artistic dynasty responsible for some of Spain's most distinctive Baroque buildings. (The family is remembered in an adjective, churrigueresque, describing an elaborately decorated style found in Spain and Latin America.)

Dating from Iberian times, Salamanca first enters the chronicles in the 3rd century B.C., when it was conquered by Hannibal. As part of the Roman province of Lusitania, Salamanca rated the title of municipality, with city walls and a bridge (still there) across the Río Tormes. Vandals and Visigoths followed the decline and fall of the Romans, and then the tide of Islam swept through. Salamanca was fought over, on and off, for three centuries until the final triumph of the Christian forces. In 1178 Ferdinand II of León assembled his parliament in the city, to which he granted special privileges. By the 16th century Salamanca was so special and splendid it was called a "little Rome".

Salamanca's two cathedrals, which throw up a thicket of spiky spires and turrets, are contiguous; you enter the old through the new. The **Catedral Nueva** (New Cathedral) is not really so modern; construction began in 1513, when Gothic architecture was going out of fashion. Though Baroque and Plateresque elements were added, it has been called Gothic's last gasp. Among the architects were two generations of the Gil de Hontañón family, father Juan and son Rodrigo. The main (west) **façade** is a study in arches upon arches, further embellished with coats of arms, statues and reliefs. Inside, the triple-naved cathedral is slightly longer than a football field. Outstanding here are the Baroque **choir stalls,** an 18th-century **organ** that sounds as good as it looks, and the 18 side chapels, most notably the **Capilla Dorada** (Golden Chapel) with 110 sculptures.

After the grandeur of the New Cathedral, the **Catedral Vieja** (Old Cathedral)

seems as intimate as a king's private chapel. Work started here in the 12th century when Romanesque architecture was giving way to new-fangled Gothic. The main **altar** (15th century) consists of 53 paintings by Nicholas of Florence highlighting a 12th- or 13th-century statue of the Virgin; above the retable is Nicholas's dramatic, detailed *Last Judgment.*

The **cloister** is an 18th-century replacement for the Romanesque original, which became a distant victim of the celebrated Lisbon earthquake of 1755. The first **chapel** on the left, the Capilla de Talavera, has an unusual Mudéjar dome; services in the old Mozarabic rite are held here. (*Mozarab* was the name given to Christians, during the period of Moorish rule in the 8th–11th centuries.) Next door, in the Santa Barbara chapel, candidates for university degrees have traditionally spent the night before the big exam praying for success, and maybe doing some last-minute studying.

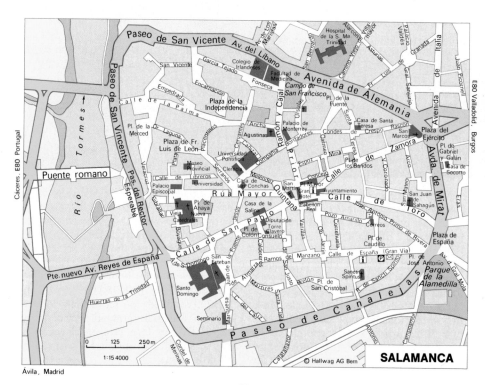

SALAMANCA

In the cathedral's old chapterhouse, a **diocesan museum** has a collection of paintings by Fernando Gallego, an underrated master of the 15th-century Hispano-Flemish style. He did some of his finest, brightest work in Salamanca. Another museum highlight is a sensitive triptych by Juan of Flanders, a contemporary of Gallego.

The **Universidad** (University) of Salamanca, founded in 1218, was one of Europe's greatest centres of learning in the Middle Ages. The 16th-century Plateresque **façade** of the main building has such intricate stonework you might think it was modelled in clay. It seethes with curlicues, cherubim, medallions, coats of arms and sculptural flourishes. In the lecture halls around a central patio, you can admire centuries of architectural and decorative details; the mood is broken only by the presence of modern audiovisual devices. And have a stroll around the **Patio de las Escuelas Menores** across the square, a spacious grassy courtyard surrounded by columns supporting wide, scalloped arches. (Salamanca is noted for a number of stately patios and cloisters, conducive to calm thoughts and meditation.)

Closer to the centre of the city, the **Casa de las Conchas** (House of Shells) is an extraordinary representative of 15th-century originality. Its exterior walls

---

The Rector Gets the Boot

One of Spain's leading 20th-century intellectuals, Miguel de Unamuno (1864–1936), had a stormy career as the head of the University of Salamanca. After teaching Greek language and literature, he became rector in 1901. In 1914 he was fired for publicly supporting the Allies in World War I. After a long, controversial interval, including exile in France, he returned to his post in Salamanca. But when the outspoken rector denounced the Franco forces in 1936, he was bounced again. Under house arrest, he died two months later.

Beyond his interests in politics and education, Unamuno wrote prolifically: lyric poetry, existentialist essays, novels and plays.

---

erupt in hundreds of scallop shells. There are few windows, indicating its initial purpose as a fortress. The patio here contains a generous collection of coats of arms tracing the family trees of the building's first owners.

Another severe building, the 16th-century **Palacio de Monterrey** is also strong on coats of arms. Its airy rectangular towers, typical of Spanish Renaissance style, have inspired many copies elsewhere within the country and in Latin America.

Zamora   *14 AB1*

Proverbially, Rome wasn't built in a day, but a Spanish saying takes a different tack: "Zamora wasn't conquered in an hour". When you see the city's position above the right bank of the Río Duero, and the remains of its ramparts, you'll understand.

Often besieged, Zamora changed hands several times during the centuries of the reconquest of Spain from the Arabs. Later it became the stronghold of the Portuguese supporters of Princess Juana, who claimed the throne of Castile from Ferdinand's wife, Isabella. Doña Juana's forces surrendered in 1475, opening the way for a unified Spain.

For a global look at this appealing historic city, cross the Duero by the 14th-century, 16-arched bridge. From the south bank you get the best view of the remarkable dome atop the **cathedral**. The Byzantine style inspired this very original cupola, roofed in curved stone tiles laid like fish scales. The Romanesque cathedral is one of half a dozen well-preserved 12th-century churches around town. Inside there is a notable retable by Fernando Gallego, as well as some unexpected, even risqué, woodcarving in the choir. In the cathedral's cloister, a **museum** highlights a prized collection of Flemish tapestries of the 15th and 16th centuries, with dramatic and often violent scenes from legend and history.

King Ferdinand I is quoted as referring to "Zamora the well-girded". Parts of

---

Workmanship by the Vanquished

The Moorish craftsmen who stayed on after the Reconquest contributed a bright chapter to the history of Spanish architecture and the decorative arts. Their style is called *Mudéjar*, from an Arabic word meaning "subjugated", a reference to the Muslims who remained in Christian Spain after the Reconquest.

Some of the obvious aspects of Mudéjar style are the geometrical designs, the horseshoe arches, the use of meticulously laid bricks, and the enthusiasm for ornamentation. Curiously, some of the very best Mudéjar buildings in Spain were synagogues.

---

the **city wall,** including impressive gateways, still surround the remains of the castle. On the north side, the intriguingly named **Postigo de la Traición** (Traitor's Gate) marks the spot where, the story goes, the assassin of the Castilian King Sancho II entered Zamora to find refuge in 1072.

Toro   *14 B1*

On the dividing line between wheat and wine country east of Zamora, the tersely named Toro (meaning, among other things, "bull") is a medieval hilltop town so well preserved that it has been proclaimed a historical-artistic monumental ensemble.

Its greatest pride is the **Iglesia Colegiata de Santa María la Mayor** (Collegiate Church), a 12th-century Romanesque classic with a two-storey turreted cupola. The west portal, which came later, is beautifully carved in Gothic style. Inside the Collegiate, the most unusual work of art is a 16th-century painting called *The Virgin and the Fly*, much studied because of the common housefly inexplicably shown at rest on a scarlet robe covering the Virgin's left knee.

Toro also has Romanesque brick churches, convents, mansions, fortifications and a 10th-century castle.

Coca Castle   *15 C2*

In Castile you expect to see castles. They come in all sizes, shapes and degrees of ferocity. None gives a more powerful impression than the brick masterwork in the small town of Coca.

In the late 15th century, the Archbishop of Seville, Alonso de Fonseca, recruited Moorish craftsmen to build him a castle in the province of Segovia. The brilliance of the architects and the artistry of the masons make this fortress the finest showpiece of Spanish Mudéjar military construction.

Three layers of walls surround an impenetrable keep, and there are towers and clusters of battlements at all levels. It's unclear why the archbishop required such awesome, if beautifully decorated, walls around his Coca retreat.

Astorga   *6 A2*

Just a couple of days before Christmas of 1886 the bishop of Astorga found himself in a seasonal no-room-at-the-inn situation. A fire had burned down his palace. Hardly had the ashes cooled when the roofless bishop, a native of Catalonia, invited a compatriot to design new quarters for him. The architect was Antoni Gaudí, the creator of Barcelona's "sandcastle cathedral".

The result, Astorga's neo-Gothic **Palacio Episcopal,** is a mad, wonderful experiment, effectively a two-tier cathedral combining pomp and fantasy. But the palace turned out so overwhelmingly palatial that no bishop of Astorga ever agreed to live in it. The building has instead been put to excellent use as the **Museo de los Caminos** (Museum of the Ways). The exhibits illustrate the pilgrim tide with maps and a hoard of saintly statues, sacred paintings and reliquaries.

A Romanesque church was demolished to make way for the present **cathedral,** begun in the 15th century in Gothic style. The Baroque façade tastefully disguises its flying buttresses, as if they were Victorian piano legs. Within, see the 16th-century retable, a towering eyeful. Two sculptors and a painter collaborated on this imposing work, and they all had the same first name: Gaspar. In the Diocesan

90

museum you can see 10th-century documents, Romanesque woodcarvings, and enough historic vestments to clothe a conclave of cardinals.

León   6 B2

The name of this prosperous modern city might suggest some wild connection with the "king of the jungle". Not so. Although *león* means "lion" in Spanish, the name actually is a corruption of the Latin *legio*—"legion"; this was an outpost of the Roman troops.

Latin is used to dignify the nickname of the city's most magnificent monument. *La Pulchra Leonina* (the beautiful Leonese) is what they call the **Catedral de Santa María de Regla**. León's cathedral, constructed in the 13th century and clearly inspired by the French Gothic cathedral at Chartres, has a glorious complement of stained-glass windows. Indeed, the top half of the walls are almost entirely glass. This worries modern engineers but floods the interior with inspiring, multicoloured light.

The west face of the *Pulchra* is surprisingly asymmetrical, with a couple of mismatched towers. Otherwise, all is harmony—a rose window high above the main portal, with three tall Gothic arches interspersed with acute mini-arches. Have a long look at the sculptural details of the middle portal, with the dramatic contrast between the happy pilgrims and the shrieking sinners in the *Last Judgment*.

Inside, crane your neck and admire the splendour of the **stained glass**: 125 huge windows and 57 other openings of various shapes and sizes for coloured light. They show the history of this art from the 13th to the 20th century.

There are tours of the **cloister,** an elegant conjunction of Gothic and Renaissance elements. This leads to a **diocesan museum,** with ancient relics, sculpture, painting and applied arts.

A few streets west of the cathedral, the **Colegiata de San Isidoro** (Collegiate Church of St. Isidore) honours an early

archbishop of Seville, noted for his voluminous and influential writings. When Seville fell to the Moors, the saint's remains were evacuated to the safety of León; his relics still attract pilgrims to this church, consecrated in 1063. On the south façade, atop all the other sculptural achievements, the saint himself is carved in stone, riding a horse as if to battle, ecclesiastical robes billowing.

Although it houses the tombs of assorted kings and princes, there's nothing funereal about the **Panteón Real** (Royal Pantheon), alongside the church. The naïve frescoes covering its arched ceilings are so wonderful that the place has been dubbed the Sistine Chapel of Romanesque art. There are uplifting biblical stories and asides picturing ordinary local people as well as animals, real and mythological. The **treasury** features some beautifully worked 11th-century caskets and an even older chalice.

The former **Monasterio de San Marcos** has a formidable Plateresque façade.

On the Road

The Way of St. James—*el Camino de Santiago*—is one of those roads that fire the imagination, like the Silk Road in China, the Old Chisholm Trail in the American West, or the Road to Mandalay.

By the 11th century, the pilgrims' way through France and across northern Spain to Santiago de Compostela had become the busiest "tourist" route in Europe. Everyone from cardinals to criminals made the trip, an exhausting, even dangerous, hike, as well as an uplifting religious experience. The pilgrims travelled in groups, the better to protect themselves from the perils along the way.

The devout French made up a substantial number of the pilgrims as well as their guides. Monks from Cluny were particularly influential in bringing Romanesque architecture to Spain. That's why many of the old churches between northern Catalonia and Galicia have so much in common.

The scallop shells—symbols of St. James—sculpted on the façade of León's San Marcos monastery identify it with the pilgrimage. The city's position as a vital way station along the pilgrim route assured its polish and prosperity.

This immensity is divided into dozens of intricately ornamented compartments, with never a dull detail. San Marcos began as a hospice for medieval pilgrims on the way to the shrine at Santiago de Compostela. King Ferdinand V ("the Catholic") poured more money in to make it a showpiece monastery for the Knights of St. James. Now it's back in the hospitality business, neatly transformed into one of Spain's most expensive *paradores* (government-run inns). Whatever the room rate, sumptuous San Marcos is worth it.

Not all of the vast ex-monastery is used for hotel purposes. Here, too, is the **Museo Arqueológico Provincial**, occupying the cloister and sacristy. The collection rounds up everything from Roman mosaics and sarcophagi to Romanesque sculptures. Note the exquisite *"Cristo de Carrizo"*, a small 11th-century ivory crucifix with touchingly human features.

For an architectural change of pace in the centre of León, see the building called "Botines", by the Catalan architect Antoni Gaudí. In spite of some original details, this once controversial construction is *not* one of his triumphs. It looks like a school building with neo-Gothic airs. It's more inviting at night though, with the white spotlights bleaching it.

A few kilometres west of León lies another Catalan contribution: the contemporary sculptor José María Subirachs has created striking, tormented statues of the disciples flanking a slim Virgin for the modern façade of the church of the **Virgen del Camino** (Virgin of the Way). Inside the church is a revered Baroque retable. The "Way" in the name refers to the well-beaten path to Santiago de Compostela, for this is the pilgrims' road.

Valladolid
15 C1

On the map, great stretches of the road from León to Valladolid appear as a straight line. This is neither slipshod cartography nor poetic licence. For many miles the N-601 goes straight through flat farmland. There is little to divert the gaze except for a few horses and sheep taking the sun. It's worth staying the course, though, for the university city of Valladolid sparkles with visual stimulation.

This is one of the hotbeds of the Isabeline style of art, expressed in extravagant, florid ornamentation. The style is named after Isabella of Castile, whose fateful marriage to Ferdinand of Aragon took place here in 1469. Valladolid was the capital of Castile until the end of the 16th century, then briefly the capital of all Spain.

Plunge right into the mainstream of Isabeline decoration at the **Colegio de San Gregorio**, founded by Brother Alonso of Burgos, Isabella's confessor. The royal coat of arms in the upper centre of the **façade** is surrounded by a circus of sculptural effects from statues and escutcheons to simulated flora. It's all so overwhelming that you're distracted, as the builders intended, from the essential simplicity of the architecture. The first impression is no flash in the pan. Inside, the double-decker **patio** is decorated almost as riotously as the front entrance. From the upper deck you get an unaccustomed close-up look at the gargoyles, four on each side—a perfect cast for a nightmare.

The college houses the **Museo Nacional de Escultura** (National Museum of Sculpture), the Prado of polychrome religious statues. If you fear a monotony of saccharine saintliness, you'll be happily

Glum faces peer through the stained glass, among the glories of 125 huge windows of León Cathedral. With rare delicacy, firemen saved the treasures during a blaze in 1966.

surprised by the variety of style and content: retables, free-standing saints, choir stalls, and even some paintings. The ceilings, too, are quite spectacular. The works range from the 13th to the 18th century, but the star here is the wood-carving genius of the Spanish Renaissance, Alonso Berruguete, said to have studied under Michelangelo. His martyrs seem to shed real tears and blood. Other important sculptors on show include Juan de Juni, an Italian-trained Frenchman of the mid-16th century, and the devout, sensitive Gregorio Fernández (1566–1636).

Valladolid's **cathedral** is a long story. Based on the remains of a 13th-century church, it was designed in 1580 by Juan de Herrera, co-author of Philip II's grandiose Escorial project. Delays kept cropping up and the cathedral never has been finished, but much of Herrera's strength still shows in the interior design. An altarpiece by Juan de Juni is the highlight of a rich ration of art within these walls.

Some famous names are associated with Valladolid. In this city several kings, including Philips II and IV, were born, and Christopher Columbus died. The arcaded two-storey house where the much-honoured explorer embarked on his final voyage has been restored. The **Casa Museo de Colón** (House-Museum of Columbus) is stocked with relics and documents from the age of discovery.

The **Casa de Cervantes** commemorates another local celebrity. Miguel de Cervantes lived in Valladolid for several years late in his literary career. His ivy-covered house, facing a peaceful, shady garden, contains furniture and books from his time. Don Quixote fans can visit the room in which he is said to have written a couple of his later, lesser-known books. Cervantes had mixed feelings about Valladolid, where he had one of his brushes with the law. The police harassed him because of a sensational murder on his doorstep; he was found innocent.

Cervantes was well travelled, as were the Augustinian monks who contributed the first-class works of art in Valladolid's **Museo Oriental**. For centuries the Augustinians worked as missionaries in Asia, and the "souvenirs" they collected range from thousand-year-old Buddhist paintings to colourful Chinese opera-style demons. The museum is inside the Augustinian monastery, at the south end of the fan-shaped **Campo Grande,** the main city park. A popular feature of this shady oasis is a small lake—really a large duck pond—from which the ducks, big and small, are more than willing to come ashore at the hint of a hand-out. Although they prefer the sweet biscuits sold nearby, a piece of bread will suffice.

Valladolid has fewer ceremonial boulevards than some other royal cities, such as León, but there is a vibrant charm about the place. For instance, the noisy and unaffected main square, the **Plaza Mayor,** is so big they could stage horse-races around its perimeter. Unfortunately, it's a traffic artery. Just about what you'd expect from the modern industrial centre of Old Castile.

Palencia   15 C1

Like the much bigger and better-known east-coast city of Valencia, Palencia was catalogued by ancient geographers. Ptolemy named the town Pallantia. Unlike Valencia, which became an important Roman colony, it repeatedly declined to be subdued or civilized by the empire. The valiant Celtiberians had less luck resisting later invasions by the Visigoths and Moors. Palencia was wiped out.

Rebuilt in the 11th century, Palencia became the political hub of Castile, where royal courts and church conclaves were held. Spain's first university was founded here at the beginning of the 13th century.

History piles up in Spain. A 7th-century chapel was built above a martyr's cave in Palencia; an 11th-century king, Sancho III of Navarre and Castile, constructed a Romanesque church on the Visigothic ruins. In the 14th and 15th centuries, a proper Gothic **cathedral** was built over *those* ruins. Today it's nicknamed *la Bella Desconocida*—the Beautiful Unknown.

The cathedral is laid out in the form of a Latin cross, with three naves. The church and adjoining museum contain a superlative array of 15th- and 16th-century works of art—woodcarvings, paintings, statues and tapestries. Among the sculptors well represented here are Pedro Berruguete, Felipe Bigarny, Gil de Siloé, Juan de Valmaseda and Simon of Cologne. Perhaps the cathedral's best-known treasure is a painting of St. Sebastian by El Greco.

Paredes de Nava   7 C3

This village, less than 25 km. (15 miles) north-west of Palencia, is the birthplace of two of Spain's finest Renaissance artists—a father and son.

Pedro Berruguete, the father, first made his mark in the Toledo cathedral at the end of the 15th century. Influenced by Italian, Flemish and earlier Spanish art, he excelled in portraiture with warm, human touches, and a mastery of space.

His son, Alonso Berruguete, learned the ropes from his father, then studied in Italy, reportedly under Michelangelo. He worked briefly as court painter for Charles V, but when business was slow he turned to sculpture. His expressive statues of saints in agony or ecstasy are among the highest achievements of the age.

The home-town church of Santa Eulalia in Paredes de Nava is adorned with works by both Berruguetes.

Peñafiel   15 C1

The castle of Peñafiel, 35 km. (22 miles) east of Valladolid, is one of a kind. From afar it looks like the age of chivalry's most improbable shipwreck. High on a lonely hilltop, the long, low, thin fort—nearly ten times longer than its width—tapers at the ends, shipshape. The equivalent of the bridge is a stern square keep.

One of the legends linked with this elegant stone castle explains its name. When King Sancho conquered it from the Moors in the 11th century, he is said to have raised his sword and sworn, "Henceforth this shall be the faithful rock *(peña fiel)* of Castile".

This castle has everything a well-made stronghold could have needed in the Middle Ages—a double set of ramparts, 30 towers, and turrets enough to give an attacker pause. In the village below, the big open plaza, mostly surrounded by houses, is ideal for bullfights.

Pedraza de la Sierra

In this isolated mountain village in the province of Segovia, the houses crowd together as if in self-defence. Despite the advantage of standing on a hill and being girdled by town walls, Pedraza still looks appealingly vulnerable. Houses with evocative names line the twisting, narrow streets. (A *parador* occupies the former House of the Inquisition.)

The castle of Pedraza has a story, too. For four years the eldest sons of King François I of France were held hostage here. Their imprisonment was a postscript to the Treaty of Madrid of 1526, which brought breathing space in the long-running feud between the French king and the Holy Roman Emperor Charles V. François eventually bought back the princes, François and Henri, for a ransom of two million gold crowns—enough to bankrupt France.

Burgos   7 D2

The one-time capital of the kingdom of Castile is an oasis of urban beauty halfway up the main road between Madrid and the French border. As one of the most significant stopping places on the Way of St. James, the city acquired centuries of experience in hospitality. When the pious pilgrim traffic to Santiago de Compostela was at its peak, medieval Burgos had more than 30 hospices and hostels. The welcome mat is still out.

What a relief—and joy—it must have been for the weary medieval pilgrims to

Flycatcher in the Cathedral

Why are all those Spaniards milling about expectantly just inside Burgos cathedral's main door, looking lighthearted rather than reverent? They are staring up at the top of the arch, to the left. They are concentrating on a clock.

Adjust your eyes to the change of light and notice the Roman-numeralled clock, surmounted by a manikin in red. It's called the Papamoscas, or Flycatcher Clock. When the hour strikes, the comic character astride the clock opens and closes his mouth.

Next to him a much smaller figure appears between two bells every quarter hour.

Jokily or otherwise, the cathedral has been telling Burgos the time for more than six centuries.

---

glimpse the delicate but prickly towers of the Burgos cathedral on their horizon. Nowadays, spotlighted at night, it's even more a beacon for travellers. The nicest approach, though, is from the south, crossing the usually lazy Río Arlanzón to the most flamboyant of the city gates. The **Arco de Santa María,** part of the city wall since the 14th century, was reconstructed in symmetrical grandeur two centuries later. As dramatic as a backdrop for grand opera, the massive gate honours, among others, Emperor Charles V and the great warrior El Cid, sculpted in niches on the front.

Along the river here, three parallel promenades follow the path of the original city wall. Trimmed trees and bushes, flower gardens, fountains and statues adorn the walks. Towards sunset all of Burgos converges here to stroll and unwind from the day's stresses, showing off their well-groomed dogs and some of Europe's best-dressed children. Although a few brave palm trees try to deny it, Burgos is hundreds of miles from the Mediterranean, where the tradition of the *paseo* was born. Yet the daily promenade couldn't be more at home.

The great **cathedral** of Burgos was begun in 1221 by order of Ferdinand III of Castile and Bishop Maurice of Burgos (said to be an Englishman). Construction dawdled on until the 19th century, though the Gothic style was sealed early in the project. The bristling, lacy spires of the west front date from the 15th century. Before you enter, walk around the complex structure and see its moods. There are ceremonial doors on four sides of the building, each sculpturally and architecturally different, with effects ranging from grand to cozy. The main **façade,** facing the Plaza de Santa María, is a stirring sight from any angle, with its high-rising balustrades and arches, statues, and a rose window with a Star of David in the middle, known here as Solomon's Seal.

This is the third biggest cathedral in Spain (after Seville and Toledo), but there's a reassuring intimacy to many of its components. The vast interior is divided into precincts by walls, fences, screens and railings; there's never a view of the whole. If you're in a rush, have a glance up at the delicately decorated octagonal dome and keep going to the far end and the **Constable's chapel.** It was designed by Simon of Cologne, son of the artist responsible for the west façade and spires. Here the most splendid golden altar, the most graceful statuary, the most uplifting cupola set the stage for the

---

Strumming guitars, a troupe of troubadours in medieval garb perform in front of the Burgos cathedral. These airy towers were a welcome landmark for pilgrims at the halfway point on their hike from France to the shrine of Santiago de Compostela.

tomb of the eponymous constable and his wife, whose effigies in Carrara marble lie atop it. The **altar** of St. Anne, with its sculptured portraits of distinguished local women, is by the German artist Gil de Siloé. His son, Diego de Siloé, designed the exquisite **golden stairway** inside the Coronería portal. Diego is also the sculptor of *Christ at the Column*, a vivid statue in the **sacristy.** High on the wall here hangs the iron-bound **coffer** of El Cid, the legendary 11th-century hero, who is buried beside his wife under the cathedral's dome.

For a sculptor's impression of the immortal Great Cid, see the equestrian **statue** of the armoured warrior, in flowing beard and cape, a few streets east of the cathedral at the San Pablo bridge. The colossal sword was called Colada, the horse Babieca. The square, the Plaza del General Primo de Rivera, is named after the pre-Franco dictator of Spain. After Franco himself died, many towns expunged his name and those of his closest collaborators from the directory of streets and squares. But conservative Burgos still honours him in the name of a riverfront avenue. Burgos was the *generalísimo*'s headquarters during the Civil War.

Burgos is an appealing city for wandering. There are stately apartment blocks with artistic touches, bustling shopping streets, inviting squares and parks, and distinguished town houses from the Middle Ages. Outstanding among them is the **Casa del Cordón,** the mansion in which Ferdinand and Isabella welcomed Columbus back from his second trip to America. Beautifully restored, it's now the home of the local savings bank.

Another noble Renaissance house, the Casa de Miranda, serves as the **Museo Arqueológico.** Three floors of exhibits, with thousands of items from the Stone Age to the Roman era, surround a neoclassical patio. Just across the street, and worth a look, the municipal food market concentrates a pretty plethora of fish, meat, cheese, fruits and vegetables. Connoisseurs can choose from among ten different types of olives.

On the western outskirts of Burgos, the **Convento de las Huelgas** was the place princesses were sent for a strict education. The institution, founded in the 12th century, soon became a powerful force in Castile, and kings were crowned and buried here. You can inspect some of the treasures of art and history—religious relics, tapestries, even battle trophies—amassed by the convent's abbesses. Behind the fortress-like walls, the complex contains a mixture of architecture—Romanesque, Cistercian and Mudéjar.

A few kilometres east of Burgos, in a forest park, the 15th-century Carthusian monastery called the **Cartuja de Miraflores** also has royal connections. Founded by King John II, it features his sepulchre (a tomb for two, with his second wife, Isabella of Portugal)—an alabaster masterpiece sculpted by Gil de Siloé. The Cartuja's many-pinnacled white granite church is bigger and more lavish than you'd ever guess from the exterior.

Santo Domingo de Silos   15 D1

Three dozen Benedictine monks live in this ancient monastery in the isolated Burgos village of Silos. In the entrance hall they sell medicinal herbs with recondite Latin names, and local honey. But, sidelines aside, the monastery's pride lies within: a two-storey cloister with pillars of capital importance in the history of Romanesque sculpture.

Monks have been drawn to the tranquillity of Silos since Visigothic times. The first, primitive monastery was rebuilt in the 10th century, only to be levelled by the Moors. A monk named Domingo thereupon undertook a whirlwind reconstruction programme, winning admiration as a miracle worker, which is how the institution comes to bear his name.

The **cloister,** which surrounds lawns and a giant, slim cypress tree, is a festival of stonework. The carvings atop the columns portray biblical personalities but also abstractions and fanciful animals.

The styles suggest that several very distinct artists were involved, but every one of the 64 columns on the ground floor is worth study. (The stonework on the upper floor of the patio, which came later, is less original.)

Just off the cloister is an **old pharmacy** with a rich library of antique medical and pharmaceutical books in several languages. Benedictine specialists looked after the health of the villagers as well as the monks. There are mortars and pestles and vessels and a still any moonshiner would covet, though it was dedicated to the distillation of medicines. Or so they say.

A short but twisting drive east of Silos takes you to a limestone gorge called the **Garganta de Yecla.** This chasm is more remarkable for its width than its depth; the walls are sometimes so close together that it's impossible to stand upright. A daring walkway has been built jutting over the rushing stream far below, putting the gorge experience, otherwise strictly for mountaineers, within the reach of almost everyone.

Logroño
8 B2

The leafy main square of this spacious modern city is big enough for a fiesta. And when it's fiesta time in Logroño you can be sure a certain amount of wine tasting goes on, day and night. This is only natural in the lively capital of Spain's premier wine region, La Rioja.

Among medieval travellers—the pilgrim road to Santiago passes through town—La Rioja was famous for its cheerful and attentive hospitality. Presumably the local wine, which has been known since the 12th century, was a factor in this fame.

Logroño is built alongside the Río Ebro, spanned here by two bridges—one of iron, the other of stone. It's essentially the same stone bridge that the pilgrims crossed. Their first stop would have been the church of **Santa María de Palacio,** which dates from the 11th century. It is topped by a tall, graceful, pyramid-shaped tower. A few streets to the south, matching Baroque bell towers mark the **cathedral,** which is considerably younger. The generously sculptured main portal, deeply recessed, is flanked by unexpectedly blank stone walls. Behind the cathedral lie the atmospheric, narrow streets of the old town.

Soria
16 B1

Spain's smallest, calmest provincial capital spreads along a poplar-shaded bend of the Río Duero. The scene is Old Castile at its most poetic. Little has changed here since the Middle Ages.

The axis of Soria runs along a pedestrian street linking the main square with a roomy, restful city park, called the Alameda de Cervantes. At the park entrance a small chapel, the **Ermita de la Soledad,** contains a treasured wooden statue from the 16th century. Exuding pathos, the *Cristo del Humilladero* (Christ of the Roadside Chapel) is a classic of Spanish Baroque art.

Across the street, the **Museo Numantino** (Museum of Numancia) specializes in relics found in the Roman ruins just north of town. Numancia was a Celtiberian city razed by its Roman conquerors after a heroic siege, then rebuilt for the glory of the empire. Time has avenged the Celtiberians, for the Roman city, too,

Red, White and Pink

The good soil, relatively mild climate, adequate rainfall and irrigation along the Ebro make La Rioja one of the most productive agricultural regions in the country. They've been making Rioja wine since at least the beginning of the 12th century. But the big boom came after a 19th-century phylloxera epidemic wiped out France's vines.

Rioja wines come in all colours—red, white and rosé—but the most prized are the full-bodied reds, considered Spain's best table wines.

Wine intoxicates the scenery. The hills north of Logroño are traced by vines planted to follow the curvature of the land. They look like tightly combed scalps.

has fallen; only fractured columns and outlines of walls survived at the site, but a reconstruction is under way.

Soria's collection of churches, in mellow toast-coloured stone, is bountiful and beautiful. Among the most important, all from the 12th century: **Santo Domingo,** with an expansive Romanesque façade; **San Juan de Rabanera,** with Byzantine touches and an early hint of Gothic; and the **Concatedral de San Pedro,** with a Plateresque portal and a Romanesque cloister.

Across the river, at the end of a romantic, tree-lined road, the **Ermita de San Saturio** is a shrine that may interest spelunkers as well as churchgoers. The octagonal church is built on a rocky outcrop above caves which were home to the worthy hermit Saturio in the 5th century. You reach the church by climbing through a series of connecting caves.

All but hidden on the left bank of the river, just north of the bridge, **San Juan de Duero** used to be a monastery of the Knights Templar. The remains of the

---

Calatayud and Martial

Just east of Calatayud, in the southerly part of Zaragoza province, archaeologists have unearthed the ancient Roman city of Bilbilis. This was the birthplace of the 1st-century author, Marcus Valerius Martialis, known by his pen name Martial.

Equipped with Celtiberian ancestry and a solid Roman-Spanish education, Martial took his wit to the imperial capital. There he became fast friends with such Roman luminaries as Seneca, Pliny the Younger and Juvenal. He shamelessly buttered up his patrons and pursued pleasure and prestige with notorious enthusiasm. A thoroughly epicurean epigrammatist, he is remembered for his much-quoted and imitated sayings—shrewd or satirical, sometimes racy, often charming.

Martial tired of the bright lights of Rome and returned to Bilbilis to spend his old age with the home folk. Nearby Calatayud, which grew up around a Moorish castle, is now a town of important Mudéjar monuments. It's a crossroads town, where two vital national highways intersect. Be prepared for a traffic jam.

---

very original Romanesque-Oriental **cloister** reveal finely carved capitals, picturing themes animal, vegetable, mineral and abstract. The church now serves as the medieval section of the Museo Numantino, with exhibits on Christian, Jewish and Islamic culture. It is closed both Mondays and Tuesdays.

Sigüenza   16 B2

What, you may ask, is a town this small doing with a cathedral fit for a metropolis and a classic fortress big enough to house a regiment under siege? It's a long story.

The **fort**, overlooking the town, started as a Visigothic castle. The Moors took it over, building a formidable *alcázar*. Reconquered by the Christian forces early in the 12th century, it became the headquarters of the bishops of Sigüenza. In the 15th century it could house 1,000 soldiers and more than 300 horses. Between wars, cardinals and kings used to be wined and dined behind these stern walls. Now it's been spruced up as a *parador*, a luxury hotel sleeping 161 guests.

At first sight the **cathedral,** too, seems to be a fortress. In the dangerous 12th century, its fiercely crenellated towers were useful for ringing bells, watching for attackers and firing back. The cathedral was begun in Romanesque style, but construction went on into the Gothic and Baroque periods. It is particularly well supplied with sculptural features. The most celebrated is the **sepulchre** of "El Doncel". Other sumptuous Spanish tombs tend to show the defunct dignitaries in perpetual sleep. But Don Martín Vázquez de Arce is sculpted reclining on an elbow, engrossed in a book. The monument was ordered by Queen Isabella to honour her young page, killed in action fighting for Granada in 1486.

The **Museo Diocesano de Arte** opposite is bigger and better than you might expect from its unprepossessing entrance. In its 14 halls you can see everything from prehistoric axes to a painting of an ethereal Virgin by Zurbarán.

Locals have been known to claim that Sigüenza's **Plaza Mayor** is one of the most beautiful main squares in Spain. It might have been in the running if the buildings on opposite sides matched, but in spite of the lack of harmony there are indeed some lovely arcaded medieval houses here.

Medinaceli   16 B2
From the main Madrid–Zaragoza road, in the southernmost part of Soria province, you can see a startling Roman arch silhouetted on a hill. It's worth the drive up to Medinaceli, a village that time has passed by.

Not that the triumphal arch from the 2nd or 3rd century is very grand, or in mint condition; its embellishments are all but gone with the wind. But it's a most unusual triple arch and the view from the summit, out over the Castilian plain, catches the heart.

While you're there, have a look at some tasteful medieval houses and a 10th-century church.

The Italian-looking name of Medinaceli is deceptive. The Romans called this place *Ocilis,* but the Arabs named it *Medina Selim,* from which Medinaceli logically evolved.

Piedra   16 C2
At last, a monastery for tourists who have had their fill of serious sightseeing. The ancient **Monasterio de Piedra** has been converted into a hotel, and the main attraction is simply the natural beauty of the surroundings.

Piedra, one of four monasteries the Cistercians founded in the kingdom of Aragon, was established in 1195. The buildings fell into disrepair after the government sold off church property in 1835. Not much is left of artistic value. For an indication of the monastic way of life in the old days, have a look at the kitchen—big enough to barbecue several cows at a time.

What's memorable here is the woodland preserve around the monastery,

something of a tropical rainforest inexplicably plunked down in northern Spain. It has waterfalls, cascades, torrents and rapids. The landmarks have suggestive names like the Horse's Tail Falls, Diana's Bath and Devil's Rock. Here is all you ever wanted to know about waterfalls; you see them from above, below and alongside. A bit of spray is inevitable, but you'll welcome it on a hot summer day.

To foster meditation, many monasteries are deliberately isolated, and some are all but inaccessible. Piedra, though, is reached by good, if twisting, roads, broad enough to accommodate all the excursion coaches. The scenery on the way changes with almost every bend, from hostile cliffs to great plains of grain, from vineyards to orchards.

Teruel   17 D2
Disaster and romance colour the story of Teruel. The Iberians got here first, but the Romans razed the original settlement in a reprisal raid. Re-established under the Moors, Teruel grew and prospered. When Alfonso II of Aragon captured the town in 1171, most of the Muslims chose to stay. A special law granted them liberal rights, encouraging the development of a mixed tradition in art, which distinguishes the provincial capital today.

Christian generosity to Teruel's Muslims lasted until the beginning of the

Farewell, Young Lovers
Once upon a time, in the Middle Ages, a young Teruel couple fell impossibly in love. Diego de Marcilla asked for the hand of the girl in his life, Isabella de Segura. To the grievous distress of them both, Isabella's father sent Diego packing; he had already chosen the lad's rich rival to be his son-in-law. Like many a loser in love, Diego joined the army.

Five years later the heroic Diego came back from the wars and wandered into the church, only to find his beloved at the altar with the other man. His heart broken, Diego collapsed and died on the spot. At his funeral, Isabella's own grief brought about an identical end. They were buried in the same grave.

16th century, time enough for the creation of lasting works of Mudéjar art. The greatest threat to these architectural treasures came during the Civil War, when the town served at length as a battlefield.

Tourists are likely to make a beeline for the Gothic **Iglesia de San Pedro** (St. Peter's Church), with a 13th-century Mudéjar tower... but not so much for artistic reasons. Adjoining the church is the **chapel** containing the mausoleum of the "Lovers of Teruel". The story of this star-crossed 13th-century couple has inspired many writers, from Boccaccio to Tirso de Molina. The lovers are commemorated in a 20th-century alabaster sculpture. Another symbol of their eternal togetherness: their bones are on view.

Teruel's **cathedral** has some intriguing Mudéjar elements, especially the finely decorated 13th-century brick tower and the lantern in the dome.

Two other local towers are considered classics of Mudéjar style. The **Torre San Martin** and **Torre del Salvador** are almost identical in design, square and divided vertically into three parts, from street-level arch to belfry. The brick and ceramic decorations on the outer walls call to mind the design of an oriental carpet.

Cuenca   24 B1

It's hot in summer, cold in winter and away from the main roads, but Cuenca has been officially declared a "picturesque site". That's an understatement. The old town is perched on a precipice above the rivers Huécar and Júcar, with medieval houses hanging over the void. Add the twisting narrow lanes, the 13th-century cathedral and even a museum of modern art and you have a busy sight-seeing agenda.

Cuenca's famous **Casas Colgadas** (Hanging Houses) date from the 14th century. Until the beginning of the present century they were known as "the Houses of the King", leading to the belief that they provided some sort of getaway for medieval kings. In the evenings, spotlights heighten the dramatic effect.

The **Museo de Arte Abstracto Español**, a collection of outstanding contemporary Spanish paintings and sculpture in the modern mode, is installed in the hanging houses. The interior decor and the view outside may distract from the works on show, but the exposition is tastefully and interestingly done.

The **Museo de Cuenca,** a provincial archaeological museum, occupies a 14th-century mansion near the cathedral. The collection starts in prehistory, goes on to Roman mosaics and statues, and gives space to local artists as a bonus.

Construction of the **cathedral,** now protected as a national monument, began right after the Reconquest, on the site of a mosque. The lovely façade was salvaged from a collapse in 1902. The original plan was Gothic, influenced by some Norman features attributed to itinerant medieval architects. Among the treasures here is a 14th-century Byzantine diptych embellished with precious stones, said to be the only one of its kind in Spain.

Albacete   24 B2

Another of the towns badly scarred by the Civil War, Albacete has almost totally recovered. Now it's a growing industrial centre noted for its steel. Not girders and

*P*recipitously ensconced on a clifftop, Cuenca is officially dubbed a "picturesque site"—which is putting it mildly. Because of its isolation, and parched weather that's usually too hot or too cold, this provincial capital has remained very provincial.

La Mancha Perspectives

Miguel de Cervantes knew what he was doing. The vast, parched plain of La Mancha, with its endless horizons and potential for blurry mirages, was the perfect setting for the adventures of his myopic knight, the immortal Don Quixote.

The home town of Quixote is never specified in the novel, but it's clearly somewhere in La Mancha. The location has to be inferred from passing references, none conclusive. Could it have been the traditional windmill village of **Mota del Cuervo** in Cuenca province? Or **Argamasilla de Alba** in the province of Ciudad Real, where Cervantes started writing the book? A modern windmill has been erected in his honour. Many a squat, whitewashed and otherwise undistinguished hamlet would love to be honoured as Quixote's birthplace.

Generally, Cervantes was a place-dropper, so we can closely follow the knight's adventures. For instance, there's no doubt about the importance of **El Toboso** (in Toledo province). In this typical village of La Mancha lived Dulcinea, the woman of Quixote's dreams. "Dulcinea's house" is open to visitors.

Aside from Quixote and Sancho Panza, windmills and castles, La Mancha is famous for its wine and cheese. The best-known wines—hearty reds and dry whites—come from the Valdepeñas region. *Queso manchego*, the greatly prized local cheese, is made from cow's or ewe's milk or both. It is produced in several varieties, from mild to rather sharp. This may call for a picnic.

pipes but scissors and knives, known for their high quality and beauty. (Or take home a souvenir Albacete machete.)

An important road junction, Albacete is surrounded by the moody scenery of La Mancha. It was founded by the Iberians, developed by Romans and later by Moors. The **Museo Arqueológico Provincial** has a big collection of prehistoric, Roman and medieval relics.

Ciudad Real *23 D2*

The name of Ciudad Real—Royal City— arouses expectations of grandeur, but don't get the wrong impression. Notwithstanding some historical royal connections, this provincial capital is very provincial.

The first king involved here was Alfonso X (the Wise), credited with founding Villa Real in 1255. It became a Royal City in 1420. Otherwise, the town's only memorable impact on Spain's history has been a period when the Inquisition was based here before moving its terror machine to permanent quarters in Toledo.

Sightseeing focuses on remains of the 14th-century town wall, specifically a Mudéjar gate, the Puerta de Toledo. There are also three Gothic churches, including the cathedral.

Somewhere in La Mancha, a farm's furrows lead towards an infinite horizon. The region's almost treeless expanses are among the least populous parts of Spain. The flat, dry but sometimes colourful landscapes inspired Cervantes; his "Don Quixote de la Mancha" was to become the best-selling novel of all time.

The Saint and the Celts

The region of Galicia, in the north-western corner of the Iberian peninsula, is a rugged land of fishermen and farmers making the most of what the ancient Romans called the End of the World. Isolated between the Atlantic tides and mainstream Spain, the Galicians preserve their own language, culture and folklore. The local music, not to be confused with flamenco, screeches from bagpipes.

Galicia

In spite of its remoteness, you couldn't say Galicia is off the tourist track. In fact, the *original* such track leads here. History's first tourists—millions of sandal-shod pilgrims—hiked from all over Europe to the supreme shrine of Spain, Santiago de Compostela.

The ancient kingdom of Galicia, around the size of Belgium or Maryland, rises from romantic sea inlets to mountain ranges susceptible to snow. More than just the altitude, it's their ancestry and isolation that give the Galicians their independent character.

The energetic Celts arrived in Galicia around the 6th century B.C., settling in thoroughly enough to put up fierce resistance to subsequent invasions by Romans (led by Julius Caesar) and Moors. Under Spanish kings, Galicia reached its prime once the tomb of St. James was discovered... at the ideal moment to rally the Christian Reconquest.

In addition to all the churches, you'll see free-standing crosses in villages and other crosses atop the stone-walled barns called *hórreos*. These granaries are built on mushroom-shaped stone stilts. They are elevated to protect the grain against rats and humidity. The crosses are extra insurance against nature's perils.

Another distinctive sight in the Galician landscape: cows and ploughs. When the cows are not being milked, they are hitched up to plough the fields or pull wagons. Though much slower and more ungainly than horses, the over-exploited cows, like the farmers they serve, do their best with what they have.

*S*tanding behind the main altar of the cathedral of Santiago de Compostela, a pilgrim touches the 13th-century image of the Apostle St. James.

⚓ La Coruña 4 C1

First, a word about the name. The English call it Corunna, the Spanish La Coruña. In the Galician language, which is very close to Portuguese, it's A Coruña. On bilingual road signs in Galicia you may see the Spanish spelling blacked out by graffiti spray. The language issue here is less intense than in Cataluña (or Catalunya), but nationalistic forces vehemently promote the use of *gallego* over Castilian.

Any way you spell it, try to put the historic port and provincial capital, La Coruña, on your agenda.

You can't get much more historic than Spain's oldest lighthouse. La Coruña's **Torre de Hércules** is said to be the only ancient Roman lighthouse still in operation. Of course, there have been some changes made since its first gleam in the 2nd century. The main, square, five-storey tower is an 18th-century design incorporating an interior staircase. If you're up to the 242 stairs, climb to the summit and take in the vistas of the city and the Atlantic.

The tower, so much a landmark that it's incorporated into La Coruña's coat of arms (flanked by six seashells suggesting St. James), stands on a peninsula near the northern tip of the city. Leading to it, the centre of town occupies a relatively narrow isthmus with a crescent beach on one side and the port on the other.

The big, proud **port** is shared by oil tankers, freighters, ferries, fishing boats and yachts. This was the point of departure for the regrouped Spanish Armada as it headed for England, and disaster, in 1588. Behind the port, the Avenida de la Marina presents shining examples of local 19th-century architecture. The **galerías** (or *miradores*) of La Coruña, glassed-in porches on the upper floors of apartment houses, are designed to warm the houses in winter and insulate them from the heat in summer. La Coruña has so many multistorey houses with these floor-to-ceiling balconies that it's sometimes called the City of Glass.

The **old town,** east of the port, contains a reasonable quota of historic churches and monasteries, winding streets and restful gardens. La Coruña's oldest church, the 12th-century **Iglesia de Santiago,** is Romanesque in style with some Gothic additions.

The **Palacio Municipal** (town hall), La Coruña's most pompous public building, is really palatial. Built at the beginning of the 20th century, it has a wide, arcaded façade and three cupolas. Many a nation's parliament would feel its dignity secure in this building's conference hall.

The North Coast

Galicia's fjord-like rías (estuaries) are sunken valleys invaded by the sea. Because of this geological coincidence, the scalloped coastline is conducive to boating, bathing and fishing.

Although the Atlantic coast south from La Coruña has the more spectacular rías, the northern indentations, called the **Rías Altas,** have their enthusiasts. ⚓ Along the inlets are unspoiled resort towns and some quiet beaches for loners or lovers.

Try to visit at least one of the attractive little towns of the Rías Altas between La Coruña and the border of Asturias. **Pontedeume** is a medieval village and old-fashioned resort with a long sandy beach; **Ortigueira** is noted for its fine sandy beach and verdant hills; **El Barqueiro,** a picture-postcard fishing village, boasts a white sand beach; **Viveiro's** historic monuments provide a contrast to the fishing port and resort atmosphere; **Foz** is popular with fishermen and bathers and claims a particularly mild climate.

El Ferrol 4 C1

A few *rías* north-east of La Coruña, El Ferrol is a naval base with a perfect, protected port. It has figured in history both medieval and modern. The main part of town has a harmonious layout dating from the 18th century, when the vital shipyards were built.

This was the birthplace of Francisco Franco; during his reign, the town's name was expanded to El Ferrol del Caudillo in his honour. An equestrian statue of the late ruler still stands in the main square. Even though he was a native of Galicia, Franco suppressed its regional aspirations in the cause of national unity. Like Ferdinand and Isabella, he even outlawed the Galician language.

Santiago de Compostela *4 B2*

Almost everybody, pilgrim or tourist, approaches one of Christendom's paramount shrines with some degree of awe. But don't expect Santiago to be a holier-than-thou town with a single solemn interest. Besides piety, so much else is going on: politics, education, commerce, tourism... even a certain amount of gluttony. Chaucer's Canterbury pilgrims would feel right at home here.

One school of thought credits Santiago as the birthplace of the European identity. The medieval pilgrims, of many languages and cultures, with nothing in common but religious fervour, came together spiritually and intellectually on the Way of St. James. This role in forming the European consciousness, to say nothing of the shrine itself, is a heavy historical burden to put on a town of less than 100,000 inhabitants. But modern Santiago seems to have no complexes; it's a well-rounded, mellow community. In the capital of Galicia, life goes on busily, often gaily, in the streets and squares among the stately buildings.

The postcard picture of Santiago, the view every pilgrim has been awaiting: the main façade of the **cathedral** looms high above the plaza, with Baroque adornments and twin towers—all the surfaces stained with rust-coloured moss. This is supposed to be the spot where a couple of 9th-century Asturian kings, Alfonsos II and III, built churches over the tomb of St. James. In 997 the whole town, including the church, was wiped out by the Moorish general al-Mansur, but he is said to have spared the tomb itself. As soon as Santiago was retaken by the Christian forces, construction of a proper Romanesque cathedral was undertaken. The European pilgrim tide was unleashed even before the cathedral was completed in 1211. The monumental Baroque **façade,** the work of Fernando Casas y Novoa, dates from the mid-18th century.

Climb the stairs from the square to the main entrance. The first surprise is just inside: the 800-year-old **Pórtico de la Gloria** (Door of Glory), a marvel of Romanesque sculpture. Crane your neck at the action stories and character studies in stone around its arches. Almost all we know about the genius who carved it is the name Master Mateo. Note the fingerprint-shaped indentations on the middle column, the result of handling by millions of the faithful.

A 13th-century polychrome statue of St. James takes the spotlight on the main altar. Don't be startled if you see hands come out of the darkness to touch the saint's shoulders or neck. They're human hands, belonging to pilgrims standing in the passageway behind the altar. A crypt below the altar contains what are said to be the saint's remains.

A Saint's Saga

Legend says that St. James the Great, one of the innermost circle of the apostles of Jesus, brought Christianity to Spain. Around A.D. 44, back in Jerusalem, the former fisherman was beheaded by order of King Herod Agrippa I of Judea—the first of the apostles to be martyred. The story goes that his followers sailed back to Spain with his body, which they buried somewhere in Galicia. After the upheavals of the Dark Ages no one could remember where the grave was situated. Early in the 9th century, a star in the sky directed some shepherds to the place. Further miracles ensued when embattled Spanish soldiers were said to have seen St. James on horseback beating back the Moors. All of which gave the Reconquest a hefty boost during its darkest days.

Modern scholars tend to scoff at the legends, maintaining that St. James never visited Spain in the first place. But in Santiago de Compostela the patron saint resists the sceptics.

The gardenless Gothic cloister leads to a **museum of tapestry** with rich old hangings, unfortunately displayed without identity cards.

Facing the Plaza del Obradoiro, opposite the cathedral's main entrance, is the **town hall**, an 18th-century neoclassical palace by a French architect, Charles Lemaur. On the north side of the square, the **Hotel de los Reyes Católicos** has a stupendous Plateresque façade. The institution was founded in 1499 to receive pilgrims. You can't put a price on history, but it's now Spain's most luxurious and expensive *parador*.

Anywhere you meander in Santiago de Compostela you're within sight of a historic church or monastery. On the secular front, the city has a charming, relaxed provinciality. The local university students, jovial and sometimes noisy, balance the sobriety of some of the pilgrims. And even when it rains, which is a familiar phenomenon in these parts, the narrow streets of the old town are full of life. Bars and restaurants bulge with patrons snacking on seafood fresh from the *rías,* washed down with the light local wines.

The West Coast
The road from Santiago de Compostela to the Rías Bajas (Lower Estuaries) goes through the legend-shrouded village of **Padrón.** This is supposed to have been the spot where the ship carrying the remains of St. James arrived. The stone to which the ship is said to have moored may be seen beneath the main altar in the local church of Santiago.

La Costa de la Muerte
Long before public relations wizards began inventing glamourous names for beach zones, there was a *costa* in Galicia. Its title wasn't calculated to lure the tourists. With awful frankness it's called Costa de la Muerte (the Coast of Death).

The uninvitingly titled *costa* is a stretch of the north-west coast encompassing fishing villages like Muxía, Camariñas, Laxe and Corme. When the ocean is calm you'd never guess that this coast has claimed more than its fair share of seafarers. The local festival in Laxe in August features a simulated shipwreck and rescue. Near Camariñas an English cemetery contains the remains of victims of the 1890 shipwreck of a British training ship, the *Panther.*

The *rías* make for a jagged coastline softened by the blue calm of the water and the warm, green curves of the hills.

Villagarcía de Arousa has a bright, cheerful appearance, but beyond the municipal gardens it's a big working port.

The highway goes right through the main square of **Cambados**—not *around* the square but through the middle—which seems a bit disrespectful to such a stately town. Note the elegant *pazos* (historic mansions). The local Albariño wine is said to be descended from vines hand-carried here by pilgrims from the abbey at Cluny, in Burgundy.

La Toja, a holiday isle of pines and palms, has been linked to civilization by a bridge for most of this century, but that doesn't seem to impair the air of total relaxation. On the mainland side is O Grove, a fishing port expanded into a popular resort.

*O*n the island of Arosa, just off the highly indented coast of Pontevedra province, live mussels are returned to the sea to grow fatter and more valuable in captivity. Galicia's seafood harvest is also spectacularly rich in scallops, oysters, crabs and lobsters.

Pontevedra

4 B2

In the Middle Ages Pontevedra was an important port and shipyard; they say the ship Columbus captained, the *Santa María*, was built here. The city preserves many a fine old building, and the squares and gardens are spacious and inviting. The major historic monument is the Plateresque **Iglesia de Santa María la Mayor** (Church of St. Mary Major), in the old fishermen's quarter. The **façade** is divided into sculptural compartments, each telling a New Testament story; the crucifixion tops the towering slab. The stone carving is attributed to a Dutch artist, very active in these parts, known only as Cornelis.

The city's patron saint is commemorated in the Baroque **Iglesia de la Virgen de la Peregrina** (Church of the Pilgrim Virgin). The curvature of the Italianate, 18th-century façade adds to the grace of the place. Nearby, the church of **San Francisco,** with Romanesque touches, was begun in the 14th century.

Two of the buildings housing the **provincial museum** of Pontevedra are connected historic mansions. There are departments of archaeology and art and, predictably, interesting exhibits on the seafaring life.

Vigo

4 B2

In this industrial city of 250,000 people, the big-time fishing boats share a splendid natural harbour with pleasure craft. Vigo was known to the Phoenicians and the Romans, and attacked by Normans, Saracens and Moors, but it didn't become Spain's leading fishing port until relatively modern times.

Vigo was formerly a mainstay of trade between Spain and its American colonies. This brought prosperity but also danger; buccaneers frequently swooped on the harbour to hijack the incoming gold shipments. Vigo also had the honour of a visit from Sir Francis Drake, renowned English naval hero (or pirate to his enemies), who pillaged the town in 1589.

Drake's band burned down the church of Santa María, subsequently rebuilt in neoclassical style as Vigo's co-cathedral. The Rua Real leads from the cathedral

---

Barnacles and Tentacles

When the tide goes out in Galicia's *rías* in the shellfish (*marisco*) season, hundreds of men, women and children bend over and start collecting a prodigious crop. It's tough work amassing a bucketful of clams, cockles, oysters, scallops and eminently edible barnacles. Between the spoils collected by barefoot scavengers and those of *mariscadores* in boats, the harvest is valued in the billions of pesetas.

One of the advantages of a holiday in Galicia is the freshness and variety of the seafood. If you tire of shellfish and fish, here is your chance to try a different type of local favourite, the intimidating *pulpo* (octopus). At fairs and fiestas it's cooked in great pots and eaten off wooden dishes.

T-shirted worshipper confesses to a sympathetic priest in the shrine of Santiago. Only about one in three nominally Catholic Spaniards goes to church regularly these days. After the Franco era, church and state were separated and divorce and birth control legalized.

*A*ctually, the rain in Spain stays mainly in
the green north-west. Near the Gorges of Sil, in the isolated interior of
Galicia, farmers have terraced the steep, fertile hillsides.
The traditional division of farms into small parcels has long hindered
the area's economic development.

are the raucous taverns crammed into the narrow Calle de Lepanto, almost in the shadow of the cathedral.

Straddling the Río Miño (here on its way to becoming the frontier with Portugal), Orense has been around since the time of the ancient Romans. They built a stone bridge now known as the Puente Romano. Actually, it's newer than it looks, dating (above the original foundations) from the 13th century. The Romans, connoisseurs of therapeutic baths, were drawn here by the hot springs.

The **cathedral,** Romanesque and Gothic, was consecrated at the end of the 12th century. Of special interest is the triple-arched **Paradise Portal** *(Pórtico del Paraíso),* an interior gateway patterned after Santiago de Compostela's Door of Glory.

Lugo *5 C2*
Enthusiasts of ancient fortifications will love Lugo, where the centre of town is enclosed by the best-preserved **Roman walls** in Spain. You can climb to the top and walk all the way around the bulging battlements, a distance of about two km. (nearly 1½ miles).

Lugo is proud of its past. In Plaza de Santo Domingo stands a Roman column topped by a huge sculpture of an eagle; the inscription, in Latin, honours Augustus Caesar, who brought peace to the empire in the age of Horace and Virgil, Ovid and Livy. Embarrassingly, though, the Roman walls failed to fend off generations of invaders: the Suevi in the 5th century, the Moors in the 8th, the Normans in the 10th, and later the Moors again. Napoleon's troops won the town in 1809.

Old Lugo is a pleasant town for strolling, with a big, tree-shaded main square, fine old town-houses, and historic palaces and churches. Work started on the cathedral in 1129 but continued so long that it includes Romanesque, Gothic and Baroque elements. There are two tall towers over the main façade and one behind for good measure.

down to the colourful fishermen's district, El Berbés. The early morning fish market is inviting for tourists and cats alike. Nearby, soak up the atmosphere at the anything-goes flea market called A Pedra.

Orense *5 C2*
Inland Galicia is more down to earth than the coast, farmers eking their living from plots of land notoriously too small to be efficient. Typically, the provincial capital of Orense is thoroughly unaffected. So

115

MIRROR ON SPAIN

Cervantes waits for inspiration at his desk in Madrid Wax Museum.

Spanish literature unerringly mirrors every step in the evolution of the country: its varied heritage, its violence and mysticism, its code of honour and harsh religious values, its alternating eras of glory and despond.

In the beginning, Spaniards bumbled through a babel of languages; Latin was the *lingua franca*. But medieval troubadours, who moved effortlessly between the warring Christian and Muslim courts, tended to choose Castilian Spanish over other dialects. Anonymous epic poems like the famous *Cantar de Mío Cid* sang the praises of Christian nobles and warriors. Late in the Reconquest, King Alfonso the Wise sponsored translations into Castilian of classical, Arab, Hebrew and Christian knowledge.

By the 14th century there was a boom in a more creative field of writing. After a spell in jail for his satirical style, **Juan Ruíz,** archpriest of Hita, wrote *El Libro de Buen Amor*, a typically lusty Spanish mixture of eroticism and devotion. Some 150 years later, *La Celestina*, a kind of Spanish *Romeo and Juliet*, appeared.

The end of the 15th century, with the Moors expelled, Spain reunited, Columbus triumphant, and movable-type printing in use, heralded Spain's *Siglo de Oro* (Golden Age). Spanish poetry soon began to match the refinement of the Italian model. But the content—religious sincerity and a profound feeling for nature—took priority over the form. One of the 16th-century literary names to remember: **St. Teresa of Ávila,** the prolific author of searching spiritual books.

On quite another level, books about *pícaros*, cynical rogues who survived through outsmarting others, were a 16th-century Spanish invention. The first picaresque novel, the anonymous *Lazarillo de Tormes*, dramatized the decaying social climate, showing the anti-hero living by his wits. The trend reached its apogee in the reign of **Miguel de Cervantes,** the greatest Spanish novelist of all time. In *Don Quixote* he presented reality on two levels: the "poetic" truth of the knight errant's fuzzy vision and the "historic" truth of Sancho Panza, more earthy and rational. Cervantes used their

116

adventures to develop a philosophic commentary on existence.

Drama came into its own with **Lope de Vega,** a theorist who was practical enough to write, or have a hand in, some 1,800 plays—action dramas, full of deceit, honour and romance. On his heels came the monk **Tirso de Molina,** creator of the infamous Don Juan. But the greatest of the Golden Age playwrights, **Pedro Calderón de la Barca,** introduced deep philosophical themes and dramatic unity.

After a couple of centuries of on-and-off decline, with literary movements coming one after another and poetry overrefined and pompous, the novel came to the fore. **Pedro Antonio de Alarcón** wrote a jolly, earthy story, *El Sombrero de Tres Picos* (The Three-Cornered Hat), and it struck a popular chord. **Benito Pérez Galdós** used the recent wars against Napoleon as the backdrop for the 46 novels of his *Episodios Nacionales*.

The Spanish-American War of 1898, which Spain lost, shook the nation into taking stock and gave rise to a literary group called the Generation of '98. The pseudonymous novelist and critic **Azorín** took inspiration from the Spanish countryside and rethought earlier literary values. The influential **Miguel de Unamuno** analysed the national problem in perceptive essays. A contemporary, **Pío Baroja,** wrote easy-to-read novels advocating social action at the expense of tradition.

In the 1930s the Spanish Civil War drove many promising novelists into political exile. But the Andalusian poet and dramatist **Federico García Lorca** stayed at home, to die a martyr. Fascinated by jazz rhythm, he presented elemental passions so intense that his characters became mere puppets, symbols of man against fate. His dramatic poetry was personal yet universal, truly modern yet solidly built on traditional foundations.

The poet **Antonio Machado,** who died in exile, explored memory and soul through recurrent symbols, seeking islands of stability in the sea of consciousness. For many Spaniards, Machado still lives; as many as 500 letters a year are delivered to a mailbox fixed to his tombstone.

In 1989 the Nobel prize for literature went to a onetime bullfighter, **Camilo José Cela.** Franco censorship rejected his stark, provocative first novel, *La familia de Pascual Duarte*.

With democracy restored, the turmoil in Spanish letters shows signs of producing new big names, even if the centre of creative gravity remains in Latin America. In the meantime, literature in the Catalan and Galician tongues, banned under Franco, steers a lively comeback course.

A poet and an essayist: Federico García Lorca, Miguel de Unamuno.

Beaches, Snowy Peaks and Improbably Verdant Pastures

The bright green of the countryside of northern Spain is the colour of a hallucination. As unreal as the tint is the tilt of the hillsides: the sheep, even cows, seem pinned to vertiginous, almost vertical fields. From this steep, bucolic backwater you can almost smell the sea, just around the corner, crashing against cliffs or caressing a sandy beach.

The Bay of Biscay—Spaniards call it the Mar Cantábrico—has a stormy reputation among sailors. But the story doesn't end with shipwrecks and battered cliffs. This corner of the North Atlantic also provides some perfectly beautiful, sometimes deserted, beaches. If the climate were more dependable ("Green Spain" is a euphemism for "Rainy Spain") the beaches and coves would be overrun with tourists.

Behind the ports and resorts and miles of seafront wilderness rises a great wall, the Cantabrian Mountains (*Cordillera Cantábrica*). The peaks shoot up over a mile and a half high—above 2,500 m.—snow and sea are all in a day's excursion.

This chapter covers a wide strip of northern Spain with at least three different personalities. The Basque Country has its own language and traditions (including what many gourmets consider the finest cuisine in Spain). Beachy but mountainous Cantabria, where industry has overtaken agriculture, was home to prehistoric artists of genius. The mountain fastness of Asturias held out against the conquering Moors.

We start our survey, as many tourists do, at the northernmost frontier crossing between Spain and France.

Basque country

Irún   *8 CI*

Even though they sell plenty of kitsch bullfight-and-flamenco souvenirs to tourists nipping over from Biarritz, the gateway to Spain's Basque Country is a bigger, more serious border town than you might expect. Most of the buildings and the wide streets were built after the destruction of the Civil War. Irún is separated from the French town of Hendaye by a natural frontier, the Río Bidasoa. Pleasure boats and visiting birds bob about in these international waters.

A whale of a beach:
La Concha Bay in fashionable San Sebastián. Only the dubious weather keeps it uncrowded.

119

Fuenterrabía *(Hondarribia)*   8 *C1*

The road signs now use the Basque name, Hondarribia, to identify this working fishing port, which retains enough charm to draw the tourists. All along the sea wall, the local amateurs cast their lines for whatever fish the trawlers may have missed. The best of the catch ends up in the cluster of Hondarribian fish restaurants. The streets of the old town are cheered by the colourful touches on the houses—wooden balconies and shutters painted red, green or blue.

Overlooking it all is a pockmarked castle (known as the castle of Emperor Charles V but said to have been built in the 10th century). Now it's been done up as a *parador*.

San Sebastián *(Donostia)*   8 *C1*

Imagine the pilgrims on their arduous way to Santiago de Compostela setting sore eyes on their first stop in Spain: San Sebastián. It must have been an inspiration, sighting the dreamy curve of this sand-and-seascape, reminiscent of Rio de Janeiro's Copacabana. Majestic scenery aside, it would have been an irresistible temptation—as it still is—to dip tired feet in the cool Bay of Biscay.

The magnificent **Bahía de la Concha** (Seashell Bay) gives the impression of a perfect semicircle, or even a 270-degree arc. At low tide the perimeter of beach stretches well over a mile. The sand is protected from the sea's mischief by the embrace of two peninsulas and the blocking action of a small island between them. Guarding the right flank, the steep **Monte Urgull** is now a municipal park scattered with the remains of a mightily fortified castle. Taking the brunt in the middle is the **Isla de Santa Clara,** a green excursion spot. On the left, **Monte Igueldo** has an amusement park, a hotel and some great views at the summit (reachable by funicular).

The main beach, **Playa de la Concha,** abuts on the business district and a zone of luxurious high-rise housing. The smaller **Playa de Ondaretta** runs out at the tennis club. San Sebastián's beaches are wholly democratic: you have to be a millionaire to afford an apartment overlooking this spectacle, but anybody can claim space on the sand; it's free.

So many festivals and special events take place in San Sebastián that you're liable to arrive to find it brimming with visitors: Carnival time, the jazz festival, or *Semana Grande* ("Big Week") in mid-August or the international film festival in September. Even off-season there's a fiesta mood, a *joie de vivre*.

The cosmopolitan atmosphere is only a little more than a century old. What had hitherto been a fishermen's village, a mercantile port and then an industrial centre was finally "discovered" when the royal family chose San Sebastián as a cool relief from Madrid's infernal summer.

San Sebastián is not a place to visit in search of historic monuments. Much of the antique aspect was wiped out in 1813 in connection with a property dispute involving Napoleon on one side and a combined British-Spanish-Portuguese force on the other. The burned-out town was promptly rebuilt with wide modern streets laid out in a New York-style grid pattern.

But in the **Parte Vieja** (Old Section), in the lee of Monte Urgull, the atmosphere still recalls an old-time fishing village. The narrow streets here are the focus for the early-evening walkabout; locals and tourists cramming the multitude of taverns, bars and restaurants. The *Donostiarras* (citizens of San Sebastián) take their food so seriously that many belong to eating clubs, known here as "Popular Societies". The members (men only) of these gastronomic academies cook gourmet dinners for themselves and friends.

The colourful old streets of the Parte Vieja radiate from the arcaded **Plaza de la Constitución**. Note the numbers painted on the balconies; when bullfights were staged in the square, the residents rented out space to spectators.

♦ Vitoria *(Gasteiz)*   *8 B2*

Sancho the Wise, king of Navarre, "discovered" this place, on a plain halfway between Bilbao and Logroño, in 1181. At the time it was a most undistinguished village called Gasteiz. Credit Sancho (number VI of that ilk) with ambitious ideas: he proclaimed it a city, gave it a rousing, victorious name, and built what became a charming walled town.

Sancho's son, known as Sancho the Strong, lost Vitoria and the surrounding province of Álava to Castile. The Castilian kings greatly expanded and upgraded the town.

The growing city of Vitoria had to wait centuries for a victory that might justify its name. In the 1813 Battle of Vitoria, the Duke of Wellington's Anglo-Spanish army trounced the troops of Napoleon's brother Joseph. An overblown monument in the **Plaza de la Virgen Blanco** (White Virgin Square) commemorates the incident.

Hats Off! The Beret Story

When you think of a beret you probably picture a French stereotype, perhaps a fisherman or an artist, with a cigarette dangling from his lips and a glass of red wine in hand. (Or, perhaps, your school uniform.) But, while the black beret is right at home in Paris or Marseilles, it's not a native style. In truth the familiar, round, flat cap is a Basque invention.

You don't have to be a farmer, fisherman or poet to wear one. You don't even have to be relaxed. In several countries, elite military units affect berets—green, red or blue—as a fraternal badge, to symbolize derring-do and exclusivity. And the police in Bilbao and other towns in the region wear bright samples of local colour—red berets, or, more correctly, *boinas*.

On the north side of the plaza, a niche on the outside of the Gothic church of **San Miguel** contains a polychrome statue of the city's patron saint. The square (actually more like a triangle) presents an admirable sample of the local balconied

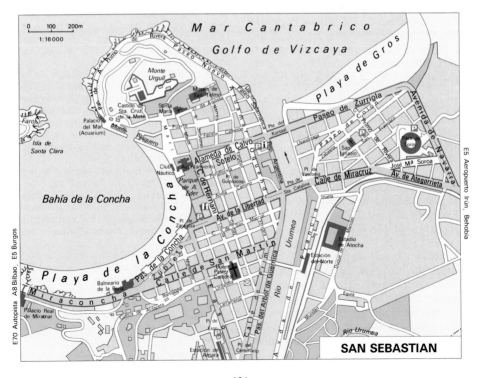

SAN SEBASTIAN

121

buildings. Elsewhere in the city, modern architects have adapted the typical sun-porched style with great success.

Just east of this plaza, the city's spacious main square, **Plaza de España**, is a classic 18th-century Spanish ensemble, with the Casa Consistorial (town hall) on the north side.

Vitoria offers a choice of cathedrals, new and old. The **Catedral Nueva**, in the modern city, is a big 20th-century rendering of Gothic style. The **Catedral de Santa María**, about 500 metres away in the middle of the crowded old town, dates from the 14th century.

The city's medieval centre is laid out in a concentric pattern, a logical design for a fortified hilltop. The streets bear the names of the trades that congregated in them—Calle de la Zapatería (shoe-makers), Herrería (blacksmiths) and Cuchillería (cutlers), for example. There are some medieval houses of great value, their walls of thin bricks alternating with equal horizontal layers of mortar. In a restored 16th-century house just north of the old cathedral, the **Museo Provincial de Arqueología** features Iron Age and Roman relics unearthed in the area. In this nicely organized modern museum, explanations are in Spanish and Basque.

Guernica
8 Bl

You've seen the picture; now see the town that inspired it. Picasso's *Guernica*, enshrined by the Prado museum, is the ultimate outcry against war. The painting was the artist's reaction to the aerial bombing by German planes of this defenceless Basque town in April, 1937. In Europe's first test of terror bombing, the casualties were in the thousands.

Now rebuilt, Guernica (Gernika) still honours the ancient oak tree in whose shade the medieval conclaves were held. A sort of Greek temple protects the stump of the historic tree, a symbol of Basque freedom. Nearby, its descendant and successor, in good health, stands behind a dignified official building called the Casa de Juntas.

Bilbao
8 Bl

The official tourist propaganda looks on the bright side, but with typical understatement, describing Bilbao's old town as an area "not without beauty". The modern part of this industrial city of more than 400,000 people—Spain's most important port—has its pleasant aspects, like boulevards and parks, to compensate for the smokestacks. The central district, full of banks as well as stores and shops, reflects Bilbao's position as the powerhouse of the Basque economy.

For tourist purposes, one sight in this capital of Vizcaya province clamours for attention. The **Museo de Bellas Artes** (Fine Arts Museum) provides a rich survey of Spanish classics plus Flemish and Italian masterpieces. After you've caught up with Goya and El Greco, Brueghel the Elder and Teniers the Younger, have a

A Tale of Three Provinces

As soon as you enter the Basque country you know you're somewhere very different. Suddenly all the signs seem threateningly foreign, in an archaic-looking typeface, with names and words full of *x*'s and *k*'s. But the language sounds nicer than it looks.

The origin of the Basque language is disputed. Although theories have linked it with Iberian or the ancient language of the Caucasus region, proof is skimpy at best. The Basques themselves think it came from nowhere foreign, but rather evolved from the language spoken by the region's original cave-dwelling inhabitants, before the first intruders arrived.

Forbidden under the Franco regime, the language (called Euskara in Basque) was clandestinely treasured as the symbol of a culture that refused to surrender. In the post-Franco liberalization Basque achieved regional equality with Castilian Spanish. Nearly all Basques are bilingual.

The Spanish Basque Country (Euskadi in the Basque language) is an autonomous region comprising three small provinces: Álava (capital Vitoria), Guipúzcoa (capital San Sebastián) and Vizcaya (capital Bilbao). Even without a word of Basque you'll be able to enjoy the music, dancing, cuisine and national sport, *jai alai* or *pelota*.

look at the upper floor, devoted to Basque and international 20th-century art. Here are luminous portraits by Ignacio Zuloaga, blue folklore scenes by Valentin de Zubiaurre, a room full of impressionist landscapes by Dario de Regoyos Valdés, and the fishermen and country folk of Aurelio Arteta. It's a unique chance to see the Basque version of the faces, scenery and way of life in their country over the last couple of centuries.

Murals, Basque-style, are devoted to political graffiti. The Basque Country has won a place as an autonomous region, but separatist forces struggle on.

Cantabria

Laredo   7 D1

West from Bilbao stretches the beach-lined Cantabrian coast with fishing villages and summer resorts little known abroad. But times are changing, and restaurants in Laredo, halfway between Bilbao and Santander, now post menus in English, French and German.

Laredo's beach, though far from town, is beautiful in the San Sebastián style, in fact, even bigger. Apartment blocks and comfortable holiday houses proliferate. The old town, with narrow, steep streets, has sprouted souvenir shops and the kind of taverns visitors seek out on long, rainy afternoons.

Because sailors from Laredo joined the expeditions of Columbus, Pizarro and later adventurers, the town's name is perpetuated in several western hemisphere communities... like Laredo, Texas.

Santander
7 D1

Successfully combining the roles of major port and tasteful resort, the sizable city of Santander looks so good because fate gave it a couple of extra chances.

In 1894 the freighter *Cabo Machichaco*, laden with explosives, blew up in the port, killing hundreds and demolishing much of the harbour area.

In 1941, a fire on the scale of the Great Fire of London ravaged Santander. Sparked by a short circuit, the flames were fanned by hurricane-force winds. Casualties were miraculously minimal, but two-thirds of the city was destroyed and 20,000 inhabitants made homeless.

For the rebirth of Santander, a far-sighted plan decreed that new buildings be held to low-rise proportions and interspersed with parks and gardens. To make life easier, they bulldozed some inconvenient hills and laid out the new streets and boulevards in a logical grid plan.

After the fire the **cathedral**, overlooking the ancient port, had to be reconstructed almost from bottom to top. It was restored to look like the medieval original, something between fortress and watchtower. The oldest part of the building is the Romanesque crypt. Other elements of the cathedral were tacked on over the centuries in the style in vogue.

Santander's top museum, the **Museo Provincial de Prehistoria,** has some fine finds from excavations around the province. Also displayed are axes, arrows, and skilfully carved staffs or batons made from deer antlers.

The antidote to Santander's clanging port, the district called **El Sardinero** gives the city its resort mood. A grand Casino is complemented by small seafood bars. The beaches, parks and gardens are spacious, though not quite the measure of the crowds that congregate on a sunny day of summer. Overlooking the sea on its own rugged peninsula, the Victorian-style **Magdalena Palace** was built for Alfonso XIII as a summer escape. It was designed with myriad architectural eccentricities.

Santillana del Mar
7 C1

In this perfectly preserved venerable village only the television aerials tacked to some of the red tile roofs reveal what century we're in. There's nothing contrived about the medieval effect. In a stone barn 30 paces beyond the main square, cows are mooing over being milked.

The name Santillana is a contraction of the name of Saint Juliana, martyred by Emperor Diocletian. "Del Mar" means "of the sea", but the village is not *on* the sea, which is a few miles north across the protecting hills.

You don't need a map to explore the narrow streets of Santillana. Just wander at will and soak up the atmosphere of the old stone houses with flowered balconies, the medieval towers and inns, and the mansions built by the "Indianos", local folk who returned, rich, from adventures in the Americas.

In front of the Ayuntamiento (town hall) stands a modern sculptor's vision of a prehistoric bison. On the stone next to it is engraved:

Santillana
Al Hombre de
Altamira

(From Santillana to the Man of Altamira.) This is the village's tribute to the cavemen of nearby Altamira, who left us a magnificent artistic legacy... featuring, of course, the local bison, long-since extinct.

At the north end of the village, the **Colegiata** (Collegiate Church) is dedicated to St. Juliana (see her statue in a niche above the Romanesque portal and the tomb inside). Built seven or eight centuries ago, the **cloister** is well worth a few minutes of meditation, if only for the beauty of the sculptural work. The capitals of the columns supporting its many arches are carved to represent biblical characters and events, or mythical beasts, or geometric doodlings.

In the **convent** at the opposite end of the village, the **Museo Diocesano** specializes in carvings of saints and angels gathered from churches around the region. The 16th-century sarcophagus of one Pedro Gonzales de Aguero portrays him lying larger than life with a sword in one hand, a bird in the other, and a faithful hound at his feet.

Altamira   *7 C1*

The caves *(cuevas)* of Altamira, a couple of kilometres inland from Santillana del Mar, contain some of the most inspiring works of art in Europe: underground art. They were painted perhaps 15,000 years ago, but that's by no means the only reason they are treasured.

These are no antique scribbles or graffiti. Like all great art, the cave paintings convey more than reality. They show the artists' intense sensitivity and soul, as well as astonishingly keen draughtsmanship.

The most sublime of the paintings occupy a part of the cave network dubbed the Sistine Chapel of prehistoric art. The bison and other muscular beasts painted on the ceiling and walls didn't get there because a few cavemen were sitting around the fire with nothing better to do. This is a special part of the cave, far removed from the living quarters, presumably a religious sanctuary. The artists would have been too close to the low ceiling to see the "big picture", yet they took advantage of the curvature and protuberances of the rock to give life and motion to their subjects. In a word: genius.

The paintings in the Altamira caves were discovered more than a century ago. Foreign experts suspected a hoax. Finally authenticated, they became a tourist attraction and money-spinner. But the very breathing of the tramping crowds threatened the survival of the art, so the caves were closed to the public in 1977. Now entry is restricted to a handful of visitors, who have to obtain permission months in advance.

Mere tourists are invited into a museum built above the caves by the Ministry of Culture. Its exhibits, and a film, explain many aspects of the geology,

Authenticating Altamira

In 1868 a hunter's dog ferreting through heavy undergrowth unearthed the hidden entrance to a cave later named Altamira. The hunter tipped off Marcelino Sanz de Sautuola, an amateur archaeologist in the region, who discovered amazing paintings deep within the caves.

In 1880 Sautuola published a monograph, "Brief Notes on Some Prehistoric Objects of the Province of Santander". The leading French experts on prehistory dismissed Altamira as either a misunderstanding or a hoax. One French palaeontologist who condescended to go down and look judged the paintings as less than ten years old. Humiliated and forgotten, Sautuola died in 1888.

But towards the turn of the century, cave paintings remarkably similar to Altamira's were discovered in France and hailed as paleolithic art. That made them official. In 1902 one of the French experts published an apology, offering posthumous rehabilitation to Sautuola and his daring vision.

archaeology and artistry involved. You can see the 30,000-year-old remains of a caveman, nicknamed "Pipo" by the locals. To simulate the cave experience, though, you have to go to Madrid, where parts of the cave have been reproduced under the gardens of the Archaeological Museum.

Picos de Europa   *6-7 BC1*

The road westwards from Santillana to Oviedo parallels the sea but rarely in sight of it. Occasionally, though, you'll see a sign, "Mirador", pointing to a lookout spot. Grab the chance to pull over and whiff the Atlantic breeze while surveying the distant seascapes. Landwards the Cantabrian countryside contributes agreeable sensations: the view of steep, green fields spattered with wild flowers and red-topped white houses, the sound of cowbells, the smell of haystacks.

Soon after you pass the beach resort of San Vicente de la Barquera, road signs offer the first of several chances to turn inland toward the Picos de Europa. This mountain range, extending into three provinces, begins scarcely 25 km. (15 miles) south of the coast.

The peaks of the Picos rise beyond 2,600 m. (8,500 ft.), so a single view may pan down from snow to blossoming olive trees. The valleys between the rugged walls of grey limestone are coloured Shangri-La green. There are three massifs, delineated by four rivers—the Deva, Duje, Cares and Sella. They make their way to the sea in many moods, flowing in refreshing brooks, shimmering in pools, or roaring through microchasms.

Utter wilderness is always near at hand here, but the main roads are in fair repair. To travel the tracks into mountain-climbing country you need a four-wheel drive vehicle. While chamois, foxes and wolves are at home up here, your closest encounter with wildlife will probably be watching the cows decide whether to get off the road.

Asturias

Covadonga 6 Bl

The most visited place in the Picos de Europa, every good Asturian is supposed to *walk* to this shrine at least once in a lifetime. Covadonga has a historical as well as religious significance.

After the seemingly invincible Moors had overrun most of the country in the 8th century, a spearhead of the Christian forces, hidden among these harsh mountains, started the Reconquest of Spain. The Battle of Covadonga in 722 was the first Christian victory in a struggle that went on for more than seven centuries.

Little is known of Pelayo, the hero who kept alive the flame of Christian Spain in this Moorish-encircled redoubt. Pelayo had royal connections; he may have been a Visigothic noble, or at least a member of the king's entourage. His statue, in knight's armour, in the main square of Covadonga is based on little more than a modern sculptor's imagination.

Across the esplanade from the statue is the basilica, an unexpectedly big neo-Romanesque church, less than a century old. Down the hill, the **Santa Cueva** (Holy Cave) is supposed to be the spot where Pelayo saw a vision of the Virgin Mary, inspiring his crusade. The cave is often jammed with pilgrims. A small 18th-century statue here, known affectionately as *la Santina* (the Little Saint), is revered as the patron saint of the principality.

Cangas de Onís 6 Bl

From A.D. 718 to 910, Asturias was the only unbowed Christian kingdom on the Muslim-controlled Iberian peninsula. The village of Cangas de Onís, now on the tourist map as the western gateway to the Picos de Europa, was its capital. Led by Pelayo, the incipient forces of the Reconquest began to push back the hitherto unstoppable invader, giving heart to Christians under the occupation and abroad.

Aside from the natural beauty surrounding Cangas, there's one man-made monument to grab your attention: a humpbacked Romanesque bridge over the Río Sella; a Christian cross hangs from its high arch.

*G*audily *garbed Basque dancers prepare for a holiday procession in the remote valley town of Oñate, in Guipúzcoa. The flat cap, called a* boina, *originated in the Basque Country, then emigrated to France, where it was called a* beret.

*E*ven in summer, pockets of snow cling to the rugged
*Picos de Europa, which stretch westward from the Pyrenees.
These well-equipped hikers reached high altitude above Fuente Dé
the easy way, by cable car. The Picos go as high as 8,688 feet
(2,648 metres) above sea level.*

Villaviciosa
6 B1

The name alone may prompt you to glance at this small town, north-west of Cangas. Does Villaviciosa really mean "vicious town"? Not at all, say the locals. The *viciosa* refers not to municipal corruption but to the luxuriant vegetation in the region.

The biggest event in its history overtook Villaviciosa in 1517. A royal armada turned up, unannounced, and the French-speaking prince who would become the Holy Roman Emperor Charles V came ashore to take his throne. Landing in this backwater was an unglamorous start to his reign; the navigators, it's reported, had been aiming for Santander. A monument in Villaviciosa has a bas-relief showing Charles coming ashore in what looks like a rubber dinghy.

Gijón
6 B1

The port and resort of Gijón, much rebuilt and expanded after Civil War damage, looks all new, but the Romans were here first. The Roman baths, dating from the

1st century, weren't rediscovered until 1903. Today's bathers head for roomy San Lorenzo beach. Since it's only 28 km. (17 miles) between the appealing sand beach and the inland city of Oviedo, there's a lot of traffic heading this way on fine summer days. Behind the beachside promenade, high-rise apartment blocks share a pleasant view.

Spaniards pronounce *Gijón* rather like the sound of a donkey's heehaw. Another evocative sound, that of foghorns, can be heard here. Gijón has a big port, from where Asturian coal is exported. The non-touristic side of the economy makes this the biggest city in Asturias (more than 250,000 inhabitants).

If you're in the market for an offbeat museum, drop in on the **Museo de la Gaita** (Bagpipe Museum), on the right bank of the Río Piles in Gijón. Bagpipes are as much at home hereabouts as they are in Aberdeen or Glasgow.

Oviedo   *6 A1*

How nice: Oviedo surrounds a central park, a perfect refuge from urban cares. With an area of 6 hectares (15 acres) the **Parque de San Francisco** may be smaller than New York's Central Park, but it has more shady trees per acre, and they are magnificent.

The political and cultural capital of Asturias was founded in the 8th century. At that early stage in the Reconquest it became the seat of King Alfonso II, but in the 10th century pomp and power followed the armies south. Happily, the end of Oviedo's royal status didn't lower the tone of the town. It still has a certain splendid something, and many a monument to prove it.

The **cathedral,** built atop the ruins of an 8th-century church, culminates in a

---

Grain on a Pedestal

"Green Spain" is also "Wet Spain", so the farmers had to find a way to protect their crops and tools. The answer is the *hórreo.* Built on either four or six pillars, according to the design, the *hórreo* keeps out rain, ground damp and vermin. These uplifted barns are more or less rustic, depending on their age, location, and the budget of the farmer. In Asturias alone more than 20,000 *hórreos* are still in use. In neighbouring Galicia, which is at least as rainy, the traditional *hórreos* are more formal and solid.

---

flourish with a tall, richly turreted tower in Flamboyant Gothic style. The original 16th-century blueprint called for twin steeples, but you'd never miss the twin. The **high altar** features an immense 16th-century retable, divided into 24 delicately carved compartments. The 14th-century **cloister,** with lovely Gothic tracery, surrounds an exceptionally lush garden.

But the most significant part of the cathedral is the **Cámara Santa** (Holy Chamber), a shrine built by Alfonso II to protect the holiest relics evacuated from Toledo in the face of the Moorish onslaught. At the entrance, notice the eloquent statues of the apostles, two to a column—outstanding sculpture from the 12th century. The Cámara Santa holds a rich hoard of works of historic, religious and artistic importance.

The city was a battlefield in the 1930s, first during an uprising by Asturian miners and then in the Spanish Civil War. In the **Museo Provincial de Bellas Artes** (Provincial Fine Arts Museum), around the corner from the cathedral, a large oil painting by Joaquín Vaquero shows the smoking ruin of Oviedo as it looked in 1942. Not even the cathedral was immune; its lofty spire was truncated.

*T*he season's harvest of maize is kept safe and dry under the roof of an Asturian farmer's hórreo.

From the Pyrenees to the Mediterranean

Smuggling isn't what it used to be. The European Community has toppled the economic wall that always divided Spain from France. The physical barrier, the Pyrenees, still stands tall though, a harshly beautiful monument to the surmountable differences between Iberia and the rest of Europe.

North-eastern Spain starts in the fastness of the Pyrenees and arcs down to the Mediterranean. Our grouping of the north-east includes Navarre, northern Aragon and all of Catalonia. It adds up to a remarkably diverse sweep of Spain, in geographical and ethnic terms. The people are mountaineers, industrialists, fishermen; depending on the location, their languages are Basque, Castilian (or the Aragonese variant) or Catalan.

Navarre   8-9 CD2

From west to east the mountains gain altitude, and the profound Basqueness of the countryside and the people begins to be less noticeable. In the middle of the Navarre Pyrenees, the most crucial of the ways through the peaks is the storied **Roncesvalles Pass**. This was the scene of

*P*amplona's festival brings fighting bulls and fearless (or foolish) young men into close contact.

a rather routine 8th-century battle later blown up into a heroic saga of knighthood in flower. What really happened was that the Basques pounced on the rear guard of Charlemagne's army there in 778. The *Song of Roland*, the first great French epic poem, retold the news as a glorious struggle against the Moors. This added a splash of glamour to Roncesvalles Pass, through which hordes of French pilgrims were to enter Spain on the hike to Santiago de Compostela.

The village of Roncesvalles, just after the pass, is quite small and simple, the kind of place where a traveller is glad to settle for spartan lodging and a hot meal. In that respect nothing has changed in many centuries. For more sophisticated facilities, it's less than 50 km. (30 miles), all downhill, to the forward-looking old capital of the kingdom of Navarre.

Pamplona   8 C2

In the 1920s Ernest Hemingway soaked up the atmosphere at the famous festival of Pamplona and wrote a book, *The Sun Also Rises* (published in Britain under the title *Fiesta*). Forty years later the locals expressed their appreciation. Alongside the Pamplona bullring stands a bust of the bearded author, perhaps the only

*In the foothills of the Pyrenees in Upper Aragon
a shepherd looks after his far-flung flock. Since time immemorial the
livestock have been kept on the move, changing altitude with
seasons to avoid climatic extremes and find the richest pastures.*

On a non-festive day, you'll just have to use your imagination. Conjure up the Pamplona of nearly two thousand years ago when, tradition tells us, the town was founded by the Roman general Pompey the Great. He wasn't at all shy about naming it Pompeiopolis after himself, and this evolved into Pamplona. There are remnants of Roman Pamplona in the **Navarre Museum** here—mosaics, columns and inscriptions.

The **cathedral** is a huge complex backing onto the ancient city wall; the defences have been integrated into a park. The overblown west façade went up in the 18th century, but the gloomy Gothic interior dates from the 14th and 15th centuries. Alongside, the beautiful Gothic **cloister** is a haven of sunshine and calm, with some notable sculpture.

Between the old and new parts of the city, Pamplona's main square, the **Plaza del Castillo,** is like the central plaza of a small town, only vastly bigger in area. There are shady trees, benches, a bandstand, plenty of space for promenading, and outdoor cafés along the edges.

The most extraordinary single building in town may be the Baroque **Ayuntamiento** (city hall), a glorious fantasy of frills, with statues of dreadful giants on the roof and plenty of balconies for festive occasions. Occasions don't come any more festive than the *Sanfermines.*

Estella 8 C2

Right on the main N-111 highway between Pamplona and Logroño is an unspoiled historic town, in its day a favourite stop for pilgrims hiking to Santiago. The Compostela connection explains Estella's array of lovely Romanesque structures.

Thanks to one of those miraculous discoveries of a holy image, in the 11th century, Estella was built at a bend in the Río Ega. The site adds much to the beauty of the town (nicknamed "Estella la Bella"); you'll see horses grazing along the river banks. Incidentally, don't try to drive across the pretty **Puente de la Cárcel**

statue in Spain in which a hero wears a rollneck sweater; the street is named Paseo Hemingway.

The running of the bulls, which pursue daring, sometimes foolhardy, celebrants through the streets, has become a perennial feature on the international television news. Fear-tinged hilarity marks this best-known aspect of the feast of St. Fermín, and if you can get to Pamplona in the second week of July, you're guaranteed some vivid experiences in exchange for your usual quota of sleep.

135

(Floodgate Bridge), so steeply hump-backed that it might gouge the bottom out of your car.

Just around the corner from a busy road, in **Plaza de San Martín,** you'll be soothed by the sound of water trickling from a medieval fountain. The tourist office is here, enviably ensconced in a 12th-century palace. At the top of a long flight of ceremonial steps the church of **San Pedro de la Rúa** (St. Peter of the Road—the "road" being the Way of St. James) has a most unusual portal, with a scalloped arch and elements influenced by both the Moors and the Cistercians. Have a look at the remains of the Romanesque **cloister.** Half of it went up in smoke in a 16th-century explosion at the castle next door; the surviving sculpture on the capitals of the columns consists of gracefully carved scenes of biblical stories and animal or vegetable life.

Another extraordinary church here, the unfinished **Iglesia del Santo Sepulcro** (Church of the Holy Sepulchre), has a superlative Gothic portal. The hilltop church, **Santa María Jus del Castillo,** was a synagogue before a medieval pogrom scarred Estella.

Just a couple of miles south of Estella, the **monasterio de Irache,** another stop on the pilgrim way, once contained a university. Its big 12th-century church looks fit enough to stand for another eight centuries. There is an interesting juxtaposition of "new" and "old" cloisters, the latter, with Plateresque details, more interesting.

Olite   8 C2
This appealing medieval town is unspoiled but for its modern main square—which somehow fits in nicely, anyway. You can't miss the local palace, the **Palacio Real,** a right royal castle with turrets, pinnacles and crenellations overlooking and surrounded by Olite. The kings of Navarre lived there in the heroic Middle Ages, until their realm was swallowed up by Castile.

Alongside the rambling palace, and actually a part of it, the **Iglesia de Santa María**, begun in the 13th century, was a royal chapel. Its sculpted portal is a distinguished example of Navarre Gothic.

Tudela   8 C3
You can see the soaring tower of Tudela's cathedral from miles away, yet once inside the labyrinth of narrow streets you may have to search for the town's principal historic monument. Built soon after the Reconquest on the ruins of a mosque, the **cathedral** is a 12th- and 13th-century classic of the earliest Gothic style. There are three monumental **portals,** the most dramatic facing west and devoted, with terrifying detail, to the Last Judgment. Among the highlights inside is the **Capilla de Santa Ana** (St. Anne's Chapel), a Baroque spree with flights of angels all the way up the walls to the top of the chapel's dome. The chapel holds the Gothic statue of Tudela's patron saint, which figures in the local festival on July 26. Save time for the Romanesque **cloister.**

La Oliva   9 D2
This was an early Cistercian monastery, renowned for its tasteful architecture and the size and scope of its library. The 12th-century king of Navarre, Sancho the Wise, and his son, Sancho the Strong, paid the bills for the church here. Of special interest is the **portal,** with some pleasing Romanesque sculptural details. The Gothic cloister is perfectly proportioned.

Sangüesa   9 D2
The ancient town of Sangüesa guards a crucial bridge across the Río Aragón, disputed during the struggle against Moors and later a crossing point on the pilgrims' way to Santiago. The church of **Santa María la Real** is built up against the river, right by the bridge. At the outset, in the 12th century, it was a royal chapel. Its south **portal** is a wonder of stone carving, if only for setting what may be a record for the number of figures sculpted per square foot.

Leyre *9 D2*

The mountain setting of Leyre monastery is as inspiring as its history, yet it's quite accessible. A well-paved road climbs from the main Pamplona–Huesca road to the monastic complex, perched between Pyrenean cliffs and a serene artificial lake far below. This monastery was the 11th-century religious powerhouse of all Navarre.

So venerable is the **church** that the original Romanesque arches are not quite perfectly curved—a treat to the modern eye, so accustomed to routine flawlessness. The west **portal** is lavishly carved, hence its Latin nickname, "Porta Speciosa" (Splendid Doorway). The sculptural repertoire here consists of saintly figures interspersed with a nightmarish parade of monsters.

Northern Aragon

The sparsely settled mountains and valleys of northern Aragon compensate for their isolation with striking scenery and regal history. Here began the medieval kingdom of Aragon, which grew to hold sway as far afield as the Mediterranean. Aragon was a key ingredient in what became the mighty realm of Castile.

Sos del Rey Católico *9 D2*

Ferdinand of Aragon, destined to become Spain's King Ferdinand the Catholic, was born in this hilltop village in 1452. Today Sos del Rey Católico is all spruced up in his honour.

It's definitely a village for walking; if you drive you'll not only lose your way (the quaint, narrow streets tend to be unnamed), but you may have to back out after a long, twisting adventure into a dead end.

The population today is less than a thousand, but the church of **San Esteban** (St. Stephen) is big enough for a congregation twice the size. Here is preserved the font in which the future king was baptized. Have a look at the **crypt**, spookily reached down a tight spiral staircase. Up top again, enjoy the **view** over the soft, furrowed green hills surrounding charming old Sos.

Jaca *9 E2*

Gateway to the Aragon Pyrenees, Jaca has been fraught with military significance for at least a dozen centuries, since it figured in one of the earliest victories over the Moors. A symbol of its strategic importance is unavoidably evident at the edge of town: an enormous, low-lying **fortress** of the classic Spanish main school of architecture. It was built during the reign of Philip II.

Jaca's **cathedral** is an 11th-century model with notable Romanesque frescoes, as well as afterthoughts like Renaissance sculpture and a Plateresque retable.

Ordesa National Park *10 A1*

Graceful Pyrenean chamois hang out here. So do wild goat, roe deer, wild boar, squirrels, and nature lovers of all stripes. The dramatic canyon of the Ordesa valley has been a national park for more than 70 years; a French national park abuts on the other side of the rocky frontier. On the Spanish side, these 16,000 hectares (40,000 acres) are officially called the Parque Nacional de Ordesa y Monte Perdido.

The Pyrenees Peak in Aragon
The tallest peaks of all the Pyrenees belong to Aragon, most pointedly the Pico de Aneto, altitude 3,404 m. (11,169 ft.). Not for nothing is this called the Maladeta (Accursed) region. Only an accomplished mountain climber could love these dangerous summits, where you can always start a snowslide, even in midsummer. Of course, they're properly poetic when seen from afar. And the Pyrenees of Aragon are equipped with international ski resorts like Astún, Candanchú and Formigal. This high above sea level, nobody could doubt that Spain is Europe's second most mountainous country, topped only by Switzerland.

Above the pine, spruce, beech, poplar and larch are inhospitable cliffs and turbulent waterfalls, altogether a filling feast of scenery. There are suggested walking tours requiring varying degrees of energy and proficiency, but anyone can enjoy the general atmosphere. Snow cuts off access to the park from about October to April.

Huesca   9 E3

The "H" in Huesca is silent, and so is the legendary bell. An old Spanish saying describes bad news as resounding like "the bell of Huesca". The story tells of the 12th-century king, Ramiro II, who invited rebellious nobles to see a great bell cast, seizing the occasion to behead them. News of the bell incident indeed reverberated throughout Aragon and beyond, but historians doubt it ever happened; among other things they say Ramiro II, a monk, was too nice a fellow to be guilty of such a devious plot.

A century or so after the alleged bell affair, construction began on the stately

trates the awful story of the bell of Huesca.

Ramiro II is buried in the church of **San Pedro el Viejo;** a coin-operated lighting system reveals the sepulchres of the monk and his kingly brother, Alfonso I. The Romanesque **cloister** here has been much restored, and in fact most of the fine carvings on the capitals have unfortunately been redone like new, too perfect to be true.

Zaragoza   *17 D1*

The unusual name, precipitating a double lisp in Spanish, can be traced back to the 1st century B.C. When a Celtiberian town on the south bank of the Río Ebro became a Roman colony under Augustus Caesar, imperial officials employed the standard, shameless overdose of sycophancy and called it Caesaraugusta. The Moors captured the town very early in the 8th century and pronounced it Saraqustah. From there it's an effortless evolution to Zaragoza (Saragossa in English).

The river, refreshed by mountain streams, is at its best here, more than halfway from its origin in the Cantabrian mountains to its outlet in the Mediterranean. The Romans constructed a bridge, often destroyed by flood or war over the centuries and rebuilt each time. The present **Puente de Piedra** (Stone Bridge), revived after its demolition at the hands of Napoleon's troops, shows elements of Mudéjar, French, Italian and Baroque architecture.

Backing onto the Ebro is Zaragoza's favourite church, one of *two* cathedrals on its skyline. The basilica of **Nuestra Señora del Pilar** (Our Lady of the Pillar) contains a small Gothic statue of Spain's patron saint. The cathedral is vast and bright and always packed with pilgrims. Across the pigeon-plagued plaza from the main entrances are religious souvenir shops (selling all sizes of statuettes of the revered image, with or without lights) and outdoor cafés.

According to tradition the Virgin Mary

cathedral of Huesca, on the site of a Roman temple and a Muslim mosque. The Gothic **façade** is divided into upper and lower halves by an unusual little projecting roof. There are three ample naves, and the alabaster **altarpiece** is a splendid 16th-century carving by Damián Forment, who was based in Zaragoza.

Across the calm square is the Renaissance **Ayuntamiento** (town hall), with corner towers and a patio, altogether a most impressive place to go to pay your taxes. A 19th-century painting here illus-

appeared here in A.D. 40, standing on a pillar. The cathedral was built in the 17th century around the jasper column in question, available for pilgrims to kiss, at the back of the elaborate **Capilla de Pilar**. The cathedral's main **retable**, as big as the side of a barn, is the greatest work of the sculptor Damián Forment. It looks intricate enough to have needed a lifetime to complete.

Zaragoza's other cathedral, **La Seo,** was built hundreds of years earlier, on the site of a mosque. Construction, in brick, lasted from the 12th to the 16th century; the architecture is mostly Gothic but there are Romanesque remnants as well as striking Mudéjar decorations and Baroque postscripts. The belfry is a 17th-century addition, chiming in with the look of the towers on the four corners of the Pilar church, a couple of hundred yards to the west.

Between the two cathedrals stands Zaragoza's most imposing civil structure, a Renaissance palace that served as the 16th-century equivalent of a stock exchange. **La Lonja** (the Exchange) brought commercial traders in from the cold. They made their deals in a most palatial triple-naved trading room. It's open to the public on special occasions.

The Moors' most lasting bequest to Zaragoza, the **Aljafería,** looks from the outside like a rendering of an ambitious child's sandcastle. But when you cross the moat (now a sunken garden) you enter the world of Muslim Spain. After the Reconquest the pleasure palace of the Moorish rulers was much tampered with, but it has been restored in splendour, with delicately filigreed arches and panelled ceilings rarely seen this far north. There are even lemon trees planted around the reflecting pools in the patio.

As well as having two cathedrals, Zaragoza possesses two tourist offices. The Aragon tourist office occupies the Zuda tower, a 14th-century Mudéjar relic between the Roman wall and the Pilar church. The municipal tourist office, across the square from the basilica, uses a mock Roman temple.

Andorra—Shangri-La in the Pyrenees

A country so small and isolated that it hasn't got an airport or even a railway station. Nor a currency to call its own: Spanish pesetas and French francs are equally valid here. Take your passport, though, for the customs men.

Andorra is the world's only country whose official language is Catalan. Spanish and French are almost universally understood, while English and German are useful in the shops. All very cosmopolitan for a backwoodsy redoubt.

Those shops are the heart of the matter. Since Andorra is free of the taxes afflicting neighbouring countries, the price of almost everything, especially imported luxury goods, comes as a refreshing surprise. Every year, millions of shoppers cross the Pyrenees to splurge on cut-price whisky, perfume and electronic gadgets. Andorra's spectacular scenery takes second place; most of today's visitors are heading straight for the bulging shops of Carrer Meritxell, the main street of the capital "city", Andorra-la-Vella. Some go on to the well-equipped winter sports resorts nearby.

The autonomous principality of Andorra has no army. Its security depends on the foreigners who rule it. After seven centuries of fiercely defended independence, power is now shared equally, and with no visible strain, by the president of France and the bishop of Urgel, just across the border in Spain. The "princes" receive a token tribute from the ministate for their trouble.

Until well into the 20th century Andorra was a lonely shepherd's domain, all but inaccessible to the outside world. Now it shares Europe's traffic problems.

Aside from the absorbing business of bargain hunting, take time for a stroll through Andorra-la-Vella, where most of the principality's permanent residents live. Visit the Casa dels Valls, a 16th-century building in which the parliament and court are housed. The nation's archives rest in a chest secured with six locks, the keys to which are held in the six parishes. In the villages are churches of admirable Romanesque design; and the countryside is as invigorating as it is rugged.

Catalonia

A dynamic region of 6 million people, Catalonia has its own history, tradition, folklore and language. (Its name is Catalunya in Catalan, Cataluña in Spanish.) From snow-prone villages in the Pyrenees to Barcelona by the sea, arguably Spain's most sophisticated city, the people are welcoming and outward-looking. In the Middle Ages the Catalans ruled a great sweep of the Mediterranean, including at one time or another Sicily, Sardinia, Corsica and parts of Greece. The empire is gone, but the memory of grandeur remains, along with the energetic, worldly outlook.

The Pyrenees of Catalonia

The rugged peaks of the Pyrenees overshadow more than just the pine forests, waterfalls and glacial lakes of a most picturesque countryside. History marks this scene with charming old hamlets, Romanesque churches and monasteries.

For raw scenery, the natural place to go is the **Parque Nacional d'Aigües Tortes y San Mauricio,** a national park of more than 100 sq. km. (nearly 40 sq. miles). Snow-capped peaks exceeding 3,000 m. (about 10,000 ft.) serrate the skyline. Chamois, ibex and wild boar cavort in these wide open spaces, but people need four-wheel drive vehicles to penetrate the park. After that, comfortable hiking shoes are essential.

Seo de Urgel *(La Seu d'Urgell)* 10 C1

Just across the frontier from Andorra, the small town of Seo de Urgel is a tourist centre with a glorious history going back to the days of the Romans. Since the 13th century the local bishop has been the co-ruler of Andorra.

The 12th-century cathedral of **Santa María,** built under Lombard influence, stands on the site of earlier churches going back to the 4th century. The Diocesan Museum keeps on show an illuminated **manuscript** of great importance and beauty—a 10th- or 11th-century copy of a commentary by the 8th-century monk called Beatus of Liébana. There are vivid action pictures of the Apocalypse.

Ripoll *(El Ripollès)* 11 D1

Wilfred the Hairy, Catalonia's first ever hero, who died bravely in battle in A.D. 878, is buried in the royal pantheon of Ripoll's ancient Benedictine **monastery.** Built in the shape of a cross, the monastery has five aisles and a transept with seven apses. The 12th-century **portal** and adjacent wall space are sculpted into a sort of storyboard of the Bible, illustrating Old and New Testament dramas. The **cloister,** from the same era, also features important stone carving. The district of Ripoll is said to contain more than 60 Catalan Romanesque churches.

Lérida *(Lleida)* 18 B1

The province of Lérida stretches from the snows of the Pyrenees to rolling grazing land and orchards. The capital city, also called Lérida, is safely in the sunny south.

The Iberians settled here, and the Romans fought over the town. The Moors moved in early in the 8th century and held Lérida for more than 400 years. You can see the Moorish influence in the **Seu Vella** (Old Cathedral), built on a promontory at the beginning of the 13th century. The **cloister,** oddly placed in front of the church, has unusual dimensions and fascinating sculptural effects. Overlooking the city here is the medieval Arab fortress of the **Zuda.** The castle suffered many misfortunes, most recently in the Civil War, but the surviving defensive walls and towers give a good idea of its one-time importance.

Poblet 10 C2

More than eight centuries ago the count of Barcelona, Ramón Berenguer IV, founded this powerful Cistercian monastery as a gesture of thanksgiving for the reconquest of Catalonia from the Moors. The royal connections brought Poblet

*Y*oung choristers of Europe's oldest music school, the
*Escolanía, participate in mass at Montserrat. For 700 years, pilgrims
have been climbing the mighty rock formations to the monastery to pay
homage to the patron saint of Catalonia; cable cars and excursion
coaches have now replaced the donkeys.*

with its rose bushes and four brooding poplars. In a peace relieved only by the trickling fountain and the twitter of birds, beauty and serenity reign in this historic quadrangle.

Santes Creus   *10 C2*

About 40 km. (25 miles) from Poblet, another great monastery sprawls among the vineyards. While Poblet is a working monastery, Santes Creus (Holy Cross) has been preserved as a museum. Thus all the buildings are on view—from the dormitories to the kitchen.

The **cloister,** a pioneering work of Catalan Gothic design, dates from the beginning of the 14th century. The **church,** begun in 1174, is austere and powerful. King Peter III the Great is buried here in a temple-within-a-church—a tall Gothic tabernacle. In addition to several tombs of lesser grandeur, the monastery reveals its regal connections in the so-called "Royal Palace"—living quarters surrounding a perfect 14th-century patio of delicate arches and a finely sculpted staircase.

Montserrat   *11 C2*

Geographically and spiritually, Montserrat is the heart of Catalonia. The ancient Benedictine monastery, tucked into extravagantly dramatic mountains, houses a 12th-century polychrome wood image of the Virgin Mary called *La Moreneta,* the little brown Madonna. This icon is so avidly venerated that you may have to queue for 15 minutes for a look. Notice her nose: long, thin and pointed; it's the same nose you'll see on half the faces in the congregation. It's a thoroughly Catalan nose.

Now that donkeys have been replaced by cable cars and excursion coaches, crowds of pilgrims and sightseers come to Montserrat to feel uplifted, one way or another. Set in a niche above the basilica's high altar (made of the mountain itself), the image is protected by glass. But a circle cut out of the shield permits

fame, fortune and historical importance. The monastery's church, as large as a cathedral, contains the **tombs** of the kings of Aragon, suspended on unique low arches in the cross vault. Here lie James the Conqueror, Peter the Ceremonious, John I and his two wives, and Alphonse the Chaste.

Poblet sprawls upon a wide-open plateau amidst fertile hillsides. The buildings were plundered in 1835 but lovingly restored. For a fuller appreciation of the monastic mood, linger in the **cloister,**

the faithful to touch or kiss the statue's outstretched right hand.

A highlight of any visit to Montserrat is its choir. The young choristers of the Escolanía, thought to be Europe's oldest music school, perform in the monastery at midday. The angelic voices sing as inspiringly as advertised.

The monks here are rarely in view, busy as they are with prayer, meditation, study in a 200,000-volume library, and down-to-earth labour. They make pottery, run a goldsmith's workshop and a printing press, and distil a pleasant herbal liqueur called *Aromas de Montserrat* sold in the souvenir supermarket.

Vich *(Vic)* *11 D2*

Vich rhymes with rich; and it's doing very well as a small industrial and commercial city surrounded by farm country.

An indication of the grandeur of the original **cathedral,** founded in the 11th century, is a seven-storey Romanesque belfry. The cathedral was rebuilt in neo-classical style at the end of the 18th century. In the 20th century a leading Catalan painter, José María Sert y Badía, covered its walls with powerful **murals.** During the Civil War the church was sacked and burned. Sert was able to return to redo his greatest work, all but finished before he died in 1945. He is buried in the cathedral. (Among Sert's other big contracts were murals for the Waldorf Astoria hotel in New York.)

Food fans know Vich for its delicious local sausages.

Gerona *(Girona)* *11 E2*

The Iberians built a fortified city on Gerona's hilltop, and over the next couple of thousand years it was often coveted and assaulted by invaders of many sorts—Romans, Visigoths, Moors, Franks and so forth. Thus its odd nickname, City of Sieges. At the moment all the threats seem contained except for an invasion of cars causing a chronic parking problem.

Although it's about 30 km. (20 miles) inland from the Mediterranean, the capital of Gerona province is by extension the capital of the Costa Brava. Beach-loving holiday-makers can easily hop over for something completely different. Aside from the history and local colour, there's the chance to shop at non-touristy prices.

You can best feel the mood of Gerona along the banks of the Río Oñar (Riu Onyar), which bisects the town (romantics find the riverfront Venetian), and up into the narrow streets of the old town. The most typical street of medieval Gerona is the steep Carrer de la Força, once the heart of the old Jewish quarter. It climbs to the base of the hill climaxed by the Gothic **cathedral,** more than 90 ceremonial steps above. This cathedral represents a remarkable feat of medieval architecture: its single nave, one of the widest in the world, creates an immense vault, like a precocious design for an aircraft hangar. The alabaster high altar has served the church since its consecration in 1038.

The cathedral's **treasury** is chock-a-block with precious articles. There are gold and silver monstrances, rare illuminated manuscripts, a statue of Charlemagne (minus his right hand), and a unique **tapestry** from the 12th century. In a room of its own, the Tapestry of the Creation summarizes the Bible for illiterate churchgoers, explaining everything, in logical order, from Adam and Eve to

*I*n Figueras, the birthplace of Salvador Dalí, the moustachioed master's influence is never far away. The Dalí museum here is the second busiest museum in all Spain.

the winds and the months. The **cloister**, laid out as a trapezoid, has delightful Old Testament sculptures.

Figueras *(Figueres)*   *ll El*
The second biggest town in Gerona province, otherwise undistinguished, happens to contain the second most visited museum in all Spain (after the Prado). The **Teatre-Museu Dalí** is just the sort of witty, surreal museum you would expect in the birthplace of Salvador Dalí. In and out of the museum, piles of truck tyres stand as solemn columns; you can't get more iconoclastic than that.

In a typically outrageous Dalí plan, they gutted the very proper municipal theatre and put far-out sculptures on stage and in the loges. An ancient Cadillac parked in the patio supports a statue of a gilt-breasted Amazon. Giant representations of hens' eggs stand on the battlements, the roof line topped by a seemingly irrelevant geodesic dome.

Shocks and little jokes aside, the institution contains a very good cross-section of Dalí's work. Even the sceptical go away admitting he was a genius.

A couple of hundred yards down the hill the **Museu de l'Empordà** includes an eye-opening collection of Greek and Roman vases, statues and implements unearthed by archaeologists in the region. Just opposite the museum a statue honours the man who was the greatest local hero until Dalí came along. He was Narciso Monturiol (1819–85), designer of a pioneering six-man submarine.

Costa Brava

The *brava* in the Costa Brava doesn't mean the coast is brave. It means wild, savage, craggy, stormy, steep. The adjective was proposed in 1908 by a Catalan poet, Ferrán Agulló, to sum up Spain's north-easternmost 214 km. (133 miles) of cliffs, coves and even beaches, backed by pines and olive groves.

With France just across the border, and the climate and all of nature so attractive, this was the first part of Spain's Mediterranean shore to achieve international fame. Since its "discovery" early in the 20th century, wrenching changes have occurred all along the Gerona coast, with bustling modern resorts eclipsing the indigenous fishing villages. However popular it has become, the fragrant Costa Brava remains a rugged adventure, even on a summer day of truce in the eternal war between the sea and the rocks.

The once-forested hills behind the pretty natural harbour of **El Port de la Selva** offered safety to prehistoric communities; flint knives, pottery and more than 70 Iron Age graves have been unearthed near here.

Miles of the coastline are visible from the ruins of **Sant Pere de Roda,** a 10th-century fortified monastery. Benedictine monks enlarged it and reconstructed existing foundations to make this ecclesiastical centre the most influential in the region. It's an energetic hike to the site on the top of Mount Vedera, rewarded by some glorious views.

Notwithstanding the crush of the crowds descending on the Costa Brava, the adventurous tourist can always find a private cove somewhere along the jagged coast. This minibeach is hidden between Tossa de Mar and San Feliu.

🏊 Cadaqués　　　　　　　　*11 E1*

This is the whitewashed Costa Brava fishermen's village everyone has dreamed of, the sort of place where you could settle in, breathe the sea air, and become an artist. Great idea, but Salvador Dalí thought of it first. In 1929 he moved into a one-roomed fisherman's house just up the coast. Later he grandly expanded his domain. It's still a great favourite with painters.

The long, eventful history of Cadaqués, marked in particular by pirate attacks, has added to the reputation of the people as indomitable characters, self-assured and independent (and the coast's most skilful smugglers). The old church was burned down by the illustrious Barbary pirate Barbarossa in 1543. The replacement, built in the 17th century, has a rich Baroque altarpiece by Pau Costa.

Rosas *(Roses)*　　　　　　　*11 E1*

From Rosas south, the character of the coastline softens from cliffs that look as if they were dynamited from the mountainside to an ample stretch of gently sloping, sandy beaches. It's so irresistible from the point of view of tourism development that the plain has acquired miles of high-rise hotels and apartment blocks.

Thanks to the contortions of the coast's geography, the **port** of Rosas faces due west; sunset-lovers gather here for the best end-of-the-day spectacle on the whole coast. Add to this the sight of the local fishing fleet returning from a day on the high seas. You can watch them auction the still-squirming seafood on little round trays.

🏊 Ampurias *(Empúries)*　　　　*11 E1*

The Greeks thought enough of the Costa Brava to build a city here. It was improved by the Iberians and then greatly expanded by the Romans. Archaeology buffs will enjoy an hour wandering through the "digs" of Ampurias—the **remains** of villas, temples, baths, the old marketplaces. Others will be content to

view the sea from the vantage point of the lovely Roman-style landscaping.

The ancient settlement was long forgotten except in local legend. The buried treasures weren't revealed until early in the 20th century. The most sensational find was a larger-than-life **statue** of Asclepius, the Greek god of medicine, sculpted in marble from an Athenian quarry. The original has been moved to the Barcelona Archaeological Museum, but a copy stands in its place in the ruined temple. Another copy is in the **museum** right on the site, which exhibits most of the local discoveries—ceramics, jewels, household items, weapons, mosaics and statues rescued from centuries of oblivion. Outside the museum, still intact on the mosaic floor, is a touching Greek inscription that has survived the ravages of time and invasions: "Sweet Dreams".

"Ampurias" figures in a number of place names along the Costa Brava, but they're just red herrings. If you're driving, look for L'Escala, the nearest resort, and then the signs for the "Ruinas".

Palamós　　　　　　　　　　*11 E2*

In 1299 the Catalonian fleet set out from here to conquer Sicily. Today the Palamós fleet casts off at dawn and returns in time for the five o'clock auction in La Llotja, the Exchange. With warships gone, the admirable bay is now shared by professional fishermen and sun-loving holiday-makers. The heart of the high-rise resort remains the inner beach of the port, where fishermen and their wives still mend their nets by hand.

Tossa de Mar　　　　　　　　*11 E2*

In dramatic cliff country south of Bagur, Tossa was an artists' colony before it became a fully developed international tourist resort. Marc Chagall called it "Blue Paradise", though the rest of us see it as white. Paintings by Chagall and other artists who frequented Tossa hang in the local museum. Brooding 12th-century walls defend the Vila Vella (old town), of which three great towers remain.

Lloret de Mar — *11 E2*

With its hundreds of hotels, Lloret is this coast's most unabashed tourist town, noted for its brash, animated nightlife. A maze of cosmopolitan shopping streets lead to the Passeig Verdaguer, an elegant seafront promenade overlooking the sweeping beach. The classic postcard view of Lloret includes a turreted castle on a rocky promontory. Quite honestly, it's a bit too perfect: a 20th-century folly.

Blanes — *11 E2*

At the southern border of the Costa Brava, Blanes is a prosperous centre of farming, industry and fishing; tourism is just a rich bonus. Nature-lovers are attracted by the wild beauty of the cliffs, and by the **Marimurtra** botanical gardens, with more than 3,000 species of trees, shrubs and flowers. Botanists and gardeners keep busy tending this dazzlingly colourful counterpoint to the sea.

Barcelona — *11 D2*

Protected by the encircling Collserola hills, Barcelona spills down a gentle slope to the sea. The capital of Catalonia is a big, sophisticated city with muscle and brains, smokestacks and flower stalls. The glory of its medieval architecture complements the audacity of its modern buildings. The citizens of this centre of banking, publishing and heavy industry read more books, see more operas, and cling more fiercely to their old traditions than the people of any other Spanish city.

Barcelona's name is said to have been coined by the Carthaginians in honour of General Hamilcar Barca, father of the legendary Hannibal. In the Middle Ages Barcelona prospered commercially, politically and intellectually. For a time the kingdom of Catalonia was the major power in the entire Mediterranean. Seeing Barcelona today, no one would doubt it.

Gothic Quarter

You can walk through 15 centuries of history in a leisurely hour in the Barri Gòtic (Gothic Quarter) of Barcelona.

Construction of the **Catedral de Santa Eulàlia** began at the end of the 13th century and lasted for about 150 years. Additions were made at the end of the 19th century. Some critics complain that the pure Catalan Gothic effect was thus ruined. But don't worry about the critics. Come back at night when the delicate **spires** are illuminated, and light inside glows through the stained-glass windows. The interior is laid out with three aisles neatly engineered to produce an effect of splendour and uplift. There are precious paintings and sculptures in the side **chapels.** So many tourists swarm through the cathedral that one big chapel is reserved, as the multilingual sign cautions, "for prayer only". The classical **cloister** is tranquil except for a large family of argumentative geese, who rule the roost here, as have their ancestors for centuries.

Museu Frederic Marés. A one-time royal palace now houses an ambitious collection of statues from the 10th century on, with the emphasis on the Spanish art of polychrome wood sculpture. The exhibits range from intricately carved miniatures to giant wall-busters.

Museu d'Història de la Ciutat (Museum of the History of the City). Far below the exhibits of old maps and documents, subterranean passages follow the tracks of Roman civilization: houses, waterworks, statues and ceramics have been excavated.

Plaça del Rei (King's Square). According to tradition, Columbus was received here on his heroic return from the first voyage to the New World. Ferdinand and Isabella, his friends at court, may have sat on the great steps of **Saló del Tinell** (Tinell Hall) to hear his report. They're pictured thus in a famous stylized painting in which American Indians brought back by Columbus fairly swoon with ecstasy at the sight of their new masters.

On the north side of Plaça de Sant Jaume (St. James's Square) stands the **Palau de la Generalitat,** home of Catalonia's autonomous government. This ceremonious 15th-century structure hides a surprise or two: the overpowering ornamentation of St. George's Room, and an upstairs patio with orange trees. Across the square, the **Casa de la Ciutat** or Ajuntament (City Hall) is even older. A sumptuous highlight is the **Saló de Cent** (Hall of the One Hundred), restored to its original glory.

But medieval life in Barcelona was not all pomp and majesty. Just to the west of the Generalitat, narrow streets with names like Call and Banys Nous mark the ancient Jewish Quarter, formerly a centre of philosophy, poetry and science. In 1391, as anti-semitic passions gripped Spain, the ghetto was sacked. At night, the bars and restaurants throb with impassioned discussion.

La Rambla

Like the sun and the shade, the tawdry and shabby share space with the chic and the charming all the way down La Rambla, Barcelona's best-known promenade. This broad boulevard meanders nearly 2 kilometres down a gentle incline from the city's hub, the **Plaça de Catalunya,** to the waterfront.

There are five sections to the Rambla,

*S*tartling *Art Nouveau mosaics and three-dimensional details embellish the façade of Barcelona's Palau de la Música Catalana, the headquarters of the municipal orchestra.*

if you go by the street signs. Actually they merge seamlessly, though, as you stroll along, the character changes. The short **Rambla de Canaletes** at the top is where, on Sundays and Mondays in season, you'll find knots of gesticulating fans replaying the games of the ''Barça'' football team. This is their recognized turf. Here, too, begin the stalls where you can buy foreign newspapers and magazines. (The farther down the Rambla you go,

the more the publications reflect the relaxation of pornography laws.)

The **Rambla dels Estudis** is popularly called the Rambla dels Oscells (of the birds) because it narrows here to become an outdoor aviary where birds of all descriptions are sold.

Birds give way to blossoms in the Rambla de les Flors, officially the **Rambla de Sant Josep**, probably the most photographed scene in the city. Two products

A camera far older than the photographer herself immortalizes a couple of tourists at the bottom of Barcelona's Ramblas. Here the shopping ranges from a guitar or a parrot to a deep-sea diving bell. Sooner or later, just about everybody turns up in the Ramblas.

enjoy a brisk trade on April 23, the day of Barcelona's patron, Sant Jordi, (St. George), which is celebrated as the Day of the Book and when it is also traditional to give girls a rose. Tickets to municipal concerts are sold or offered and information about museums and current exhibitions is available at the city's Department of Culture.

The heart of the Rambla is the **Pla de la Boqueria**. Set back from the street, a giant red pepper stands under a stained-glass medallion hanging over the entrance to the overflowing market. The centre of the *pla* is paved with a mosaic by the painter, Joan Miró. The **Gran Teatre del Liceu** is a monument of the Catalan *Renaixença* (renaissance), built in 1844.

The street entertainment starts in the **Rambla dels Caputxins**, You'll encounter jugglers, fire eaters, pavement artists, violinists, "human statues" and a varied assortment of eccentrics. Note the naïve painted angels floating over the doorway of the old Hotel Oriente.

The final promenade leading to the harbour is the short **Rambla de Santa Mònica**. The area is the beat of prostitutes and policemen on the lookout for pickpockets and bag-snatchers. The warren of alleys to the right is the **Barri Chino**, or Chinatown, once notorious for forbidden sin. Now that many erstwhile sins are no longer forbidden, it has lost much of its interest and customers, though it's still no place for a midnight stroll. The Carrer dels Escudellers on the other side of the Rambla is the gateway to a district of cabarets, bars, flamenco shows, and restaurants. Nearer the port, a passage leads to the **Museu de Cera**, the wax museum. The Rambla ends at the **Plaça Portal de la Pau**, Gate of Peace Square, with the **Monument a Colom**, as the great navigator, Columbus, is called in Catalan.

Montjuïc

The modest mountain called Montjuïc was developed for the Barcelona world's fair of 1929. It's being transformed again

as the heart of the 1992 Olympic Games. (You can hardly avoid portents of the Olympics; the image of the Games' mascot, a cartoon of a smiling mongrel named Cobi, can be seen everywhere in town.)

In the centre of the fairgrounds is the terrace of the **Fuente Mágica**, truly a "magic fountain". Saturdays and Sundays from 10 p.m. to midnight, the fountains perform a ballet of rising and falling jets bathed in a mist of changing colours set to music. Some 260 combinations are programmed.

Prominent on the hill, the domed **Palau Nacional**, built for the 1929 fair, houses one of the world's greatest collections of medieval art. The **Museu d'Art de Catalunya** begins with 10th- and 11th-century Catalan religious paintings that bear a striking resemblance to ancient Byzantine icons. See the 12th-century wood carvings from church altars, and magnificent frescoes of the same period, rescued from the walls of crumbling old churches.

The prehistoric items in the **Museu Arqueològic** come mostly from Catalonia and the Balearic islands. Many Greek and Roman relics were unearthed at Empúries (Ampurias), up the coast, and there are displays from Barcelona's own Roman days.

The **Fundació Joan Miró** features bright modern architecture and a riot of paintings, sculptures, drawings and tapestries by the Catalan artist Joan Miró (1893–1983) making this as happy a museum as you're ever likely to see. The intense Catalanism of the place extends to the titles of the works, given in Catalan and occasionally also in French, but never in Spanish.

Take along your sense of humour when you visit the chirpy Fundació Joan Miró in Barcelona.

Gaudí and "Eixample"

In Catalan, *eixample* means extension or enlargement. In Barcelona it means the new city that grew beyond the medieval walls in the 19th century, elegant, tree-lined boulevards of distinguished buildings. Even when the Modernist architects failed, they added character to a forward-looking city.

The greatest of Barcelona's *art nouveau* architects was Antoni Gaudí (1852–1926), whose enthusiasts come here on pilgrimage. Here are typical Gaudí projects you can see in one outing, starting in the old town and working out through the "Eixample":

Palau Güell. Just off the bustling Rambla, this palace keeps its biggest innovations out of public view, but the rooftop chimney array is so original that it relieves some of the severity.

Casa Batlló. Gaudí's sensuous curves in stone and iron, and his delicate tiles, conflict with the house next door by another brilliant architect, Puig i Cadafalch. That's why this part of the Passeig de Gràcia is often called the "Block of Discord" (a pun in Spanish).

Casa Milá. Gaudí fans love its undulating façade, adorned with wrought-iron work, and the roof terrace with weird formations covering chimneys and ventilators.

Parc Güell. This incomparably inventive park started out as a suburban real estate development, but it failed. Only two houses were sold (Gaudí bought one of them). The park delights young and old with its gingerbread-type houses, cheery use of tiles, and huge serpentine bench bordering the main plaza (picture below).

Temple Expiatori de la Sagrada Familia. Gaudí's unfinished Holy Family church, the "sandcastle cathedral", is an extravagant hymn to one man's talent and faith. Many Catalans see this stupendous, controversial church as an extension of their own faith and strivings; their donations keep the construction work going. When Gaudí died (run over by a Barcelona tram) he left only sketches of what he had in mind, leading to the haunting question: how would he have carried forward this project? No matter. Where else can you stand in a roofless cathedral and watch it being built? Before your eyes descendants of the great Catalan stonecutters are shaping the faces of angels.

Poble Espanyol ("Spanish Village"). For the 1929 fair they built this 2-hectare (5-acre) Spain-in-a-nutshell exhibit, showing off the charms and styles of the nation's regions, in full scale but superconcentration.

More Barcelona Museums

Museu Marítim. In Barcelona's enormous medieval shipyard, the Reials Drassanes, great sailing ships were built. There's a full-sized reproduction of the victorious flagship of the Battle of Lepanto (1571), as well as a 15th-century atlas once owned by Amerigo Vespucci.

Museu Picasso, Born in Málaga, Picasso came to Barcelona at 14 to study. His talents, even at that early age, are strikingly clear in informal sketches, cartoons and doodles on display in three contiguous 13th-century palaces in the Carrer de Montcada. A large exhibition here is devoted to a series of 58 paintings he donated to the museum, including 44 bizarre variations on the Velázquez work, *Las Meninas.*

Costa Dorada

The fine golden sand for which the Costa Dorada is named extends almost without a break along more than 250 km. (over 150 miles) of calm Mediterranean shore. Technically it starts north of Barcelona and stretches all the way down the coast of Catalonia to the delta of the Ebro.

Sitges *11 C2*

Natural beauty, liveliness and dignity combine to make Sitges an internationally admired resort. The children-friendly beach is nearly 5 km. (3 miles) long. The parish church, on a promontory, was built between the 16th and 18th centuries, but sacked during the Civil War.

The **Museu Romàntic** is an old aristocratic home decorated in 19th-century style and full of the fascinating things of the era—furniture, clocks, music boxes and a large family of antique dolls.

Tarragona *18 C2*

Strategic location, mild climate and wine were the advantages that drew the Romans to Tarragona in the 3rd century B.C. It became the capital of Rome's biggest Spanish province, grand enough for an emperor or two to spend the season. The advantages are unchanged.

For a close-up tour of the ancient city wall, see the **Passeig Arqueològic** (Archaeological Promenade). The foundation of the wall is composed of uncut stones weighing up to 35 tons each. The fortifications above were much remodelled and strengthened over the centuries. The views from here over the countryside and the sea are stirring.

The **Museu Arqueològic** is a modern, well-designed exhibit of delicate mosaics, ancient utensils, pre-Roman, Roman and Spanish coins. A much-restored 2,000-year-old fortress next door contains additional archaeological items, including a classy marble sarcophagus found in the sea.

A Roman **amphitheatre** was built into the hillside beside the sea. Modern excavations uncovered an early Christian church on the site. Across town, near the central market, the **Roman forum** is a well-kept open-air museum. On the edge of town, the **Necròpoli i Museu Paleocristià** (Necropolis and Palaeo-Christian Museum) was a cemetery for Tarragona's early Christians. You can walk along observation platforms looking down upon hundreds of graves, urns and even bones. The adjoining museum displays some

Hand in Hand in Catalonia

The stately *sardana,* the national dance of Catalonia, evokes an uncommon affection and interest among the people. The music may grate at first, because of its hints of Arabic woodwinds and the trills of Italian operetta. It also endures longer than one would have thought possible: just four lines of music repeated without mercy for up to ten minutes. It's a rugged workout for the dancers, who link hands, young and old together, friends and strangers. Anyone can join in.

5th-century sarcophagi sculpted with astounding skill.

In a city said to have been converted to Christianity by St. Paul himself, the **cathedral** is bound to be awesome. Begun in 1171 in Romanesque style, the project shifted gears to Gothic for most of the rest. But there are later touches in Plateresque and Baroque. The **main altarpiece** is a splendid alabaster carving by the 15th-century Catalan master Pere Johan. Nineteen chapels fill the sides of the church; they range from the unforgettably beautiful to 19th-century kitsch. The **cloister** is so large that there is little shade. Notice the sculptural feature known as the Procession of the Rats, a wry fable carved 700 years before the invention of Mickey Mouse.

Salou   18 C2

High architectural standards and well-kept gardens enhance this cosmopolitan resort's claim to be the Playa de Europa (Beach of Europe). The 3-km. (2-mile) beach is bordered by a lavish promenade with solid rows of stubby palm trees and masses of colourfully arranged flowers.

The Ebro Delta

Just past the small port of L'Ampolla begins the lush, tropical Ebro Delta, measuring more than 260 sq. km.—100 very flat square miles. It was created from the mud travelling down the great river all the way from Zaragoza. As the river continues its reclamation work, the delta expands perceptibly each year. A rich rice-growing district, it's also a rallying point for migratory birds.

Tortosa   18 B2

Straddling the muddy Ebro, Tortosa was a key bridgehead for the Romans. Julius Caesar awarded Tortosa the title of independent municipality. The elaborate fortress at the top of the town belonged to the Moors, who held out there at length during the Christian Reconquest. The **cathedral** is a classic case of Catalan Gothic.

San Carlos *(Sant Carles)* de la Rápita
18 B2

At the bottom end of the Costa Dorada, the eccentric 18th-century King Charles III decided to build a port of international significance. The city-planning brainstorm never came off... except for the gigantic **main square** he designed. It is so enormous, and the town itself so small, that there aren't enough shops and offices to fill its perimeter. Impertinently, the main road to Valencia goes right down the middle of Charles's melancholy plaza.

*A rice farmer shares the Ebro Delta with the
migratory birds, who attract serious hunters in season.
Attempts to turn the River Ebro into Aragon's outlet to the sea
have been dormant for years. As for the rice, it will go into paella,
one of the masterpieces of east coast cuisine.*

20TH-CENTURY MASTERS

Spain's greatest 20th-century artists were multi-media geniuses who created everything from paintings and engravings to ceramics and movies. They found their muse in the hungry Paris days and lived long, remarkably productive lives. Picasso died at 91, Miró at 90 and Dalí was 84.

The century's artistic titan, Pablo Ruiz y **Picasso** (1881–1973), went through phases from blue to pink to black and invented many a school of art. Born in Málaga, he spent his early years in La Coruña and Barcelona. From the age of 20 he signed his works with his mother's maiden name. Thanks to his inexhaustible output and controversial fame, Picasso's underlined signature became almost as familiar worldwide as the calligraphy of Coca-Cola. His tempestuous private life (shared by a series of seven women) was often reflected in his work, joyous or haunted. Perhaps his most revolutionary phase was Cubism, in which he fragmented the subject and reassembled its parts.

Picasso soon turned to other styles, but Juan **Gris**, another Spaniard in Paris, made Cubism his life. In 1906 Gris moved into the ramshackle house Picasso and other Bohemians occupied in Montmartre. When the frail, shy Gris died at the age of 40, Picasso was a pallbearer.

During the Spanish Civil War Picasso created his most unforgettable painting, the vast canvas dedicated to the bombing of the Basque town of Guernica. Picasso always refused to comment on its meaning, but the picture tells its own story of the horror and

Unfinished business: the studio of Joan Miró, Palma de Mallorca.

agony of war. At the opposite edge of the emotional spectrum, Picasso is also remembered for a happy image: a few inimitable brush strokes evoking the dove of peace.

Joan **Miró** (1893–1983) met his Frenchified countryman Picasso in Paris and spent many years in France, but he never lost his Catalan roots. Born in Barcelona, he had to struggle to become an artist. His parents forced him into the business world, but after he suffered a nervous breakdown they allowed him to go to art school. In Paris he dallied with the Dadaists, painted something like naïve art, then found his own patch of surrealism. In the 1920s he knew all the intellectual celebrities in Paris, from Ezra Pound to Henry Miller, from Max Ernst to Ernest Hemingway (Miró's unlikely sparring partner at a boxing club). The world warmed to his increasingly luminous colours and deceptively haphazard, childishly rendered forms. His dreamy, sometimes nightmarish abstractions were instantly identifiable as Miró, and in 1941 he was a star of New York's recently built Museum of Modern Art. Like Picasso, his versatility extended to ballet design, ceramics and sculpture.

Salvador **Dalí** (1904–1989) lived so outrageously that his art was often obscured by flashes of what looked like charlatanism. Even before his first trip to Paris in 1927 his surrealistic style was recognizably Dalí. While collaborating with Luis Buñuel on the shocking film, *Un Chien Andalou*, Dalí met Gala, who was to become his wife and all-purpose model. Although Dalí lived most of his life in Catalonia, the moustachioed monarchist disdained Catalan nationalism. His will bequeathed everything to Spain.

Dalí's classical draughtsmanship appeased audiences otherwise repelled by what he had done to the objects in his paintings. His melted watches, eviscerated bodies and unearthly landscapes captivated Europe, then America (where he took refuge in World War II). His astonishing pictures and provocative public relations stunts made Dalí a household name. History will have the last word on his stridently self-proclaimed genius.

A huge 3-D optical illusion by a whimsical Dalí; Picasso feeling blue in Barcelona at age 22.

Orange Blossoms and Golden Beaches

You can thank the Romans and the Moors, who lingered for centuries in eastern Iberia, for the ravishing beauty of the scene: fragrant, flowering almond, olive and citrus orchards. This long strip of lush scenery is sandwiched between endless beaches and aloof mountains. Nature's drama is always at hand.

For touristic purposes the shore divides into *costas* as poetic as the "orange-blossom" coast, and as prosaic as the "white" and "warm" coasts. The use of image-conscious names signals that the holiday trade makes hay along this part of the Mediterranean. But not all the development is as intense as that of the Costa Blanca's skyscraper boom town, Benidorm; many other resorts have barely been discovered.

To provide a diversion from sunbathing, on the beach or by hotel pools, we present some alternatives: typical fishing villages, castles, and historic cities with important cathedrals and museums... a sightseeing itinerary as full as you could want, and all within easy reach of the sands. Starting at the top, just beyond the Ebro Delta.

These Castellón fishwives are so busy mending the nets that they turn their backs on a splendid sight, the Peñíscola peninsula, topped by its 14th-century castle.

Costa del Azahar

The Orange Blossom Coast begins just south of the Tarragona border. In the province of Castellón it stretches for 112 km. (70 miles) down a coast exceptionally well endowed with beaches. Why call it Orange Blossom? (*Costa del Azahar* doesn't exactly trip off the foreigner's tongue.) The orchards come down practically to the beach: oranges as far as the horizon. They grow enough citrus fruit here to wipe out scurvy around the world. This is one part of Spain where, if you ask for orange juice at breakfast, it's almost certain to be freshly squeezed.

Vinaròs   *18 B2*
This big, working fishing port has an unusual French connection in its history. In 1712 the Duke of Vendôme, who commanded Philip V's army in the War of the Spanish Succession, died in Vinaròs. Not in battle but, it's said, at table, after eating more than his fill of the delicious local fish.

Benicarló   *18 B2*
This little town has an old castle and a pretty 18th-century church, with an

octagonal bell tower and magnificent front door.

When the sizable local fleet of trawlers returns to the port, a siren announces the big event of the day, the fish auction. If a tray of prawns looks less than fresh, a fisherman's deft kick shows how lively they really are. The buyers maintain poker faces until the prices in the backward auction decline to an interesting level; a miniature Wall Street frenzy.

⚓ Peñíscola   18 B2

The name, accented on the second syllable, may be a corruption of the Latin for "peninsula". Peñíscola's tiny peninsula—a big rock, really, rising above the sea—contains a medieval castle, gardens and a hamlet of whitewashed houses within its walls. As in many towns along the coast, tourist facilities spread from the nucleus to exploit the almost limitless beach potential; the resort area tends to overwhelm the native core.

The **castle** was built by the Knights Templar on the ruins of a Moorish fortress. It had its era of glory thanks to a distant religious schism: Church councils bounced Pope Benedict XIII, formerly Cardinal Pedro de Luna of Aragon, from his always tenuous papacy early in the 15th century. He found asylum in Peñíscola, where he holed up in contemplation until his death. The castle's layout is so complicated that Pope Luna could easily have misplaced a couple of bishops. There are restored ramparts, tunnels, a church, a Gothic hall, and areas suitable for parades. And sensational sea views.

Castellón *(Castelló)* de la Plana   25 D1

The provincial capital grew at its present location after the area's reconquest from the Moors in 1233. Historic buildings here include a cathedral restored after being terribly damaged in the Civil War, an octagonal 16th-century clock tower and the 18th-century town hall. The city's outlet to the sea, El Grau, is a busy port; nearby beaches have caught the eye of property developers.

Sagunto   25 D1

As the Costa del Azahar crosses into Valencia province, the concentration of historic sites picks up. The ramparts crowning the town of Sagunto bear witness that the centuries have been fraught with turmoil and significance here.

Sagunto was the tinderbox that ignited the Second Punic War. In 219 B.C. the young Carthaginian commander Hannibal attacked the Roman town of Saguntum, apparently in disregard of a treaty. The populace held out heroically during a cruel eight-month siege, but Saguntum finally fell. When Hannibal refused demands to pull out, the Romans declared all-out war. They recaptured Saguntum, rewarded the survivors for their loyalty and redeveloped the town on a grand scale. But the incident prompted Hannibal to set off on his incredible march across the Alps to the heart of his enemy's empire.

You can observe the importance of Saguntum at the **Roman theatre,** largely restored, built into the hillside. Delegations of school children test the theatre's acoustics with screams; otherwise it's all very evocative of ancient Rome.

Alongside the theatre a modest **archaeological museum** delves back into Iberian sculpture, Roman ceramics, mosaics, inscriptions and statues, and medieval relics.

Sagunto's **acropolis,** which sprawls for hundreds of yards atop the hill above the town, shows signs of half a dozen civilizations, starting with the Iberians. But most of the fortifications are Moorish. The panorama from this vantage point, called the Castell de Sagunt, sweeps from the citrus orchards to the sea.

Valencia   25 D1 ⚓

An infinity of orange trees surrounds Spain's third biggest city, erstwhile capital of a kingdom. With its crowded historic centre framed by parks and gardens, Valencia is as spirited as the song of the same name.

The city can claim to be more than

2,000 years old. According to the Roman historian Livy, "Valentia" was founded in 138 B.C. The Visigoths displaced the Roman Empire here in A.D. 413, followed three centuries later by the Moors. The city flourished as the capital of a far-flung Moorish kingdom until the Spanish superhero El Cid captured it at the end of the 11th century and became Duke of Valencia. But the Moors retook control after less than a decade and stayed in place until the final Reconquest in 1238 by James I of Aragon. Valencia remained a kingdom under Aragon until the merger with Castile in 1497.

No sooner had Christianity been restored than plans were laid for **La Seo** (the cathedral). Construction continued, on and off, for centuries, resulting in a very varied final effect. Just when you thought all cathedrals looked alike, Valencia's brilliant change of pace sets you straight. The concave main portal, rather cramped, is a Baroque effort,

How Those Oranges Grow

In the extraordinarily fertile region called the Horta de Valencia, surrounding the city, millions of orange trees grow and grow. There are three juicy harvests per year. The secret of citrus success is the balmy climate, but the orchards require irrigation. Channelling the river Turia, the Romans organized the first irrigation system here, which was expanded and perfected by the Moors.

For a thousand years disputes over the exploitation of the available water have been settled by the Water Tribunal, which still convenes every Thursday at noon on the steps of the apostles' portal of the metropolitan cathedral. No lawyers, no briefs, just oral decisions (in the Valencian dialect) which are honoured by all.

while, around the corner, the **apostles' portal** is a French Gothic beauty. The third doorway is Romanesque. A trademark of the cathedral, and the city, is a tall octagonal **tower** called the Miguelete or Micalet, a Gothic treasure designed

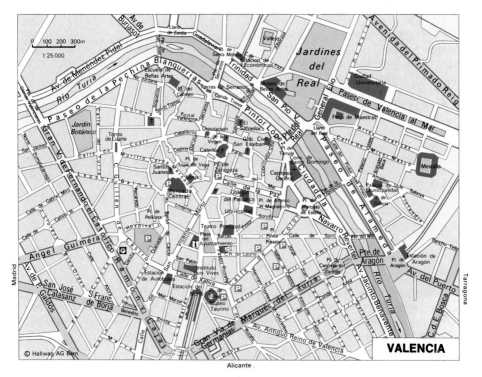

© Hallwag AG Bern

VALENCIA

165

in 1381. The literal highlight inside is a Flamboyant Gothic lantern, a periscope of windows thrust skyward to brighten everything in sight. Above the altar in the old chapterhouse, a chalice from the Roman era is claimed to be the Holy Grail.

In the plaza facing the cathedral and the attached basilica of the Verge dels Desamparats (Our Lady of the Forsaken), a fleet of white pigeons—white ones only—assemble for almost nonstop feeding by well-wishers; packaged pigeon feed is sold in the square.

A sort of commercial cathedral is the **Lonja de la Seda** (Silk Exchange), a 15th-century masterpiece of civil Gothic design. This is where Valencia's medieval silk merchants haggled in a setting that would ennoble any stock market in the world. The main hall, with thin spiralled pillars supporting ogival arches, is superb. Across the street, the central market, an early 20th-century iron market, is a hotbed of contemporary commerce—enticing fruit, vegetables, fish and meat for the kitchens of all Valencia.

Valencia's most unusual museum is housed in an astonishing old palace. The **Museo Nacional de Cerámica** has assembled more than you might think it was possible to know about the history of ceramic art. Among the highlights are hundreds of inspired glazed tiles (*azulejos*) and tile ensembles. Children love the three 18th-century coaches parked on the ground floor, including the Rolls Royce of carriages, which transported the palace's owner, the Marquess of Dos Aguas. The exterior of the palace is an overwhelming 18th-century Rococo extravaganza; it may be no accident that the architect went mad.

In an unprepossessing palace on the edge of the park called Jardines del Real, the **Museo de Bellas Artes** has the definitive collection of 15th-century Valencian art. Influenced by Flemish or Italian techniques, Valencia's medieval artists produced impressive religious paintings, shown here in abundance. Also noteworthy is a Velázquez self-portrait, sincere and unsmiling with moustaches upstanding. The next room contains a little festival of Goya—serious portraits and amusing anecdotal paintings and drawings.

What started as simple festive bonfires a few centuries ago has evolved into Valencia's unique carnival, the *Fallas*, a week of revelry climaxing every March 19, St. Joseph's day.

What makes Valencia's celebration so unusual is the amount of talent, effort and money that goes into the hundreds of satirical effigies on floats destined for the flames. The fireworks, costing millions of pesetas, are such a sure-fire success that there are daytime previews, louder than a battle, and smokier, too.

Gandía   25 D2

Several times a day guided tours visit Gandía's **Palacio de los Duques,** now a Jesuit college. This was the birthplace of a saintly 16th-century duke of Borja (the

*E*ven a white wedding fails to distract the fleet of well-fed white pigeons always begging from the tourist crowds outside the Valencia cathedral. For a bird's-eye view of the cathedral and the city surrounding it, you can climb to the top of the octagonal Miguelete tower; a modest admission fee is charged.

Italian branch of the family, the notorious Borgias, went down in history for other reasons). The duke (1510–72) became a priest as a middle-aged widower and led an expansion of Jesuit operations through Europe and the western hemisphere. He was canonized in 1671.

There are miles of beaches just beyond the town popular with locals and tourists alike. A beach festival is held in mid-August.

Costa Blanca

It wasn't a public-relations genius who first dubbed the Mediterranean coast of Alicante province the Costa Blanca. Some 2,500 years ago, Greek traders founded a colony here and named it Akra Leuka, White Headland. The brilliant light, the hot, dry climate and the miles of fine sand beaches make the White Coast one of Spain's liveliest tourist zones.

Benidorm! The name has come to symbolize packaged tourism at its most intense, with economy-minded vacationers holed up in high-rise stacks of cubbyholes or elbow to elbow on the beach. In fact, the customers enjoy it and often come back year after year for more of the same. You'll find unlimited possibilities for jollity; however, this is not the place to go for solitude.

The beaches sprawl to the north and south of the industrial town of **Denia**, named after a Roman temple to the goddess Diana (the temple remains on view in the town hall).

The family resort of **Jávea** was described as "environmentally nearly perfect" by the World Health Organization. The coast from here extends rockily to eastward-thrusting **Cabo de la Nao,** with fine sea views.

Calpe is a former fishing village at the base of the **Peñón de Ifach,** a volcanic mini-Gibraltar. Non-climbers content themselves with two fine sandy beaches.

In the lively hilltop village of **Altea,** life continues almost unchanged in the face of the tourist tide. From here you can see the alternative: Benidorm's soaring skyline of mass tourism.

Benidorm   25 D2

Say what you will, Benidorm is one of the great success stories of international tourist development. Take an obscure fishing village with a desirable climate and 7 km. (4 miles) of golden sands and... let there be skyscrapers! This is where the action is, as cosmopolitan as smorgasbord, sauerkraut and "tea like mother makes it". Benidorm knows what the package-tour invaders want and provides it cheerfully and efficiently, round the clock.

The original fishermen's quarter still exists. It rises to a promontory from which you can look back at the crescent beaches to the north and south and the wind-sculptured mountains behind. Offshore, the Isla de Benidorm is an unofficial bird sanctuary.

Villajoyosa   25 D2

Houses painted blue, pink, red or yellow line the palm-lined esplanade near the old fishing port. In the last week of July the resort drops everything for one of those Moors and Christians fiestas—parades, cannonades and a recreated naval battle, commemorating a 16th-century defeat of Algerian pirates.

Alicante   31 E2

With a population of more than a quarter of a million, Alicante (Alacant in the Valencian dialect) is a typical bustling Mediterranean port, and that includes the palm trees, promenades and outdoor cafés. A bonus is a spacious beach (Playa Postiguet) right next to the harbour.

Alicante's history looks down at you from the **Castillo de Santa Bárbara,** atop cliffs that squeeze the city towards the sea. The castle not only appears invulnerable; you wonder how it ever got there at all. Somehow the Carthaginians built the first fort on this hilltop, in the 3rd century B.C., and it was greatly expanded by subsequent regimes. You can drive up the steep, winding road to the summit or take the lift built into the hillside across the busy coast road from the beach. The fort is illuminated at night, and so is the 30-storey hotel downtown competing with it for skyline honours.

Horizontally impressive is the multi-balconied, Baroque **Ayuntamiento** (town hall). Just inside the main door, at the base of a ceremonial staircase, is a plaque marking the official "zero point" or sea level, from which all altitude in Spain is measured.

*I*nland from Benidorm, the townsfolk of Alcoy dress up every April to commemorate a 13th-century battle in which St. George is said to have helped defeat the Moors. The spectacle is such fun that nearby hotels are booked up long in advance.

*E*verywhere along the sea, the views are marvellous.
On the promontory of the old town of Benidorm, where
a castle once stood, vacationers rest their feet and gaze out across
the unruffled Mediterranean in the general direction of the coast of
North Africa. So this is the birthplace of European culture!

introduced by the Carthaginians. Today many tens of thousands of elegant palms surround the city on three sides. Wherever you may be in Spain on Palm Sunday, the fronds you see come from Elche. As for the dates themselves, you can taste them anywhere, but more memorably beneath graceful trees as tall as houses.

The restful **Parque Municipal** has superb palm trees as well as a citrus alley and a noisy frog pond. The tourist office is on the edge of the park.

The **Palacio de Altamira,** a former royal holiday residence, is now a national monument.

In Elche's prettiest precinct, the **Hort del Cura** (Priest's Garden), grows celebrated palm trees as well as pomegranate and orange trees and a small cactus forest you'd hate to be lost in. Star attraction is a seven-branch male palm tree of exceptional age, girdled together to hold it upright. Overlooking the grove's lily pond is a replica of the mysterious, ancient *Dama de Elche* (Lady of Elche); the original sculpture is featured in Madrid's Archaeological Museum.

Orihuela 31 D2

About halfway between Elche and Murcia, but out of sight and sound of the busy N-340 highway, the small city of Orihuela is best known for its fertility. The Río Segura irrigates its citrus orchards and a palm grove, as well.

The old university, on the northern outskirts, was constructed in the 16th and 17th centuries. It's now a school, the **Colegio de Santo Domingo**. You can visit its cloisters and beautifully tiled refectory.

The Gothic **cathedral,** begun in the early 14th century, with spiral rib vaulting and ornamental grillwork, is considered one of the region's finest. Ask to see the admirable Velázquez painting, the *Temptation of St. Thomas Aquinas,* displayed deep in the cathedral behind a series of locked doors. The vogue at the time was to make all humans look angelic, but the angels in this celebrated work look human.

In the modernized halls of a 17th-century palace, the **museum of 20th-century art** specializes in Spanish works, including Miró, Picasso and Dalí. Next door, between Calle Mayor and Calle Jorge Juan, is the 14th-century **Iglesia de Santa María**, on the site of a mosque.

Elche 31 E2

On many road signs, the town's name is a terse *Elx*, as the Moors called it. Centuries before the Muslim occupation Elche was famous for its **date palm trees,**

173

Costa Cálida

Even the water is warmer on the Warm Coast. The water in question is that of the **Mar Menor**, the "Little Sea", a vast lagoon almost entirely sheltered from the open Mediterranean. The shallow isolation of the Mar Menor means high salt and iodine content and water temperatures that in winter average a tolerable 18° Celsius (65° Fahrenheit).

Resort facilities have multiplied on the sandy breakwater walling off the Mar Menor, called La Manga (the Sleeve). A boost for tourism is the nearby airport of San Javier. Nature has closed off the 170 sq. km. (65 sq. miles) of the lagoon so effectively that contact with the open sea has to be maintained through a system of canals and floodgates. The fish use these channels for commuting, and the local fishermen are ambush specialists.

The coast south-west of Cabo de Palos turns rugged and rocky.

Cartagena   31 D2

The principal port on this coast—and an important naval base—is the compact, bustling city of Cartagena. Its name refers to the Carthaginians who captured Cartagena a couple of thousand years ago. The almost landlocked harbour is so well protected that Andrea Doria, the 16th-century Genoese admiral, remarked that the Mediterranean had only three safe ports: June, July and Cartagena.

The high point of the city is the **Castillo de la Concepción**, a fort dating back to Roman and perhaps even Carthaginian times. Near the main square below, the big, cigar-shaped object on view is a submarine of Jules Verne vintage. The local

Prickly succulents compete for attention with flowers and date palms in Elche's Hort del Cura.

inventor Isaac Peral launched it in 1888, ten years too late for a world first.

Immediately west of the Castillo are the ruins of the 13th-century **Iglesia de Santa María Vieja**. The portal has been restored, but the columns and Roman mosaic floor are authentic.

Murcia   31 D2

The capital of the Costa Cálida is an inland city of pleasant boulevards and narrow old streets. A rich oasis since Moorish times, the city was the capital of a *taifa* or breakaway kingdom. After the Reconquest, Castile annexed the kingdom of Murcia to gain access to the Mediterranean.

Built on the ruins of a mosque, Murcia's 14th-century **Catedral de Santa María** is a face-lifted Gothic building sporting a lovely, concave Baroque façade. Alongside, though invisible from some vantage points in the crowded city, the 18th-century bell tower tapers grandly to a final cupola and turret. Outstanding inside the cathedral is the 16th-century **Capilla de los Vélez** (Chapel of the Vélez family), with all manner of florid decoration, as well as two small paintings by Lucas Jordán. Elsewhere in the cathedral you can see polychrome wood **sculptures** by Francisco Salzillo (1797–83), a Murcia artist of Italian descent. His *pasos*—sculptural ensembles carried through the streets in Holy Week processions—are admired for their realism and pathos. To round out your acquaintance with this local hero you can visit the Salzillo Museum (at Calle de San Andrés, 1), crammed with his carvings.

Calle de la Trapería, the old town's principal shopping street, now a pedestrian mall, runs north from the cathedral. The street's highlight is the **Casino de Murcia**, a private club, not a gambling facility, in an altogether astonishing 19th-century building. The entrance hall to this splendid folly is a copy of the Hall of Ambassadors in Seville's Alcázar. Cherubs look down from the ceiling of the lavish ladies' lavatory.

The Spain of Sunshine, Passion and Poetry

From the peninsula's highest mountains to the shores of the Mediterranean and the Atlantic, Andalusia's diversity contains everybody's idea of the "real" Spain: white villages among the olive groves, cities of architectural splendour and timeless traditions, and booming beach resorts. Southern Spain is the home of flamenco, gazpacho, the bullfight, Spanish poetry, and those sultry beauties with flashing black eyes.

Andalusia (Andalucía in Spanish) is an autonomous region composed of the eight southernmost provinces, adding up to one-sixth of Spain's total area and population. Perhaps the happy climate explains why this land has been inhabited for at least 25,000 years.

The civilizing Romans built roads and aqueducts; they brought their language, their laws, and, eventually, Christianity. But the most profound foreign influence on Andalusia came from the Moors, whose occupation of this area lasted longer than in any other part of the country. Muslim-controlled Andalusia enjoyed prosperity, technological advance, intellectual attainments, and tolerance. After the Reconquest, the south played a leading role in Spain's Golden Age of discovery and empire.

The headdress and earrings are for special occasions, but the smile is an everyday adornment.

Our coverage of Andalusia's most memorable sights begins at the seaside before moving inland for the treasures of the nation's most storied cities.

Costa de Almería

The largely inaccessible coast of Almería province, the easternmost part of Andalusia, seems a world away from the bustle of the neighbouring Costa del Sol. Almería has seen relatively little resort development. Except for underwater fishermen, few tourists have come near its lonely, rocky coves.

But **Garrucha** has a long beach and a yacht harbour. A couple of kilometres inland, **Mojácar** is a charming white village on a hill. You can't miss the Moorish influence in the cubic houses, some with domes.

The main road from Murcia to the provincial capital of Almería steers clear of the coast, offering instead extraordinary inland scenery. **Sorbas** is a town in the middle of nowhere, the more so since it is surrounded by the sinuous bed of the

Río Aguas. High above the cliff face, the white houses seem to hang in the sky. The countryside becomes red and slightly menacing. Near the little town of **Tabernas,** with its Moorish houses and castle ruins, solar power is being exploited on a big scale. The scenery is so engrossing that in the area called **Mini-Hollywood,** American and Spanish film companies have shot a number of cowboy films. Not far away from this Dakota-like setting, the sand dunes are convincing enough to serve as the backdrop for desert films.

Almería 30 BC3

Like the other towns with names starting in "al"—Albacete, Algeciras, Alicante and all—Almería spent formative centuries under Moorish rule. *Al-Mariyah* is Arabic for "mirror", perhaps a reference to the mirror-clear waters of the Gulf of Almería.

The **Alcazaba,** an 8th-century Moorish fortress, overhangs the town and the port. The stronghold is even bigger than it looks from below: 35 hectares (87 acres) of mostly ruined fortifications and a garden

*S*urrounded by the fertile hill country of inland
*Andalusia, a white village stands out as if the target of a celestial
searchlight. The Moors ruled here for centuries, setting the
pattern for narrow streets of whitewashed houses concealing cool,
flowered patios.*

179

where everything from geraniums to cacti grows. The buildings in the inner redoubt were all but levelled by a 16th-century earthquake. But the crenellated ochre outer walls and a section of the turreted ramparts stand firm.

Just inland from the harbour front stands the forbiddingly fortified Gothic **cathedral.** You can blame the Barbary pirates for the architectural constraints. Completed in the mid-16th century, this bastion of the faith bolstered Almería's seaward defences in a nervous age.

Heading to the port, the **Paseo de Almería** is the ideal street for strolling and shopping, with outdoor cafés to vary the pace.

Costa del Sol

The Costa del Sol promotion board believes this is the best of all possible *costas*. It enjoys 326 days of sunshine per year, the board assures us, adding: "But the remaining 39 days are just as nice".

Even if you're not wearing rose-coloured glasses, you'll have to admit the climate of the Sun Coast is pretty close to everybody's ideal. Thus, even though the beaches tend to be narrow and grey, this sprawl of resort hotels, holiday villages, *urbanizaciones* and time-share developments continues its cosmopolitan growth. Everybody wants a piece of the action, a place in the sun. Today's tourist is tomorrow's resident, and so, for better or worse, the bonanza rolls on.

Our coverage of the coast continues from east to west through the provinces of Málaga and Granada.

Almuñécar   *33 E2*
The double life of Almuñécar bounces between the beach and the old town above, inviolate on its small hill, topped by a Moorish castle. Almuñécar has always been famous for its red pottery; you can still see the artisans at work. The town was founded by the Phoenicians, who called it "Sexi".

Nerja   *33 E2*
East of Málaga, where the beaches are less expansive than to the west, only one big international resort has been developed: Nerja. Hotels and hostels cluster around Nerja's **Balcón de Europa,** a palm-fringed promenade built atop a cliff that juts out into the sea, with beaches to port and starboard.

The **Cueva de Nerja**, a cave 4 km. (2½ miles) east of town, was discovered in 1959 by a group of boys out hunting bats. Evidence, including wall paintings and tools, shows that the stalactite-encrusted cave has been inhabited, on and off, since Cro-Magnon days.

Málaga   *33 D2*
More than 3,000 years ago Phoenician traders founded Malaka, the future Málaga, at the strategic spot where the Río Guadalmedina joins the Mediterranean. Later the settlement grew under Carthaginians and Romans. In the invasion year of 711 the Moors seized Málaga and built it into one of Andalusia's great cities. Almost at the end of the Reconquest, in 1487, it was finally returned to the Christian fold after a dreadful siege of three and a half months.

Tourists from beach resorts all along the coast head for Málaga for a taste of the real Spain: twisting, narrow streets, waterfront promenades, an old Moorish fortress, and bullfights on Sundays.

The ancient fort atop pine-clad **Gibralfaro** (Lighthouse Hill) looks down on the bullring; whether there's a *corrida* or a pop concert, the sound zooms right up. The **view** from Gibralfaro reaches from the Mediterranean horizon to the stony mountains north of the metropolis. Much ravaged by wars and the centuries, the redoubt is just a shell filled by a wild garden. A footpath leads uphill from the Paseo del Parque to the summit, but pickpockets and worse have been known to lurk along the way; to be on the safe side, go by taxi, bus or car.

The **Paseo del Parque,** on land reclaimed from the sea, parallels the waterfront. Tall palm and plane trees, bougainvillea, aloes and geraniums luxuriate in this tropical garden alongside the clean, modern port. Midway along the avenue, Plaza de la Aduana gives on to the **Alcazaba,** a Moorish fortress. Across from the entrance lie the partially excavated ruins of a Roman theatre. It's a bit of a climb up the hillside to the Puerta del Cristo (Gateway of Christ), where the first mass was celebrated after the Reconquest. Higher still, the former royal palace of the Moors contains a modest museum of archaeology.

Málaga's **cathedral** is known as the "little lady with one arm" because it has one tall tower and the forlorn stump of another; work on the second "arm" stopped in 1783. Under construction for three centuries, the Renaissance building incorporates Baroque and neoclassical elements.

The **Museo de Bellas Artes**, nearby in Calle de San Agustín, shows, among

other things, Málaga through the eyes of local artists. The most celebrated of them, Pablo Picasso, has a room of his own here. The museum also preserves some of the furniture from the house (still standing in Plaza de la Merced) where Picasso was born in 1881.

Torremolinos
33 D2

With its beaches, bars, restaurants, nightclubs, discos and throngs of tourists, Torremolinos can claim to be the fun capital of the Costa del Sol. From the beach of La Carihuela, a few remaining professional fishermen still set out at dawn in their gaily painted wooden barques. The catch, fried, ends up on the tables of the lively seafront restaurants.

Mijas
33 D2

A sidetrip into the hills from Fuengirola goes to the picturesque village of Mijas, where the appearance of a typical corner of rural Andalusia has been preserved,

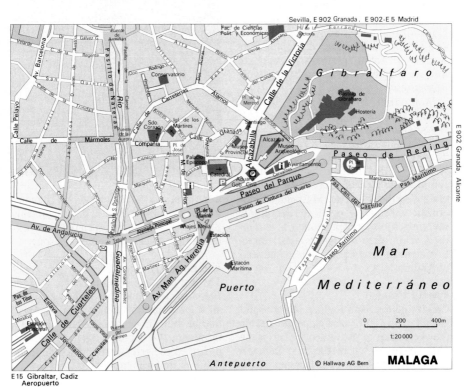

surrounded by modern villas and developments. Except for *burro* (donkey) "taxis", traffic is barred from the core of the village, with its steep streets of whitewashed houses. The souvenir shops overflow with woven goods, tooled leather and ceramic articles of all kinds. Mijas has Spain's only *square* bullring, dating back to Moorish times.

Marbella
32 C3

Isabella of Castile is credited with coining the name Marbella (from the Spanish for "beautiful sea"), an improvement over Salduba (Salt City), as the Phoenicians called it. Royalty and celebrities still gravitate to what has become the aristocrat of Costa del Sol resorts. Prices are accordingly higher than anywhere else along the coast. But the standards are superior in accommodation, service and cuisine.

Marbella encompasses 28 km. (17 miles) of beachfront, built up with exclusive hotel complexes, and a marina with parking space for hundreds of pleasure craft. North of the main road, in the old town, small shops are scattered through the warren of twisting streets. There are historic churches and a storybook Moorish fortress.

Monuments of the new Marbella cling to the hills on the western outskirts. If you glimpse a slightly enlarged copy of the Washington White House, it's the holiday residence of the king of Saudi Arabia. Within hailing distance can be found a whole galaxy of princely palaces. On a neighbouring rise, Marbella's modernistic mosque is open to the public every afternoon except Friday. Five hundred years after the Reconquest, direction signs in Arabic are again to be seen in Andalusia.

Puerto Banús

Call it Spain's Saint-Tropez. A thousand yachts crowd the marina, some so big they bear flags of convenience. This is the kind of resort where the first item on the "appetizers" menu is Russian caviar

and the second is Scotch salmon. Beyond restaurant row there's a line-up of chic nightclubs and shops—open nights, weekends and holidays in the high season.

Estepona
32 C3

The last of the big resorts on the western flank of the coast, Estepona provides all the essentials—beaches, golf courses, marina—in an engaging small-town atmosphere. Of Roman origin, Estepona preserves the remains of Moorish fortifications and watchtowers.

Algeciras
32 C3

The Moors landed here in 711; you can see their influence in old Algeciras. Otherwise it's all business in this high-rise town, an international gateway prospering from coast-road traffic and the ferry and hydrofoil links with Tangiers, Morocco, and the Spanish North African enclave of Ceuta. Probably the best thing about Algeciras is the view across the bay to Gibraltar's memorable silhouette. The highway westwards climbs sharply, offering some thrilling seascapes.

Although there's a certain formality at the posh resort of Puerto Banús, shoes are not really obligatory for wading.

Bobbies on the Rock

Beery pubs and tea rooms instead of wine and *tapa* bars, helmeted bobbies in place of Civil Guardsmen: Gibraltar is a sort of fun-house mirror image of Britain just beyond the Costa del Sol.

A lot of history hangs over the narrow, controversial peninsula of only 6 sq. km. (2½ sq. miles) called the Rock *(el Peñon);* a British colony one-tenth the size of Manhattan island. The ancients considered it one of the Pillars of Hercules, marking the limits of the known world. (The other pillar was across the strait in Morocco.) In 711 the Moorish invasion of Iberia started here, led by Tariq ibn Ziyad, who named the peninsula after himself: *Gibel-Tariq,* Tariq's Rock, whence the modern "Gibraltar".

Spain reconquered Gibraltar in 1462, only to lose it to Britain in the 18th-century War of the Spanish Succession. As a crucial base for the Royal Navy, "Gib" won honours in several wars. Spain, now a partner of Britain in the European Community and NATO, would like to regain sovereignty, but the Gibraltarians overwhelmingly profess allegiance to the United Kingdom.

For more than 15 years Spain blockaded the border. Since 1985, though, it's been easy to visit Gibraltar for sightseeing, duty-free shopping and round-the-clock casino gambling. Most tours take in the ruins of the Moorish castle, the view from the Europa Point lighthouse, historic Trafalgar cemetery, and the apes' den for a look at Gibraltar's famous Barbary apes. According to local superstition, if these tailless macaque monkeys ever leave, British dominance will end. When the primate population declined during World War II, Winston Churchill himself stepped in, and the frisky apes have received special rations ever since.

Costa de la Luz

The Atlantic-facing coast of southern Spain, called the Coast of Light, runs from the Strait of Gibraltar up to the Portuguese border. Seafaring folk who know the whims and perils of the open ocean share this shore with a relative trickle of tourists. This remote side of Andalusia, which seems a long way from the elegance of some Mediterranean resorts, has much to offer in the way of folklore, history and seafood.

Tarifa   32 BC3

Africa is only 13 km. (8 miles) away from Tarifa, Spain's southern extremity. Morocco's Rif mountains hang on the horizon like a spectre. Parts of the old Moorish walls still stand, along with the 10th-century fortress. It's now known as the **Castillo de Guzmán el Bueno,** after Alonso Pérez de Guzmán, a 13th-century Christian commander, who chose "honour without a son, to a son with dishonour". Thus did Guzmán the Good sacrifice the life of his own son, held hostage, rather than surrender Tarifa to the besieging Moors.

From the castle ramparts you can look over to the Rock of Gibraltar.

Cádiz   32 B3 ⚓

Rolling Atlantic waves crash against the rocky defences of this narrow peninsular city, basking in a certain sunny subtropical allure. Prosperous high-rise districts overflow from the slightly frayed historic centre of the ancient seafaring town.

The Atlantic Ocean shaped the history of Cádiz. It was founded about 3,000 years ago by Phoenician traders from Tyre. Christopher Columbus, too, valued the excellent harbour, from which he departed on his second and fourth voyages to America. Later, when treasure-laden Spanish fleets were wont to take refuge here, Cádiz was attacked by Barbary pirates and Sir Francis Drake and sacked by the Earl of Essex. The Spanish and French fleets sailed from here in 1805 to fight the British just to the south, off Cape Trafalgar. A French sniper bagged Lord Nelson, but Britain prevailed.

In 1812, while Napoleon's troops besieged the city, the first Spanish constitution was proclaimed here. The delegates met in the **Oratorio de San Felipe Neri,** a domed church in the maze of the old town. You can hardly see the building for the memorial plaques vying for prominence on the façade.

The Baroque **cathedral,** overlooking the ocean, has a landmark dome glazed yellow. Its lavish treasury features a monster-sized monstrance made of a ton of silver. In the crypt is the tomb of the very Spanish composer, Manuel de Falla, who was born in Cádiz in 1876 (and died in Argentina in 1946).

Sanlúcar de Barrameda   32 B2

Columbus's third trip to the Indies started here, where the Guadalquivir meets the Atlantic. So did Magellan's round-the-world expedition. Vineyards on the hills near this fishing port produce Manzanilla, a rich wine similar to sherry. The sea breezes are supposed to supply Manzanilla's special tang.

Doñana National Park   32 AB2

Three environments share the Parque Nacional de Doñana, this big, wild conservation zone: sand dunes, piney areas and marshes. Up until recent times, royal hunting parties used to fan out over the region, shooting exotic birds, deer and wild boar. Now the wildlife—including more than 250 bird species, transient or permanent—is protected. Among the rarities: imperial eagle, lynx, purple gallinule and crested coot.

Four-hour guided tours in four-wheel-drive vehicles start from the reception centre at El Acebuche. For details and reservations, phone (955) 43 04 32.

El Rocío   27 D3

One of the biggest, most enthusiastic religious festivals in Spain takes place in the obscure community of El Rocío ("the Dew"), on the edge of Doñana National Park. The Whitsun (Pentecost) pilgrimage attracts more than a million colourful participants from all over Spain; they come by car, tractor, horse carriage, ox cart, on horseback or afoot. What brings them all to this inconspicuous town is a religious statue to which miracles are attributed. The relic, the *Virgin of the Dew*, is said to have survived the Muslim occupation hidden in the marsh.

Columbus Country

The Río Tinto area around the industrial port city of Huelva is where Christopher Columbus started his travels. You can follow his trail in the area:

Near refineries on the road from Huelva to La Rábida, a giant waterside **monument** sculpted by Gertrude V. Whitney gives an impression of Columbus at the helm. (Mrs. Whitney [1877-1942], the daughter of the tycoon Cornelius Vanderbilt, also established New York's Whitney Museum.)

The Franciscan monastery at **La Rábida** is one of those "Columbus Slept Here" places. In fact, he seems to have spent a lot of time in La Rábida waiting for Ferdinand and Isabella to approve his project; the monastery's prior, who also believed that the world was round, intervened on his behalf. Monks take visitors around the Mudéjar-style monastery several times a day (except Mondays), so you can visit the cozy chapel where Columbus prayed.

In anticipation of the 500th anniversary of the Columbus adventure, a broad new boulevard leads into the pleasant little town of **Palos de la Frontera**. This is where Columbus is said to have stocked up with water and headed for America. In the meantime the river has long since silted up, and Palos is surrounded by farmland. A monument marks the water source, and they're digging a canal several hundred yards from there to the river.

Columbus recruited crewmen in the nearby town of **Moguer**. It's also the birthplace of the Nobel prize-winning poet, Juan Ramón Jiménez (1881-1958). Pertinent quotations from his works are immortalized on tiles affixed to walls all around the town.

Ayamonte   27 C3

The Costa de la Luz, and Spain, end at the Guadiana river, the border with Portugal. The frontier town of Ayamonte is bigger than you might expect. The Ayuntamiento (town hall) has a classic patio with palm trees, a fountain, arches and tiled walls—all open to the sky. From the *parador* on a bluff above Ayamonte you get an eye-filling view of the white town, the meandering river, and, across the way, Portugal looking curiously flat. The self-consciously regal Portuguese town of Vila Real is only 15 minutes away by ferry.

Inland Andalusia

Beyond the beaches, Andalusia can climb to breathtaking heights; continental Spain's tallest peak, the Mulhacén (3,482 m.—11,424 ft.), is here. But the population concentrates in the lowlands, especially in the fertile triangle of the Guadalquivir valley. Our survey of the towns and cities of inland Andalusia takes a leisurely circular route, clockwise, starting in the hills north-west of Marbella.

Ronda 32 C2

Clinging to a clifftop sundered by a deep gorge, Ronda is a strong competitor for the title of Spain's most dramatically sited town. The dizzying emplacement has always appealed to strategists. The ancient Iberians settled here and then the Romans dug in. Under the Moors Ronda proved impregnable for well over seven centuries.

The **gorge** that cleaves the city, called the Tajo, plunges 150 m. (nearly 500 ft.) down to the surly Río Guadalevín. During the Civil War, hundreds of Nationalist sympathizers were hurled to their deaths in the abyss, as recalled by Hemingway in his novel *For Whom the Bell Tolls.*

For the best prospect of the Tajo and the patchwork of fields beyond, catch the view from the **Puente Nuevo** (New Bridge). It has spanned the ravine for more than two centuries, leading to the **Ciudad,** the old Moorish enclave. Ronda's Moorish kings—and Christian conquerers—used to live in the **Palacio de Mondragón.** Beyond the Renaissance portal, spacious courtyards with horseshoe arches and Arabic inscriptions reveal the real origins of this stately structure.

Ronda's chief mosque survives a street or two away as the church of **Santa María la Mayor.** The minaret was converted into a bell tower, and a Gothic nave was tacked on to the original structure.

Across the chasm again in the post-Reconquest part of town called Mercadillo, Ronda's neoclassical **Plaza de Toros** (bullring) is one of the oldest in Spain. A Ronda man, Francisco Romero, spelled out the rules of bullfighting in the 18th century; his father is said to have "invented" the red rag that provokes the bull. This ring is all but venerated as the cradle of the *corrida.*

Arcos de la Frontera 32 B2

Another hill town in an extraordinary spot, Arcos de la Frontera, also attracted ancient Iberian settlers. The *frontera* in its name recalls the fact that it was on the medieval border between the forces of Christians and Moors.

At the top of the hill are the town hall, two churches and a *parador.* The fourth side of the square, a railing at the edge of a cliff, offers a stupendous view over rural Spain at its best—rolling hills of orchards, olive groves and vineyards and, directly below, the life-giving Río Guadalete. Roam the steep, narrow streets of the old town, with its Moorish and Gothic buildings.

Jerez de la Frontera 32 B2

Old wines and young horses bring fame to Jerez, the biggest town in the province of Cádiz.

Sherry, the English name of the locally produced wine, is a corruption of "Jerez". A few of the many wineries, or *bodegas,*

*A*t fiesta time in Jerez, a few casks of sherry are bound to be consumed. Most visitors to the town make a beeline for Domecq or Gonzalez-Byass to tour a bodega, *with free samples.*

In the rolling hill country of Andalusia, the late 20th century has brought sweeping changes to agriculture, thanks in large part to bold irrigation projects. But the colour of the farmhouses is still white.

Drake forcibly brought sherry to the attention of the English public. In a raid on Cádiz, the swashbuckling Drake seized nearly 3,000 barrels of the admirable aperitif. Known as "sack" or "sherry-sack", it soon graced all the fashionable tables of London.

. Shakespeare thought highly enough of sherry to praise it at length. In *Henry IV, Part Two*, high-living Sir John Falstaff ends a long monologue extolling sherry with this endorsement: "If I had a thousand sons, the first human principle I would teach them should be to forswear thin potations, and to addict themselves to sack."

As for the horses, the Royal Andalusian School of Equestrian Art *(Real Escuela Andaluza de Arte Ecuestre)* has the smartest, prettiest, lightest-footed mounts you've ever seen. Every Thursday at noon the Jerez riding school puts on a beautifully orchestrated show by horses that strut, goose-step, leap and dance; dogs and cameras are forbidden. The rest of the working week, midday training sessions may be watched. Best of all, try to make it to Jerez for the annual spring horse show.

By way of historical monuments, the 11th-century walls of the Moorish **Alcá-zar** are now surrounded by gardens. Below the hilltop fortress, the 18th-century **Colegiata** contains, appropriately, a precious image of *Cristo de la Viña* (Christ of the Vineyards).

in Jerez invite tourists (weekday mornings only) to see how sherry is blended and aged in dark, aromatic halls. At Pedro Domecq they're proud to show off historic casks; visitors have ranged from the Duke of Wellington to Princess Anne and Plácido Domingo. Gonzalez-Byass treats tourists to the tricks of its wine-tippling mice. The hospitality of the *bodegas* is as generous as the bouquet of their wines: every tour ends with a comprehensive tasting session.

Just over 400 years ago Sir Francis

Seville   *32 B2*

Romantic, spiritual, sensual Seville is as grand as an opera. Certainly it has inspired more operas than any other city: *The Barber of Seville, The Marriage of Figaro, Don Juan, Fidelio, Carmen...* You can visit the sweatshop where the irresistible Carmen worked, rolling cigars on her thigh.

Seville has many faces—Moorish and Christian, stately boulevards and narrow alleys, tranquil gardens as fragrant as orange blossoms and cafés as noisy as an argument. But they're all parts of the

*A*rabesques in old Seville: the spacious Patio of the Doncellas (ladies-in-waiting) in the Alcázar is a Renaissance impression of the Moorish style. In the 14th century, Peter the Cruel recruited Mudéjar architects and artisans to redo an old Moorish palace. Expansions, repairs and revisions went on intermittently for several centuries, resulting in some mixed metaphors. But, in a word, it's sumptuous.

heart and soul of Spain. Capital of flamenco and the bullfight, birthplace of Velázquez and Murillo, Seville is the fourth-biggest but most Spanish of Spain's cities. (But beware another superlative: its pickpockets and petty thieves are notorious throughout the country.)

The history of Seville leaps from success to success, under the Romans, the Visigoths and the Moors. After the Reconquest Seville won a monopoly on trade with newly discovered America. During this Golden Age, the slogan went: "Madrid is the capital of Spain but Seville is the capital of the world."

In 1401 the Great Mosque of Seville was razed to make way for a colossal **cathedral** which became the largest Gothic church in the world. There are five naves and more than 30 chapels, including the Plateresque **Capilla Real** (Royal Chapel), last resting place of the 13th-century "King Saint" Ferdinand III, who delivered Seville from the "infidel". Closed off by an 18th-century grille, the High Altar is so beautiful it's worth squeezing up against the screen for a good look. An ornate 19th-century **sarcophagus** near the south entrance is said to contain the remains of Christopher Columbus, well travelled even in death. (He died in Valladolid in 1506 and was reburied in Seville. The rest of the posthumous journey is fogged by historical confusion, but the bones were shipped off to Santo Domingo and maybe Cuba. After the defeat in the Spanish-American War, his presumed remains sailed back to Seville.)

Alongside the cathedral, the celebrated **Giralda** tower, once a minaret, is the city's lofty symbol. It's a hike up 34 flights of ramps and one of steps to the top of the 98-metre (322-foot) tower, but

---

Springtime in Seville

Since the 16th century, the most solemn week in the Christian calendar has been the occasion for tremendous manifestations in Seville. The **Semana Santa** (Holy Week) **processions**, with masked penitents in black pointed hoods, ornate candle-lit religious scenes carried on the shoulders of the faithful, and plaintive music, fill the streets for eight days, Finally, jubilant church bells signal the relief and joy of Easter.

Soon after the pageantry and fervour of Holy Week, Seville drops everything for the **Feria de Abril** (April Fair). Andalusia's most colourful celebration is a kaleidoscope of flamenco, bullfights, horses, flowers and wine.

---

you can stop along the way for a breather and unusual views of the cathedral's pinnacles and the cityscapes beyond.

The **Alcázar** of Pedro the Cruel is a sumptuous monument from the 14th century. The ceilings and walls of its halls provide a concise if overpowering concentration of Mudéjar abandon. But unlike the Alhambra in Granada, this rambling palace was built under Christian kings who valued Moorish skills. Beyond the richly embellished salons and apartments, the terraced **gardens**, scattered with pools and pavilions, are superb in their own right.

More Mudéjar sensations await in a typical 15th-century Andalusian palace, the privately owned **Casa de Pilatos** (Pilate's House). The elegant patio, oddly, has niches for the busts of Roman emperors and similar dignitaries.

As for that *femme fatale*, Carmen, the royal tobacco factory she worked in—an enormous, square, 18th-century structure behind a moat—is now the campus of the **University**.

La Cartuja, an island in the Guadalquivir, is being spruced up for the 500th

---

*F*lowers brighten everyday life in the narrow alleys of Seville, the world capital of flamenco. The local form of the dance, called the Sevillana, is also popular in Madrid.

anniversary of the first outing to America. Columbus is said to have planned his voyage during a stay at the island's Carthusian monastery. La Cartuja is the site of Seville's EXPO '92, the first universal exhibition since Osaka in 1970.

Córdoba
29 C2

Two distinct Golden Ages, centuries of political power and cultural attainment, account for Córdoba's glow of greatness. The first big break came under the Romans; the second, even bigger, under the Moors.

The birthplace of the intellectual Seneca family, Córdoba was the capital of Rome's Hispania Ulterior. It became the biggest Roman city on the Iberian peninsula. In the Middle Ages, indigenous Christians and Jews helped Córdoba blossom under Muslim rule as a centre of culture, science and art. By the 10th century, the capital of the caliphate was as big and brilliant as any city in Europe. Two of Córdoba's 12th-century native sons were Averroës, the Muslim philosopher and physician, and Maimonides, the Jewish philosopher and physician; both were all-round intellectual superstars.

After the Reconquest, the Spaniards customarily levelled mosques and built churches atop the rubble. In Córdoba, happily, they spared one of the world's biggest and most beautiful mosques. But then they built a cathedral inside it. The result is called the **Mezquita-Catedral.** The original Great Mosque, begun in the year 785 by Emir Abd-er-Rahman I, grew to its present humbling proportions under the 10th-century leader al-Mansur.

A high wall surrounds the sacred enclosure. You reach the mosque through the ceremonial forecourt with its fountains and orange and palm trees. Inside, in the half-light, an enchanted forest of hundreds of **columns** seems to extend to infinity. The columns of marble, onyx or jasper are topped by arches upon arches, in red and white stripes. At the end of the main aisle, tendrils of stone twine around the 10th-century **mihrab** and the *mak-*

sourah before it, the enclosure where the caliph attended to his prayers. Almost hidden in the very centre of these acres of beauty is the **cathedral,** a spectacular sequel in Gothic and Baroque styles, pointedly rising far above its surroundings. The Emperor Charles V told the sponsors, "You have destroyed something unique to build something commonplace". (But the mahogany choir stalls are splendidly carved.)

South-west of the mosque, on the river, the **Alcázar** was actually built by a

Christian king, Alfonso XI. There are pleasant patios, Roman relics, terraced gardens and, best of all, **views** from the ramparts.

To absorb the full flavour of Córdoba there's no substitute for wandering the narrow streets and alleys of the **Barrio de la Judería** (Jewish Quarter), in which a small 14th-century synagogue can still be found. You'll need all your peripheral vision not to miss glimpses of cool, flowered patios, so perfect they seem show windows for traditional Spanish life.

Retaking Córdoba from the Moors, the Christian forces spared one of the world's most beautiful mosques, but added "improvements" and called it a cathedral.

Jaén 29 D2

The province of Jaén, east of Córdoba, enjoys some of Spain's happiest scenic contrasts: harsh mountains staring down at undulating hills covered with olive groves and luxuriant valleys refreshed by giant irrigation projects.

The provincial capital, Jaén, spreads beneath an ancient Moorish castle, now a *parador*. The cathedral has a vast Renaissance façade, which contrasts with the narrow streets and little squares. The provincial museum specializes in archaeology, notably Iberian and Roman relics. For a closer look at 11th-century life, see Jaén's **Arab baths**, among the most extensive anywhere in Spain.

Baeza 29 D2

Not many towns of 15,000 inhabitants can inventory more than 50 worthwhile historic buildings, but charming Baeza is very special. It played an important role in the Moorish period, then prospered after the Reconquest. All's quiet today: the main square, much too big for a town this size, is surrounded by a hodgepodge of architecture, ranging from agreeable to distinguished, with no shortage of cafés and farm equipment stores. Just off the square, the **Fountain of the Lions,** composed of recycled Ibero-Roman statuary, marks the Plaza del Pópulo. The tourist office, in a 16th-century mansion, has maps of suggested walks through Baeza's prized **ensemble** of golden stone churches, monasteries and palaces.

Úbeda 29 D2

Nearly twice the size of Baeza, Úbeda is just as engaging, but more pompous. This was an important headquarters during the Reconquest; many of the Spanish nobles involved in the struggle liked Úbeda well enough to build palaces.

The town's 16th-century moneybags, Francisco de los Cobos, built the **Sacra Capilla del Salvador** (Sacred Chapel of

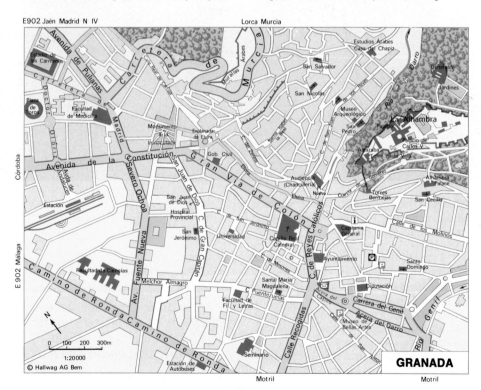

GRANADA

the Saviour), still a private chapel (but open for visits). The one-time Palace of Dean Ortega, on the same square, became one of the first of Spain's state-owned tourist hotels; the old town is so undefiled by commercial infringements that you might miss the understated "Parador" sign. Beyond is the Renaissance **Palacio de las Cadenas** (Palace of Chains), the name referring to its decorations, now the town hall. Opposite, in the 13th-century church of **Santa María de los Reales Alcázares**, they replaced the patio of a mosque with a Gothic cloister. Those are some of the monuments on just *one* of several historic plazas in Úbeda. The whole town is a joy.

Granada   29 D3

Two things make Granada inspiringly different: its site on the slopes of the snowcapped Sierra Nevada; and the time warp in its past. For more than two centuries, while the rest of Spain was build-

ing Gothic cathedrals and heating up the Inquisition, Granada remained a more than self-sufficient island of Islam encircled by the unfinished Reconquest. Moors seeking refuge from vanquished Córdoba and Seville swelled the population, pitching in to make medieval Granada ever grander. When Ferdinand and Isabella accepted the keys to the vanquished city in January of 1492, they found such splendour that they added some extravagances of their own.

Of the Moorish monuments that once crowned the heights of Granada, only one remains—a sprawling complex of fortifications, palaces and gardens from the 13th and 14th centuries. The ochre-red citadel of the **Alhambra** suffered centuries of vicissitudes and years of neglect, but it shines as the most magnificent medieval palace the Arabs ever built—anywhere.

You enter through the former council chamber *(Mexuar)* and a patio into the

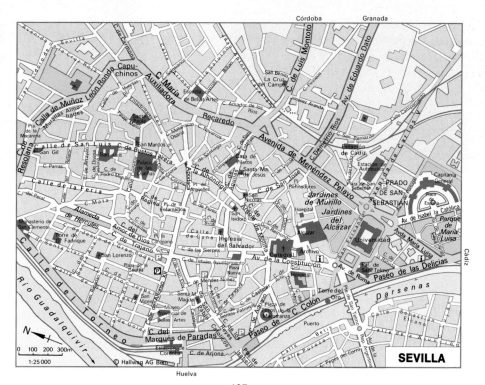

197

The Moorish king who surrendered Granada to the Christians wept when he looked back at this sight: the Alhambra's towers backed by the snowy Sierra Nevada. Overleaf: intricacies of the Patio of the Mexuar, leading into the "official business" area of the medieval Alcázar palace.

Arabian-Nights **Patio de los Arrayanes** (Court of the Myrtle Trees). The reflecting pool, a focus for photographers, is populated by a pack of plump goldfish. In the **Salón de Embajadores**, the royal audience chamber, the walls, five storeys high, are decorated with the most finicky Arabic filigree and calligraphy. At the centre of the elegantly arcaded **Patio de los Leones** (Court of Lions) stands a fountain supported by a dozen spitting lions of stone. Splendid rooms radiate out on every side.

A section of the Alcázar was razed to make way for the **Palacio de Carlos V** to give Charles V a Renaissance roof over his head. The design, a perfect circle in a square, is by Pedro Machuca, a student of Michelangelo. The more interesting of two museums here, the **Museo Nacional de Arte Hispano-musulmán,** features some exquisite examples of the local Moorish arts and crafts, from an inlaid throne to wonders of ceramics.

Of the **Alcazaba,** the oldest part of the Alhambra, only the outer walls and towers survive. Still, the **view** from the top—the Torre de la Vela (watch tower)—is the kind of prospect wars are waged for. It reaches from the snowy mountains to the lovely forested hills, down to the tile-roofed warrens of old Granada, and the plain beyond.

The **Generalife**, first of all, is not the name of an insurance company. The name (pronounced khay-nay-rah-*lee*-feh) comes from the Arabic for "architect's garden" or perhaps "sublime orchard". The king would seek refuge from the pomp and protocol of the Alhambra next door, to muse among the fountains, trees, flowers, and the romance of an inimitable view over his realm. In the grounds of the summer palace, oleander, rhododendron and roses thrive, fountains play and cascades tumble.

In the centre of town, Granada's white and gold cathedral, designed by Diego de Siloé, is as imposing as ordered. But the freestanding **Capilla Real** to one side steals its thunder. The Renaissance chapel serves as the **mausoleum** of the Catholic Monarchs. Behind a glorious wrought-iron screen, the white marble effigies of Ferdinand and Isabella lie on the right-hand side of the chancel, with those of their daughter Joan the Mad and her husband Philip the Fair on the left. Look into the crypt below to see the simplicity of their actual lead caskets. Under glass in the **sacristy** are Ferdinand's blunt-tipped sword, with a small gold handle a child could barely get a grip on, and Isabella's jewelless crown.

Land of the Conquistadores

Stranded halfway between the sea and the nation's power base, Estremadura (Extremadura in Spanish) has always languished as an economic backwater. Its most valuable export has been its talent. The region's ambitious, courageous young men left their home on the range and crossed the sea to make history.

Estremadura

This wide open land of the Spanish west was the birthplace of the *conquistadores,* the adventurers who opened a new continent. Among the celebrated native sons *(extremeños),* Cortés colonized Mexico, Pizarro conquered Peru, and de Soto went on to discover the Mississippi. Nowadays young men leave Estremadura for the same economic reasons, but they usually choose to make their fortune less dangerously, in Madrid offices or northern European factories.

Estremadura's heyday came in the time of ancient Rome. Along with all of present-day Portugal, the region belonged to Roman Lusitania. The capital of this promising province was the small city of Mérida, then grandly known as Augusta Emerita in honour of the emperor and his legionaries who settled there. Archaeology fans can have a field day.

Two refreshing rivers—the Guadiana and the Tagus—flow through the region on their way to Portugal and the Atlantic ocean. Great efforts have been made to tap the rivers for irrigation, but beyond these green spots Estremadura remains a parched country. It's still underpopulated except for the migratory flocks of sheep among the holm and cork oaks; if you like to eat lamb, just reach for the nearest menu. The farmers also keep pigs and make ham and sausage that have achieved a national reputation.

The definition of Estremadura ("land beyond the Río Duero") was flexible in the Middle Ages, when it encompassed a much larger area than the modern boundaries. For our survey we stretch the borders to include a couple of charming, historic towns just across the line in Salamanca province. But we've arranged this chapter in south-to-north order, starting in a part of the region indistinguishable from Andalusia.

In Estremadura, far-sighted storks make themselves at home on the best vantage point of the old walled city of Cáceres.

*F*or centuries the "best and brightest" of
Estremadura's young men emigrated in search of economic
opportunity or adventure—for instance, conquering the Americas.
In modern times, enterprising irrigation schemes have greened the hills
here, but little else has changed for some traditional farmers.

By way of special events of more than local interest, the Zafra cattle fair in the first week of October is always festive. It's been going on here since ancient times.

Badajoz
21 D2
This close to the Portuguese border, you're as likely to find baked codfish on the menu as lamb stew. Because the ancient Romans founded it at a sensitive strategic location, Badajoz (now the biggest city in Estremadura) has often figured in war stories, most recently and tragically in the Civil War.

The ancient **Puerta de Palmas** gateway, a small fortress in itself, leads to the walled city, with its narrow medieval streets. Another arch used to bar the way to the gardened **citadel** on Orinace hill, overlooking the Guadiana river. This is where the rulers of the Moorish kingdom of Badajoz held forth.

The **cathedral,** with its heavy walls and pinnacled tower, was built in the 13th century. The Gothic architecture was later modified with Renaissance effects. Inside are highly regarded choir stalls, paintings, tapestries and tombstones.

Mérida
21 E2
In the Plaza de España, the main square of this vaguely tropical-looking little city, just about every school of architecture is represented, none with first-class honours. You'd never guess this sleepy town was once an imperial capital dubbed the Rome of Spain. But you'll understand when you see the monuments the empire left behind.

The town was founded in 25 B.C. It grew rich and influential as capital of the province of Lusitania. After the fall of the Romans and an unedifying parade of barbarians, the Visigoths further enhanced the city. But in A.D. 713 it fell to the Moors. The caliph, disappointed by his new subjects' revolutionary stirrings, set in motion the town's five centuries of decline.

The partially restored **Teatro Romano**

Zafra
21 E3
The white houses of Zafra recall its Moorish origins. So does the design of the town's medieval castle, previously an *alcázar*, now a *parador* for tourists. What with its 15th-century cylindrical towers and crenellations the first impression isn't very hospitable, but the interior is bright and welcoming. The *parador* is named "Hernán Cortés" in honour of the conqueror of Mexico. He stayed in this castle before his excursion to the New World.

seats over 5,500 spectators. For acoustics and visibility the design has never been bettered. Mérida's theatre was built in the 1st century B.C. under the sponsorship of Agrippa, the son-in-law of Emperor Augustus. The show—tragedy, comedy or mime—went on until late in the 4th century A.D. Under new management, classical Roman and Greek plays are again being produced here... an inspiring way to spend a summer evening under the stars.

The elliptical **Anfiteatro,** next door, was designed to hold 15,000 fans of gladiatorial combat and chariot races. (The arena has far more seats than the theatre because action shows always drew bigger crowds than the more intellectual offerings.)

Just across the street from the park leading to the theatre and arena is an unexpectedly big, modern museum. No mere local project, this is the **Museo Nacional de Arte Romano.** On show are statues (a bust of the emperor, of course), vases, even paintings discovered on the podium of the arena. Numismatists point to a number of novelties among the locally minted coins.

Around town are many other Roman monuments, most notably the ruins of Spain's only remaining Roman circus; what's left of a patrician villa next to the arena; a temple to Diana; Trajan's Arch; an aqueduct; and a bridge half a mile long, with 64 granite arches, across the Guadiana. The **hornito,** "little oven", is a small temple where a 13-year-old martyr, Santa Eulalia, is said to have been burnt alive by the Romans. In Mérida they sell accurate reproductions of Roman relics, honestly labelled as copies. Nobody claims they've just been excavated, and nobody is peddling coins dated "26 B.C.".

Guadalupe   22 B1

From afar, the turrets, spires and crenellations of the rambling monastery announce an impressive shrine. Physically as well as economically, the institution

totally dominates the very small town spread at its feet; the main square of Guadalupe descends from the monastery's steps. The narrow streets of the village, whose prosperity has always depended on the pilgrim traffic, wear a welcoming smile. Bird cages and pots of flowers enliven the balconies of the old houses.

Everything here revolves around a small religious image. The dark-skinned wooden statue of the Virgin of Guadalupe was considered miraculous enough to win battles and inspire overseas discoveries. When Columbus brought back a couple of token American Indians, they were baptized here to symbolize the Christianization of the New World. Columbus also named the Caribbean island Guadeloupe after this town.

The **monastery** complex (its full name is *Real Monasterio de Santa María de Guadalupe*) covers an area of 2 hectares (about 5 acres). There are so many irregularities and extensions that the floor plan looks like a kindergarten pupil's collage. The Flamboyant façade, flanked by stern, square, defensive towers, offers some airy Mudéjar stonework. The church—officially a basilica by order of Pius XII—was begun in the 14th century and enlarged in the 18th. One of the sculptors who worked on the main altarpiece was Jorge Manuel Theotocopuli, son of El Greco.

To see the rest of the complex, including the revered statue and the riches around it, you have to join a tour. The guides tend to speak only Spanish, but some exhibits are labelled in English as well. You'll see the 15th-century Mudéjar

Sculpture on the corner of Conquistador Hernando Pizarro's mansion in Trujillo illustrates the subjugation of the New World.

The Story Behind the Statue

Spoilsport experts say the venerated effigy of the Virgin of Guadalupe was carved at the end of the 12th century. But according to legend it's well over twice as old.

In the medieval version, the statue had been carved by St. Luke himself. Then, late in the 6th century, it's said, the icon stood in the private chapel of Pope (later Saint) Gregory the Great in Rome. The pope sent the statue to Seville, but just before the Moors overran the city in A.D. 711 the relic was evacuated northwards. It was buried for safekeeping alongside the Guadalupe river, but in the chaos of those days it was lost.

Next chapter: In the 13th century a shepherd named Gil Cordero had a miraculous vision: the Virgin herself directed him to the spot where the statue was buried. Soon a shrine was built, then a chapel, a church, and eventually the vast citadel-monastery. The elaborately dressed and crowned statue has attracted millions of ordinary pilgrims, primarily from Spain and Spanish America, as well as celebrities from Ferdinand and Isabella to Pope John Paul II.

cloister, an embroidery museum, the Gothic cloister, and the chapterhouse and sacristy, with a remarkable collection of paintings by Zurbarán, among others.

Trujillo   *22 A1*

The hilltop skyline of Trujillo, seen from afar, is one of those storybook sights that revive the spirits of the tired traveller. Up close, the town is even nicer. Although Spain has historic towns with far more imposing architecture, Trujillo's main square must win the prize for relaxed charm. The eccentrically shaped and tilted **Plaza Mayor** is a happy conjunction of distinguished and ordinary buildings.

The most elegant building here, on the south-west corner of the square, is the **Palacio del Marqués de la Conquista,** built by Pizarro's half-brother (and son-in-law), Hernando. Along with seals of honour on the walls, look for the bas-relief portraits of Francisco and Hernando and their South American Indian brides. With their historic escutcheons, portals, windows and patios, half a dozen

palaces around the town reward close study.

Diagonally across the square, you can't miss the bronze **statue** of Francisco Pizarro, scourge of the Incas. He and his horse wear armoured helmets. Behind them, the town clock looks out from the corner tower of the Gothic church of **San Martín;** storks nest above it, evidently immune to the jolt of the gongs. If you want to explore the long, dark nave of this church, paved with historic tombstones, mind the step: halfway to the altar the floor level suddenly rises.

The Romanesque and Gothic church of **Santa María la Mayor,** up the hill, was built on the site of a mosque. It has an admirable retable in Hispano-Flemish style by Fernando Gallego. On the balcony, note two VIP-sized stone seats, built for the Catholic Monarchs, Ferdinand and Isabella. They came here for the funeral of Juan II of Aragon.

On the hilltop, the heavily fortified **castillo** began as a Roman fort and later became a Moorish *alcazaba*. Above the keyhole-shaped main gate, in a glassed-in niche, stands the *Virgin of Victory*, the local patron. The view over Trujillo from here is the best in town.

Cáceres   *22 A1*

The old walled city of Cáceres, capital of the province of the same name, is one big national monument, a magnificent assembly of mellow stone churches, palaces and towers.

Before it became a feast of medieval architecture, Cáceres was a Roman town called Norba Caesarina, founded by a proconsul called Gaius Flaccus. During the very Dark Ages, barbarians rampaged through the town, after which the Moors moved in. They rebuilt the Roman wall, which looks now much as it did then. Control over Cáceres seesawed between the Muslims and the Christians in the 12th and 13th centuries. On April 23, 1227, the town became part of the kingdom of León.

You're bound to gravitate to the **Plaza**

Mayor, along the town wall. It's the centre of local life, especially at the hour of the *paseo.* The crowd bulges into the side streets; conversations reverberate; husks of chewed sunflower seeds shower like snowflakes onto the pavements. As night falls, the historic buildings are illuminated, providing an unduly dignified backdrop to the very relaxed ritual.

The skyline used to be more vertical. Many an aristocratic or nouveau-riche family crowned its mansion with an ego-expanding fortified tower. But they were truncated late in the 15th century by order of Queen Isabella. Later the rules were eased, so there are heights enough to interest a number of storks. One of the most visible towers is part of the Toledo-Montezuma mansion, formerly the home of a local man who married the daughter of the Aztec emperor.

Go through the Arco de la Estrella (Star Arch) into the **old town** and climb at leisure among the often-rough stones of the medieval mansions, towers and churches. Be alert for the details: heraldic shields, Renaissance windows, filigreed roof decorations; you may catch a glimpse of a pretty patio. The Casa de las Veletas (Weathervane House) has been turned into a strikingly good provincial **museum** of archaeology and ethnology. In the basement is an 11th-century Moorish cistern; it still needs draining.

Alcántara
21 D1

In its day, the **six-arched bridge** over the Tagus near here was world renowned for its elegant engineering. The Romans built it in A.D. 106 during the reign of the Spanish-born Emperor Trajan. The bridge, with extraordinarily high arches, is 194 m. (636 ft.) long and altogether so impressive that the town was named after it: al-Qantara is Arabic for "the Bridge".

The name of the town in turn was given to the order of knights who defended their fortress here against the Moors in the 13th century. The knights became the Order of Alcántara. With a membership up to 100,000, it figured prominently in two centuries of struggle for the reconquest of Spain.

East of Alcántara the Tagus has been dammed, giving the landscape a dramatic facelift. Beyond its contribution of beauty, the lake multiplies the area's recreational possibilities.

Plasencia
22 A1

When King Alfonso VIII of Castile liberated this hilltop town from the Moors in the 12th century, he renamed it Plasencia, and fortified it with a city wall enhanced by 68 towers. Plasencia's significance has slipped since then, but the bristling silhouette still stands. The old mansions and churches retain their historic allure.

The **cathedral** works its architectural way from Romanesque to Gothic. It rates among Estremadura's most significant churches for its rich ornamentation, starting with Plateresque embellishment on the exterior. The choir stalls, carved to illustrate Bible stories and scenes from medieval life, are the work of Rodrigo Alemán.

In the old town are aristocratic houses and full-blown palaces, as well as narrow streets lined with white houses for ordinary people. Tuesday is market day in Plasencia, as it has been since the 13th century. Like the country folk who flock to the market, it's all very rustic and unspoiled.

La Alberca
14 A2

Donkeys at work traverse the main street of this unpretentious national monument, just north of the Estremadura border in León region. The atmosphere is warm with peasant charm. The upper storeys of the whitewashed houses overhang the narrow streets, flowers brightening the flimsy-looking wooden balconies. You may see the bean harvest spread out to dry in the middle of La Alberca's unassuming Plaza Pública, a far cry from the grandeur of main squares elsewhere. Black-clad housewives wait patiently behind trays of pollen and

*A religious procession trudges along a narrow
street of Cáceres. In this pious city the military order of Santiago was
founded in the 12th century; its knights protected pilgrims
on the way to Santiago de Compostela.*

in the Reconquest here, then settled down in the area. The shrine of the *Virgen Morena* (Dark Virgin), a statue discovered in the 15th century, is a popular goal of modern-day pilgrims.

Ciudad Rodrigo   *13 E2*

You can walk all around the town here, literally. Take the path atop the medieval defensive wall encircling Ciudad Rodrigo. The perimeter measures more than 2 km. (over a mile), an irregular oval shape, and the sentry route is uninterrupted.

Ciudad Rodrigo's Plaza Mayor is a shambling affair, neither a square nor a triangle. It is distinguished by the **Casa Consistorial**, the town hall, a 16th-century arcaded palace with a belfry. A smaller palace on the square has come down in the world; its ground floor serves as a general store, where farmers' wives come in search of detergent, shampoo and a whisper of gossip. There are, however, perhaps a dozen worthy old mansions in the town with interesting features—escutcheons, grillwork, stonemasonry, a patio.

The exterior of the **cathedral,** begun in the 12th century, is full of fine sculptural details, especially around the west portal. Inside, the choir stalls are richly carved by the same Rodrigo Alemán who won the Plasencia contract. The Rodrigo in the name of Ciudad Rodrigo is another fellow completely, Count Rodrigo González Girón, who gave the town a big boost in the 12th century.

The best-known landmark of Ciudad Rodrigo is an archaeological monument beyond the walls. **Las Tres Columnas** (the Three Columns), in a triangular configuration, seem to have made up the corner of a Roman temple.

Here in the border country, so close to Portugal, the countryside is very sparsely settled. Cowboys tend rambling herds among low, generous oak trees, shaped just like the tiny plastic trees used in architects' models of landscape. The cows enjoy the shade.

home-made nougat and honey; the "soft sell" is as sweet as the product.

Only 15 km. (9 miles) west—and up-hill—from La Alberca, the **Peña de Francia** is a peak with a Dominican monastery (closed in winter) at the summit. A paved road winds to the top (altitude 1,723 m.—5,653 ft.), spreading at your feet an incomparable view of all of neighbouring Castile and more.

This far from France, the name of the peak ("Rock of France") is a puzzler. It's suggested that French pilgrims joined

THE CONQUISTADORES

They came from the harsh soil of Estremadura and went forth ruthlessly to explore and exploit the New World. Many of the Conquistadores, who launched Spain's Golden Age in the 16th century, grew up virtually as neighbours. They came from small towns no farther apart than New York and Philadelphia or London and Birmingham. They braved the unknown—and unimaginable hardship and danger. A few returned rich and bemedalled. Most of the other notables died in Spanish America, victims of hostile receptions or the intrigues of their own countrymen.

Francisco **Pizarro**, born in the 1470s in *Trujillo*, is said to have worked as a swineherd before signing on for early expeditions to the Caribbean and South America. He thrived as a colonist in Panama, then set forth down the uncharted Pacific coast to Peru. In a battle with the primitively armed Incas, Pizarro captured their ruler, Atahualpa. Having accepted a huge ransom

Hometown statue of Francisco Pizarro.

in gold and silver paid for Atahualpa's release, the Spaniards executed him. The Inca empire fell apart and Pizarro, known as the Great Marquis, became the not necessarily beloved ruler of Peru. Rivalries among the colonial masters seethed. In 1541, in his palace in Lima, the city he had founded, Pizarro was assassinated.

Fame and fortune in the New World was a family affair for the Pizarros. Francisco's half-brother, **Gonzalo,** after helping subdue the Incas, explored Ecuador. He made history as the leader of the first revolt by colonists against Spanish rule. But the viceroy captured him and he was decapitated. Two other brothers, **Hernando** and **Juan**, joined the Pizarro family business. Juan perished in an Indian siege. Hernando, the governor of Cuzco, was the only one of the four to retire. He died peacefully, of old age, back home in Estremadura.

The first European to set eyes on the Pacific, Vasco Núñez de **Balboa,** was born around 1475 far from any sea in *Jerez de los Caballeros,* Estremadura. Balboa became an explorer almost by default. A career as a pioneer farmer in the Caribbean failed and, to flee his creditors, he stowed away on a ship to Panama. From there he contrived to be put in charge of a daring expedition westwards through jungle and swamp. In September, 1513, from a mountain top, he sighted the "South Sea", which he claimed for the King of Castile. The rest of his career was anything but pacific. Intrigues among the colonists put him in the dock on trumped-up charges of rebellion and high treason. By order of his own father-in-law, Balboa was beheaded in 1519.

The small Estremadura town of *Medellín,* in Badajoz province, was the birthplace, in 1485, of the conqueror of Mexico, Hernán **Cortés**. Well educated, the son of a distinguished family, he sowed some notorious wild oats before sailing for the Caribbean at the age of 19. From Cuba, which he helped conquer, Cortés led an 11-ship expedition to the east coast of Mexico. The local Indians, soon subdued, presented the Spaniards with a gift of 20 maidens. One of them, renamed Doña Marina, became the interpreter, political adviser and, eventually, mistress of Cortés.

Scuttling his fleet to discourage defec-

Vasco Núñez de Balboa gets his first glimpse of the Pacific Ocean.

tions, the Conquistador marched his troops to the Aztec capital, the rich, beautiful city of Tenochtitlán. It was a three month ordeal, through jungles and over mountains. The Aztecs, who had never seen horses, much less guns, were awed into submission. Cortés took the ultimate hostage: Montezuma, the gentle ruler of a barbaric society. The final conquest of Mexico, more complex and costly than anticipated, took another year. King Charles V, who received a generous slice of all the Mexican gold, promoted Cortés to the rank of a marquis and Captain-General of New Spain. But the later years were anticlimax, and the great Conquistador died in obscurity in 1547.

Francisco **Orellana** helped a fellow *Trujillo* man, Pizarro, conquer Peru. Next he founded the city of Guayaquil, Ecuador. In 1541, searching through thick and thin for El Dorado, he became the first European to explore the Amazon River, which he named. On the way back for a second visit, Orellana's ship capsized and he was drowned. By an ironic twist of politics, the lands he mapped for Spain now belong to Portugal.

Born in *Villanueva de la Serena*, Estremadura, around 1500, Pedro de **Valdivia** explored Chile. He founded the cities of Santiago, La Concepción and (at last surmounting the modesty problem) Valdivia. A couple of years later his forces lost a battle with a revolting tribe of Indians. Captured, Valdivia was very slowly tortured to death.

Balboa's brother-in-law, Hernando **de Soto,** seems to have been born around the year 1500 in *Jerez de los Caballeros*. Rich and well educated, he took part in the conquest of Central America. As an officer in Pizarro's Peruvian operation he became the friend of the Inca chief Atahualpa. When Pizarro betrayed the king, de Soto, disillusioned, went home to Estremadura. But adventure called, and he mounted a thousand-man expedition to the southern part of North America. In the course of explorations all the way from Florida to Oklahoma, de Soto's band were the first Europeans to explore the Mississippi river. De Soto survived many a battle and hardship but he fell victim to a fever. They buried him in the river he had put on the map.

Spain's Holiday Seas
For All Seasons

The empire, once intercontinental, has slimmed to realistic, democratic dimensions, but Spain still shows the flag in the Mediterranean and the Atlantic. Its two alluring archipelagos, now autonomous regions, have found their vocation: the tourism business, in a big way.

In the western Mediterranean, the Balearics comprise a sunny cross-section of holiday possibilities, from mountainous Majorca, its beaches crammed with tourists, to low-slung, sleepy Formentera. In the Atlantic, just off the coast of North Africa, the volcanic Canaries thrive as a semi-tropical escape from winter. Within each of the archipelagos every island has its own character and fierce local pride.

The Balearics

Foreigners have been making themselves at home on the Balearic Islands since the Carthaginians settled down about 25 centuries ago. The Romans ejected them, but soon the Dark Ages intruded: Vandals, Byzantines and Saracens, followed by the Moors. Since the Reconquest in

*A*t *Canary Islands longitude, you can swim in the Atlantic all year. But winter is chilly in the Balearics.*

the 13th century things have been generally quiet, barring the incursions of the Barbary pirates and, more recently, swarms of jet transports packed with pale-faced tourists.

Majorca *19*
For decades, Majorca (Mallorca in Spanish) has been Europe's playground. The most popular holiday island in the Mediterranean is about the size of New York's Long Island. There are two distinct regions, so you can switch from a beach holiday to the mountains, and back again, on the same day.

Well over half of the total population of Majorca lives in the animated and cosmopolitan capital city, **Palma de Mallorca**. Before the serious sightseeing, start on Palma's tree-shaded central promenade, called **Es Born** in the *Mallorquí* dialect of Catalan. This elongated plaza, once the scene of jousting tournaments, is the hub of the city's social life. At the top of Es Born is Avinguda Rei Jaume III, the street of sleek, expensive shops.

The **Palacio Almudaina** was once the residence of the Moorish kings. After the Reconquest it was rebuilt for the medieval kings of Majorca (briefly an autonomous kingdom). Catch up on your

215

Balearic history in the museum housed in one wing of the palace.

Overshadowing the delicately arched and covered balconies of the palace is **La Seo,** the massive Gothic cathedral. According to legend, King Jaime I ordered its construction after a brush with fate in a terrible storm at sea in 1229. The job went on for hundreds of years. Unlike most Spanish cathedrals, this one has an open plan with a continuous view from end to end; the choirstalls have been moved out of the way.

High above the beachside suburb of El Terreno stands a sturdy symbol of Majorca, the cylindrical keep of the **Castillo de Bellver**. In its own pine-wooded park, the fortress has commanded the sea and land approaches to the city since the 14th century. Until 1915 it served as a break-proof jail-with-a-view.

Out around the island, Majorca is riddled with caves, suggesting an original way to escape the hot sun. A two-hour guided tour of the popular **Cuevas del Drach** (Dragon's Caves), stretching for more than a mile, takes in all the expertly lit, fanciful shapes, with names like Ruined Castle and Diana's Bath. At Lago Martel, a large underground lake, when the lights go out a boatload of musicians arrives, playing overwrought classics.

The **Cuevas de Hams** (Caves of the Hooks) show nature in a more whimsical mood. The seemingly impossible shapes of stalactites and stalagmites have been formed by centuries of dripping water fanned by vagrant air currents.

The experience of a third Majorcan cave, the **Cuevas de Artá**, so impressed one visitor, Jules Verne, that he sat down and wrote *Journey to the Centre of the Earth.*

Majorca's coast couldn't be more varied—long white beaches with or without high-rise hotels, tiny coves, and cliffs to take your breath away. For stupendous scenery it's hard to match the cliffs of **Cabo Formentor**, the northernmost projection of the island.

Inland, a favourite tourist destination is the former Carthusian monastery, **La Cartuja**, at Valldemossa. During the bleak winter of 1838 it served as the love-nest of the Polish composer Frederic Chopin and his mistress, the French novelist George Sand. Majorca inspired Chopin to compose beautiful music, but his companion likened the islanders to barbarians, thieves and monkeys. The couple fled Majorca, and their creditors, in the spring. You can visit the monastery's cell No. 2, where the couple lived.

*O*ver hundreds of years the indefatigable farmers of
Banyalbufar, in western Majorca, have transformed a harsh hillside
into a carefully tended flight of fertile terraces. Tip for tourists: below
the village hides a small beach.

Minorca
19 C1

On Minorca (Menorca in Spanish) the second-largest Balearic island, the sedate capital, Mahón, overlooks one of the world's finest deep-water harbours. Across the island, its rival, Ciudadela, the former capital, takes itself less seriously. Between them, in countryside now lush, now rock-strewn, Minorcan life just slumbers on.

Mahón *(Maó* in *Menorquí)* has been much fought over, and occupied by the French and, for much of the 18th century, the British. In addition to some local dialect words borrowed from French and English, vestiges of this mixed-up past are Georgian architecture and sash windows, a gin distillery, and *salsa mahonesa*, which we now call mayonnaise. An archaeological museum in the Casa de la Cultura digs into themes as diverse as Phoenician and Aztec relics.

Ciudadela *(Ciutadella),* on the west coast, has its own fine harbour. The white-washed streets of Minorca's ecclesiastical capital radiate charm. **Ses Arcades,** the street leading to the 14th-century Gothic cathedral, is all archways and completely Moorish.

Around the island are hundreds of **prehistoric sites,** including the imposing *taulas* shaped like the letter T. These Bronze Age structures are presumed to have held some religious significance. How the vast stone blocks were lifted into position is a weighty mystery in itself.

Ibiza
19 A2

The White Island, a favourite with film stars, artists, and the last of the hippies, packs in the package tourists. Beyond the beaches, Ibiza merits attention for its unique cultural and even zoological attractions. (The big-eared Ibizan hound, a hungry-looking dog as common here as any cur, can trace its history back thousands of years.)

Ibiza *(Eivissa),* the island's capital city, presents a charming view from the sea. Its ancient walled town, **Dalt Vila,** grows up a hillside, with all the houses white-washed (by official decree). Ibiza's **fortifications,** 16th-century bulwarks atop the remains of Moorish walls, are almost completely intact. Within are wide-open plazas and a maze of narrow alleys, steep cobbled streets, curious dead-ends and unexpected vistas.

Colonized by Carthage in the 7th century B.C., the island held on to the old traditions long after the Romans vanquished Hannibal. The capital has two **archaeological museums,** one opposite the cathedral and the other beyond the walls in the lower town. They add up to a truly great treasury of Carthaginian art, especially thanks to the terracotta statuettes.

Across the island, the tourist capital of **San Antonio (Sant Antoni) Abad** is a skyline of high-rise hotels and holiday apartments around a breathtaking bay cluttered with yachts, fishing boats, ferry-boats, and even freighters.

Formentera
19 A3

Airportless and all but waterless, little Formentera is "doomed" to escape the skyscraper culture. Still, the tourists crowd onto the ferries from Ibiza, four nautical miles away, to enjoy unimpaired horizons and endless topless beaches.

*M*inorca's second city, Ciudadela, may have been founded by the Phoenicians. The fortifications were built to fend off the 16th-century raids of the Barbary pirates.

Formentera is flat enough to explore by bicycle. There is also a bus: just one, painted bright orange.

Canary Islands

Seven specks scattered over 300 miles of the Atlantic, the Canaries are as varied as the beaches of Bali, the terraced mountains of Nepal, the pasturelands of Ireland... or the hellfire of Hades. It took the Spaniards the best part of the 15th century to subdue the islands' original inhabitants, the Stone Age Guanches.

Tenerife

The largest of the Canaries, Tenerife is as lush as any tropical paradise—except for dramatic volcanic zones and Mount Teide, at 3,718 m. (12,198 ft.) the highest mountain in all Spain. In a single Tenerife day you can pick bananas, throw

*L*ooking for your place in the sun? There's plenty of elbow room at Maspalomas on the south coast of Gran Canaria. The dunes are reminiscent of the Sahara, just a short hop across the Atlantic in Africa, but all creature comforts are available here.

snowballs, swim in the Atlantic, and go to the opera.

Puerto de la Cruz, the high-rise tourist centre, is across the island from the capital, Santa Cruz de Tenerife. Just outside "Puerto", the **Botanical Garden** was founded by royal decree in 1788. In fact, the whole island is an outburst of botanical beauty; even the roadsides are fragrant with honeysuckle and mimosa.

A cablecar goes nearly to the summit of **Pico del Teide** (rhymes with lady). This is fire-and-brimstone country, lonely and desolate, where only one flower, a curious blue violet, has ever been known to grow.

Gran Canaria

When Columbus stopped here on his first trip to the New World, Gran Canaria was just about the end of the known world. Now the island has the largest city in the Canaries, sophisticated nightlife, and miles of glorious beaches.

With a population of some 360,000, **Las Palmas de Gran Canaria,** the capital city, is a major commercial and historical centre, a cosmopolitan resort and a vital seaport all rolled into one. **Puerto de la Luz,** the huge modern port, is host to more than a thousand ships each month, from proud cruise liners to rusted tramp steamers. **Casa de Colón** (Columbus's House) was the governor's residence when Columbus slept there in 1492; now it's a museum.

Near the south coast, the **dunes of Maspalomas** constitute a mini-Sahara of great beauty. Another natural wonder is the **Bandama crater,** an extinct and totally tame volcano with lovely farmland inside its huge depression.

Lanzarote

If you like volcanoes, Lanzarote will warm your heart. The island's lunar surface is pockmarked with more than 300 volcanoes. Amazingly, onions, tomatoes, melons and grapes spring from the arid black ash.

For a riotous bit of tourism, try the camel ride up and down the **Montañas**

de Fuego (Fire Mountains), a sort of national park of volcanic desolation. Fires still glow just a few inches beneath the surface. Elsewhere there are unusual caves, excellent beaches and endearing white villages.

Fuerteventura

The sandiest of the Canaries, Fuerteventura is only a stone's throw from the Sahara—and looks it. Beaches still outnumber hotels. On the north coast, **Corralejo** is a brochure photographer's dream: golden strands sinking gracefully into the bluest of blue seas.

Gomera

This small, mountainous island was the last stop for Columbus before he left for the unknown. He said his final prayers at the church of Nuestra Señora de la Asunción (Our Lady of the Assumption). The **Torre del Conde** was the home of the Count of Gomera (murdered by Guanches) and his beautiful widow, Beatriz de Bobadilla. How well Columbus knew her is a matter of conjecture, but he liked Gomera enough to touch base in 1492, '93 and '98.

La Palma

Green and touchingly beautiful, La Palma rises steeply to a summit 2,423 m. (7,950 ft.) above sea level. **Santa Cruz de la Palma,** the island's port and capital, is a clean, bright metropolis in miniature. From a vantage point in the **Caldera de Taburiente National Park** you can look down into what's called the world's largest crater. Not to worry; it's long extinct.

El Hierro

The smallest Canary is a genuine getaway island, with a rocky coast and few tourist facilities. The whole north-western coastline, called **El Golfo,** is actually the inside of a volcanic crater, half of it sunk beneath the sea. Don't miss El Hierro's nightlife: watching the sun set over the endless ocean, the sky unmarred by power lines or TV aerials.

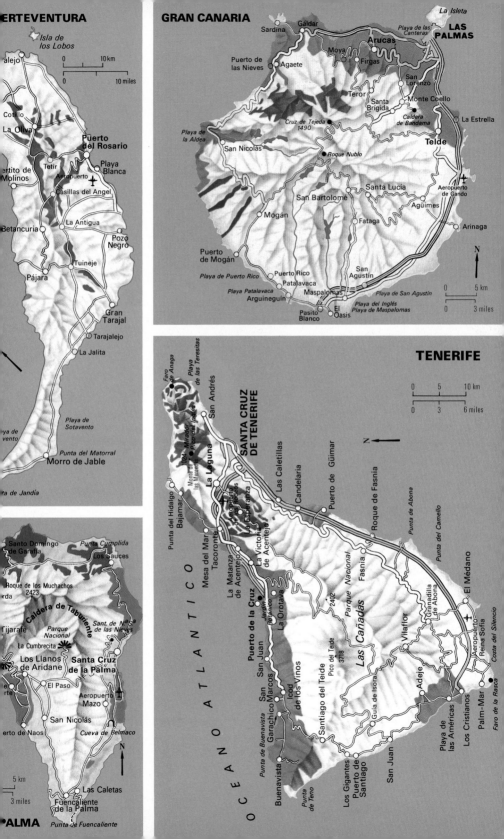

Where the Action Is, by Land and by Sea

What to do after, before and between all that sightseeing? In Spain the options are all inviting: a vigorous sporting life, the excitement and challenge of shopping, entertainment for highbrows and everybody else, and some of the world's most colourful festivals.

Sports

With its seas and mountains, Spain brims with sporting opportunities, strenuous or relaxing, summer or winter. You can ski in the mountains and swim in the sea on the same day. Slighting polo, hang-gliding and some other minority pursuits, we offer a brief survey of the principal possibilities.

Most visitors to Spain regard **swimming** as an integral part of a holiday. There are hundreds of miles of sandy beaches (choose between fine, golden sand or coarse black), and pebbly and rocky ones, too. Many areas have coastlines conducive to **snorkelling**. Masks, breathing tubes and flippers are on sale in all the resorts. In season, many of the best beaches are packed with tourists, but with a little enterprise you can still discover nearly deserted coves. The main tourist beaches offer a whole range of facilities—restaurants, bars, changing rooms, showers, deck-chairs and parasols. Some beaches are reserved for nudists. On busy beaches, flags are hoisted to advise swimmers of sea conditions: a green flag means it's safe for swimming, while red means danger.

Measures have been taken to combat the problem of polluted water and beaches. But if you prefer freshwater swimming pools, more and more can be found, either in hotel complexes or water parks, which have swimming and diving pools, water slides and other amusements. Madrid alone has 60 open-air swimming pools, to be found within sports centres *(polideportivos)*. The La Elipa and Pilar complexes even have nudist zones.

Scuba diving prospers particularly off the Costa Brava, the Costa Almería and the Balearic islands, with their rocky coasts and clear water. Diving centres operate in several resorts. They can arrange for the necessary diving permits, provide boats, equipment and, in some cases, tuition. In the unlikely event that

In all seriousness, eagle-eyed players compete in an unusual local version of the all-Mediterranean game of bowls.

225

you find any submerged archaeological relics, they must be handed in to the *Comandancia de Marina*.

The main resorts have facilities for **water-skiing** and the ecologically purer sport of **windsurfing**. (Tarifa, on the breezy Strait of Gibraltar, is considered one of the world's windsurfing capitals.) Shop around rival schools first to compare prices. And, as you skim across any bay, keep an eye out for bobbing heads; in some resorts swimming and skiing areas overlap.

For **boating** enthusiasts, most tourist beaches have a variety of craft for hire; some of the large hotels have sailing boats available. Prices vary considerably from resort to resort. More serious sailors will find marinas all along the coasts; Catalonia alone has two dozen yacht clubs and sporting ports. Big regattas take place among the Balearics and in the Bay of Cádiz.

Fishing from rocks along the coastline is popular, but results are better if you hire a boat and head for open water. If you're accompanied by a local fisherman you'll find what you're looking for more quickly. Cheap fishing tackle is available in most resorts.

You don't need to go to the seaside to fish; a *Mapa de Pesca Fluvial*, map of river fishing, issued by the tourist board, shows where to hook what catch—theoretically, anyway. It also gives details of season dates and licences.

Sports Ashore

Spain offers a superb variety of **golf** experiences, with more than 90 courses around the country. Not every pro is a Severiano Ballesteros, but the quality of instruction is generally high. There are about a dozen courses in the surrounds of Madrid; nearly all resort towns have a golf course within driving distance. If golf figures prominently in your holiday planning, ask the *Real Federación Española de Golf* for a detailed map of Spain showing every golf course, with the facts about each of them. (For a list of

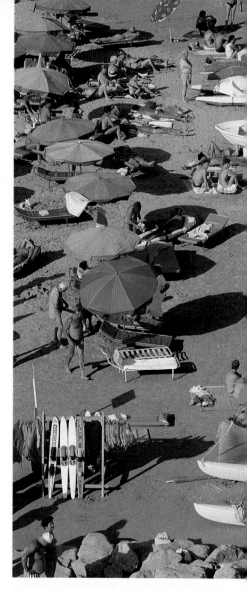

national sports federation addresses, see page 278.)

Many hotels, apartments and villa complexes have their own **tennis** courts, but in the busy tourist season you may have to book a day ahead. Some hotels have professionals who give lessons. Beyond the resorts, there are hundreds of tennis clubs around the country—nonmembers can often rent a court—as well as municipal tennis installations.

For **hunting and shooting** enthusiasts, Spain's national preserves provide a

*O*n the beach at Paguera, Majorca, everything
you need is right at hand, from umbrellas and deck chairs to pedal boats
and water skis. Closer to the capital, Palma, the beaches become
more crowded.

A grown-up way to play in the sand in Spain.
The rules of the game are the same as at home but the scenery may be anything from palms to pines to snowcapped mountains. In the Canaries an 18-hole course skirts the crater of an extinct volcano.

resort travel agencies advertise riding excursions, with transport to and from the ranch and a country meal included. For the experienced and saddle-fit, there are often two- to four-day mountain treks.

You may not immediately think of Spain for a **skiing** holiday, but, along with neighbouring Andorra, it attracts an increasing number of snow-sports devotees. The top resorts feature sophisticated ski-lifts and testing runs that can match the best in the Alps. And you stand an excellent chance of getting a suntan, whether in the Pyrenees or at Europe's most southerly ski resort, in the Sierra Nevada. For a skier's map of Spain, contact any Spanish tourist office or the National Federation of Winter Sports (see page 278).

Spain's No. 1 spectator sport, **football** (soccer), is a perfect excuse for a family outing. Matches are usually held in the evenings; the animated post-mortem goes on, over cigars and *coñac*, far into the night. Tickets are sold at the stadium but when internationally known teams like Real Madrid or Barça are playing, you may have to get them well in advance.

On another level, for those who fancy a game themselves, resort hotels sometimes organize a staff versus guests match.

Off the Wall, Like a Shot
For a rousingly different experience, go to a *frontón* to watch the ancient Basque ball game, *jai alai*, also known as *pelota*. Players use woven straw scoops to combine the functions of glove and catapult, snagging the whizzing ball and blasting it back against the far wall at speeds up to 200 kilometres per hour (125 mph). You will catch on to the rules of the game quite easily. However, the system of betting, which engrosses most of the audience, is likely to remain a mystery. Bookies negotiate the odds by hand signals and slang, tossing receipts to their clients inside tennis balls. Even the referee, on the dangerous side of the protective screen, has been known to place a discreet bet during the match.

wealth of targets, from wild boar to wolf. For details about permits and laws concerning import of arms, fire off a letter to the national hunting federation (*Federación Española de Caza*) in Madrid, or check with a Spanish tourist office.

Even before the days of El Cid, **horse-riding** was a Spanish speciality. Numerous ranches cater to tourists, providing a quiet seaside jog or, for more advanced riders, good horses, skilled instruction and interesting cross-country rides. Some

Shopping

Modern Spain has long since climbed out of the bargain basement; the more European the country becomes, the higher the prices seem to soar. Still, the new abundance means a broader choice, offering the careful shopper more chances of finding genuine value for money. And you can't miss all those very Spanish souvenirs, frivolous or meaningful, clamouring for the tourist's attention.

For a quick survey of what Spaniards are buying, browse through the big department stores—el Corte Inglés and Galerías Preciados. They have branches in almost every sizeable town, with easy-to-find souvenir and gift departments; you can wander on to fashions, furniture or whatever interests you. For orientation, check the multilingual directories posted at the entrances. In some stores polyglot employees are stationed behind information desks to help foreigners with their shopping. Unlike most Spanish businesses, these chains stay open nonstop across the lunch-and-siesta break until about 8 in the evening.

More than a dozen cities have branches of Artespaña, the official network of showplaces for Spanish artisans. They stock classy handicrafts—from artistic ceramics and furniture to a full suit of armour.

The shopping choices are predictably wider in the big cities, which also have the advantage of more reasonable prices than the resort areas. For regional specialities the best buys are on the spot: the biggest choice of Toledo steel, clearly, can be found in Toledo; your bottle of sherry will be more meaningful if you buy it at the bodega in Jerez.

For exclusive fashions and jewellery, the top shopping streets are Madrid's Serrano and Castellana and Barcelona's Passeig de Gràcia, though the trendy overspill goes far beyond. Upmarket resorts like Marbella and San Sebastián also offer lavish opportunities for luxury shopping.

Antiques abound in Madrid's Rastro (which also serves as a transit camp for some unbelievable junk). Barcelona's near equivalent to the Rastro is the Els Encants flea market. Good-natured haggling over the price is all but obligatory in open-air bric-a-brac markets. And while you're there, beware of pickpockets.

A note on taxes: the Spanish government levies a value added tax ("IVA") on most items. Overseas tourists can be refunded the IVA they pay on purchases over a stipulated amount, but some paperwork is involved. Shopkeepers, who have the forms, can explain the procedures. The rebate is supposed to catch up with you after you've returned home. (In any case, keep all your shopping receipts handy to show to the customs men.)

Best Buys in Brief

Alcohol. For liquid souvenirs, look for bargains in brandy, sherry, table wines and quaint local liqueurs like the herbal concoctions in Galicia and anisette from Chinchón, in decorative bottles.

Antiques. Let the buyer beware among the tempting, theoretically authentic antigüedades: paintings, polychrome sculptures, illuminated medieval psalters, hand-made rugs, furniture, porcelain and crystal. At very least you can always take home a rusty old door key suitable for a haunted house, or a kitchen iron of undeniably pre-electric vintage.

Artificial pearls, from Majorca, are so cleverly made that not even experts can tell the difference until they feel the smoothness (the real ones are rougher).

Capes. Madrid's fashion-conscious young men have adopted the traditional black elegance; women's models are as glamorous as ever.

Ceramics. Each region produces its own distinctive shapes, colours and designs, traditional or cheerfully modern. Among the standouts: the blue-and-white classics from Manises, near Valencia; the blue-and-yellow products of Talavera de la Reina; and avant-garde ideas from Sargadelos, Galicia. Or take home a hand-painted, illustrated *azulejo* (wall tile).

Damascene. Study the intricacies of inlaid gold designs in steel—knives, scissors, thimbles, jewellery. This art, begun in Damascus, lives on in Toledo.

Embroidery. In many a village the women spend their days at the kind of needlework their grandmothers taught them: handkerchiefs, tablecloths, pillowcases. And look for lace mantillas, those lightweight shawls for covering shoulders and sometimes heads... as Spanish as their name.

Fans. The collapsible kind, as fluttered by *señoritas* over the centuries, are illustrated with hand-painted scenes for every taste.

Fashions. Madrid has become a hotbed of fashionable innovation, its young designers turning heads all over Europe. Barcelona also bears watching. And regional fashions make their mark, notably the Ibiza look in resort wear. You can even buy a real flamenco dress; they come in a rainbow of colours. For men: custom-made shirts and suits. Off-the-peg children's clothes are charming but expensive.

Foodstuffs. You can take home an aftertaste of Spain, mostly sweet—almonds (roasted or sugar-glazed), dates, figs, *turrón* (nougat), *chochos* (cinnamon jawbreakers from Salamanca), *membrillo* (quince paste), or locally celebrated pastries. Olives, too.

Glassware. On the island of Majorca

231

A *16th-century figurine peers, not quite angelically, at prospective buyers in a Toledo antique shop. At the other extreme of the shopping possibilities (page 231), there's an endless choice of wineskins for every tourist's taste.*

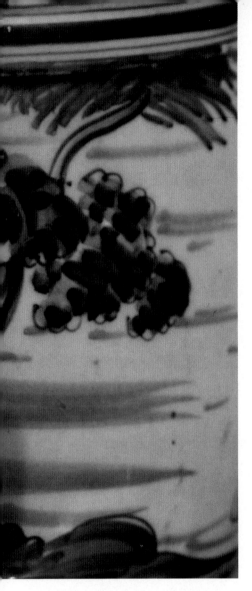

bracelets by itinerant artisans to expensive silver or titanium necklaces in sophisticated modern designs, Spain can satisfy most tastes.

Knives. For a pointed present, penknives, daggers and swords from Toledo, where the Crusaders bought theirs.

Leather. Top-flight raw material, processing and workmanship account for the renown of Spanish leather products at their best. Whether you're looking for a sturdy wallet or the handbag of a lifetime, you'll find exactly what you want. Also fine gloves, belts, coats and shoes.

Paintings. Gone are the days when Spain's best artists lived in exile. In the current air of freedom and creativity, the muse is back. Madrid has developed into one of Europe's leading contemporary art markets, and Barcelona has dozens of galleries; other provincial centres follow the trend.

Rugs. From the south come inventively designed, meticulously woven, colourful floor coverings: tiny throw-rugs or big, thick carpets. Some are so original they're worth putting up as wall hangings.

Trinkets. Millions of tourists keep coming back for the same old novelties— sets of toothpick-sized swords, plastic-lined wineskins, castanets, bullfight posters (with your name as matador) and, irrationally, imitation Mexican sombreros. If all this turns you off, don't give up hope: every season brings new knick-knacks.

Valencian porcelain. Lladró collectors can stock up; less detailed models (not seconds) from the same workshop go under the name *Nao*.

Woodwork. Spanish carvers have been whittling sublime statues, altars and choirstalls for centuries. Look for reproductions of classic saintly figures. Downmarket, there's no shortage of Don Quixote statuettes. And olive wood makes salad bowls, pepper mills, chess boards and beads. If portability is irrelevant, consider Spanish furniture—reproductions of classic styles or enterprising modern designs.

glassmaking is a tourist attraction. If you miss the demonstration, you can see the results of all the huffing and puffing— blue, green or amber bowls, glasses, pots and pitchers—in stores all around the mainland.

Hats. Just for fun: a broad-brimmed Andalusian hat or a bullfighter's; a Basque beret, or a wickerwork sombrero.

Ironwork. Heavy on the baggage scales, but wrought-iron lanterns, candlesticks and lamps are a bright idea.

Jewellery. From cheap but decorative

Entertainment

The challenge here is keeping the pace. Since Spaniards don't usually start thinking about a leisurely dinner until nigh onto 10 p.m., the nightlife tends to keep going far later than in other countries. The sleepless "cats" of Madrid are Europe's champion night-owls; smaller Spanish cities aren't far behind. From opera to girlie show, from flamenco to disco, every kind of entertainment is on tap. But you need enough time and energy.

Madrid by Night

Take your choice: a nightclub with dancing girls, an "intellectual" café, a dark tavern staffed with professional drinking partners, a deafening discotheque, a coffee bar with "live" classical music, a jazz club, a folk-music spot, or an imitation of an English pub. There's even audience-participation flamenco dancing. It's all happening in Madrid.

Travel agencies run Madrid-by-Night tours, taking in a couple of the top floor shows. Normally, the all-inclusive price covers dinner and a quota of drinks. (Similar package deals are available in other big cities and resorts.)

Madrid is one of 18 Spanish cities and resorts with a gambling-and-everything casino (actually the Casino Gran Madrid is half an hour out of town on the N-VI highway.) You can invest in roulette, blackjack, chemin de fer and other adult games until 4 a.m. On your way in they'll ask to see your passport.

A bouncy version of flamenco enlivens a fiesta. Overleaf: bullfight icons in a Madrid restaurant.

Flamenco

Throbbing guitars, snapping fingers, stamping heels, and songs that gush from the soul put the passion in flamenco, Spain's best-known entertainment. Many songs resemble the wailing of Arab music —which may be a clue to flamenco's centuries-old origins, although "flamencologists" are divided on the derivation.

Flamenco nightclubs attract local enthusiasts as well as tourists who don't usually go to nightclubs or stay up late. The anguished chants and compelling rhythms generate an electricity that crosses all frontiers of nationality or language.

There are two main groups of songs: one, bouncier and more cheerful, is known as the *cante chico*. The second group of songs, called *cante jondo*, deals with love, death, all the human drama, done in the slow, piercing style of the great flamenco singers.

Purists say the talent in a *tablao flamenco* in Madrid is rarely up to top standard. The show-biz version available in coastal resorts is even less authentic. For the real thing, you have to go to flamenco's birthplace, Andalusia, and search out the specialist bars and small clubs frequented by Spanish connoisseurs.

Cultural Activities

Spaniards take **opera** very seriously; consider José Carreras, Plácido Domingo, Victoria de los Ángeles, Teresa Berganza and Montserrat Caballé. However, only Barcelona has a proper opera house, the Gran Teatre del Liceu, described as the finest theatre in the world when it opened in 1857. The crisis is to be eased in time for the 1992 anniversary festivities: Madrid's Teatro Real will be reopened as an opera house after extensive renovations, and Seville will dedicate a new Teatro de la Maestranza.

Madrid is the home of **zarzuela,** the uniquely Spanish form of operetta, first presented in the 17th century at the palace of La Zarzuela, the royal family's residence. These musical plays come in two varieties, light-hearted and serious. Even if you don't understand the language, an evening of zarzuela will entertain and enlighten.

For **concerts,** Madrid's new Auditorio Nacional de Música is the home of the Spanish National Orchestra. In Barcelona major concerts take place at the wildly *art nouveau* Palau de la Música Catalana. Concerts and recitals in cities often take place in historic surroundings, such as churches and palaces.

Spain's tradition of **drama** is long and glorious; Lope de Vega wrote or co-wrote something like 1,800 plays, and Tirso de Molina, who created the character Don Juan, turned out hundreds. Spanish and foreign plays, classical and contemporary, can be seen in theatres all over the country. Madrid alone has dozens of theatres, often offering two performances per night.

Television and other distractions have drastically cut the size of the Spanish **cinema** audience. Almost all the foreign films shown commercially in Spain have been dubbed into Spanish. But in the big cities a certain number of cinemas show foreign films (usually controversial or "art" films) in the original version, with Spanish subtitles. If your Spanish is adequate, catch up on the works of contemporary film-makers like Victor Erice, Carlos Saura and Pedro Almodóvar.

The *Fiesta Brava*

Even among Spaniards, bullfighting excites controversy. Is it an art, a spectacle, a metaphysical experience... or ritually choreographed slaughter? However you judge the *fiesta brava,* the bullfight has long been a symbol of Spain— flamboyance and fate, and violence with grace.

The Spanish writer and philosopher José Ortega y Gasset, much concerned with the soul of Spain, wrote of "the tragic friendship, going back three millennia, between the Spanish man and the brave bull". In truth, nobody can say when the first Spaniard fought the first bull. Something anticipating the bullfight was known among the ancient Celtiberian people. The first operating bullrings were the amphitheatres that had crumbled after the fall of the Roman empire; elsewhere in Spain, bullfights were held in the town square.

The rules of bullfighting were codified in the 18th century (see Ronda, page 186). It was never meant to be a sport, for no one regards bullfighting as a contest between equals; it's one man's wits against the brawn and instinct of a specially bred beast. The odds are weighted heavily against the bull, for whom the conclusion is foregone. Yet, every time the *torero* enters the ring, he knows his own life is in danger. (Some of the most admired bullfighters have been martyred by brave bulls. The municipal museum of Córdoba is largely devoted to the life and death of a local hero, Manolete, fatally gored at the age of 30; elsewhere in town he rates a triumphal statue.)

Starting, traditionally, at exactly 5 o'clock in the afternoon, the scenario of the *corrida* is straightforward. To the accompaniment of a fanfare of trumpets and clarinets, the *matadors* and their teams arrive in fanciful, even effeminate uniforms. (Don't call the *torero* a *toreador,* please; it's a word invented to suit the lyrics of Bizet's *Carmen.*) After the opening procession, the first bull of the afternoon enters the ring. The fighter sizes up the bull's intelligence and agility and begins to tire him using the big red and yellow *capote.* After these preliminaries the *picador,* a mounted spearman in Sancho Panza costume, lances the bull's shoulder muscles.

In the second *tercio* (the second of the drama's three ritual acts) the deft *bandarilleros* risk a goring as they stab long beribboned darts into the animal's shoulders.

In the final, fatal *tercio* the matador taunts the bull with the small, dark-red *muleta* cape, eventually dominating him. Finally, as the panting bull awaits the inevitable, the matador unveils his sword and lunges for the kill.

Depending upon the skill and courage shown by the matador, he may be awarded an ear, two ears or, rarely, the top prize, two ears plus the tail of the bull he has just despatched. If he has disappointed the audience, he is likely to be sent off in silence or with catcalls.

Bullfight fans consider a *corrida* an extemporaneous poem about the mystery of life and death. Critics condemn the spectacle as the most barbarous form of cruelty to animals. To assuage the opponents, it's been suggested that Spain adopt the rules of neighbouring Portugal, where the bull leaves the ring on his own four feet. But many a devout supporter of the *fiesta brava* would reply: "Over my dead body".

236

FESTIVALS

The Spaniards gave the world the word *fiesta*, but others can only try to imitate their holiday enthusiasm, that special combination of faith and pageantry, often leavened with levity. No Spanish village is too small to produce a stately saint's day celebration. And no city is too big to forget its roots in religion and history. So many festivals go on all over Spain that you're almost bound to stumble upon one in your travels. But the major events are well worth planning for. Hundreds of *fiestas* are officially deemed most worthy of touristic interest. Here's a sampler:

January: *San Sebastián* Saint's day parades.

February or **March:** *Santa Cruz de Tenerife* and *Cádiz* Carnival processions.

March: *Valencia* "Fallas", fireworks and bonfires of satirical effigies.

March or **April:** *Málaga, Seville, Valladolid* Holy Week processions.

April: *Seville* April Fair, parades, bullfights, dancing; *Alcoy* (Alicante) Moors and Christians "battles". *Madrid* Teatro Alcalá Palace, Flamenco festival, performances, exhibitions, films, etc.

April/May: *Madrid* Dance festival, international and national troupes.

May: *Jerez de la Frontera* Horse Fair; *Almonte* (Huelva) Pilgrimage of Rocío; *Sitges* International theatre festival.

At the Jerez "Feria del Caballo" the horses are dressed to the nines.

June: *Toledo* Corpus Christi processions; *Alicante* St. John's Day, fireworks and bonfires; *Badajoz* Flamenco festival.

July: *Pamplona* St. Fermín festival, bull runs and bullfights; *Granada* music festival; *Marchena, Seville,* Guitar festival; *Alcalá de Guadaira, Seville,* (2nd fortnight) Flamenco festival; *Barcelona* "Greek festival", daily performances of theatre, dance, song and cinema. Barcelona flamenco festival held concurrently; *Tarragona* Dance festival; *Mérida* Theatre festival.

August: *Ribadesella* (Asturias) International kayak races, processions; *La Alberca* (Salamanca) traditional Assumption commemoration.

September: *Jerez de la Frontera, Logroño* Wine harvest festivals, *Barcelona* Merced festival, music and folklore; *Rioja* Plectrum music festival.

October: *Zaragoza* Pilar Festival processions and folklore.

December: *Málaga* "Los Verdiales" 28th Dec., show of festive and humorous music.

Unadulterated Delights of Spanish Cuisine

The adventure of eating in Spain recalls a less complicated age, when food everywhere tasted good, was wholesome and didn't cost a fortune. Here and now Spanish meat and sauces are savoury and appetizing, the fish fit for a feast, and the fresh vegetables transport your palate to the farm. You can dine well whether you choose candlelit luxury or a bargain-priced country inn.

Just because Spanish food is satisfying and filling doesn't mean it's unrefined. You have to admire the complexity and originality of concoctions like *paella* and *gazpacho* and almost anything *a la vasca*. Each region has its gastronomic strengths, from the seafood creations of the north to the rice platters of the east to the succulent ham of the south. And for every dish there's usually an honest local wine to match.

Like much of the world, Spain is suffering a proliferation of *hamburgueserías*, *pizzarías* and fast-food emporia. But the overall prospect for the visiting gourmet in search of healthy, tasty food remains heartening.

In a colourful Barcelona restaurant the customers transit the kitchen on the way to their tables. The menu is enormous but seafood springs to mind.

Where to Eat

In the resorts, the food may be described as "international cuisine", a euphemism for the mediocrity of compromise: no matter what country you come from you can't claim that it's inedible or offensive. But it's certainly unexciting. For meals to remember you'll have to break out of the tourist rut, hunting down the restaurants where Spaniards and resident expatriates eat. There you'll savour the authentic atmosphere as well as the food.

For Spaniards the most insignificant meal of the day is **breakfast.** Typically this means a spartan eye-opener of *café con leche* (half expresso coffee, half hot milk) and a pastry at the counter of a local bar. Most hotels offer breakfast, though it's not normally included in the room rent. Some *paradores* and luxury hotels have weighty buffets with an inviting variety of hot and cold foods for a fixed price; elsewhere a croissant and coffee is the rule. But, in deference to foreign habits, most hotels and some cafés can provide a *desayuno completo*: orange juice, eggs, toast and coffee.

Lunch is what you want to make of it.

The Snack to End All Snacks

A *tapa* is a snack you can eat with your fingers, or impaled on a toothpick—anything from marinated olives to garlic-fried mushrooms, from meatballs to a cold slice of Spanish omelette. Some specialist bars, called *tascas*, have a whole counter full of hot and cold appetizers, a Spanish version of smorgasbord (though not self-service). Confronted by such temptations, it's easy to lose your head and eat more than you planned. You may not only lose your appetite for dinner, you could find you've spent more than a good dinner would have cost.

The atmosphere in a *tasca* is ever-changing. One minute the place is empty, the next the crowd is fighting for space at the bar, the counter-men are shouting to encourage business, and debris is piling up on the floor. Don't be shy about tossing your olive stones, mussel shells and used paper napkins on the floor. If you don't, the waiter will!

You can simply point to whatever *tapas* you want; you don't have to know the Spanish names. In fact, in a few cases, it might be better not to know what it is that looks and tastes so delicious... unless you're a fan of snails, baby eels, tripe, squid and marinated anchovies. The code is simple: one helping is called a *porción;* a large serving is a *ración;* if that's too much, order a half-serving, a *media-ración.*

For most *tapa* enthusiasts the food is more important than the drink: house wine or chilled draught beer served in small glasses.

If you're too busy to take a long break you can snack in a café, or sit at the counter of a *cafetería* for a fast *plato combinado,* one of the set dishes. A *merendero* is an unpretentious eatery stocked with fresh fish. In *restaurantes* a leisurely lunch rarely begins before about 2 p.m. A *menú del día* (day's special) usually lists three courses available with bread and wine (or beer or mineral water) at a reasonable set price. Cheap alcoholic refreshment—from *aperitivo* through table wine to brandy—is universally available in Spain; taken under the hot sun, it may convince you of the benefits of the siesta. But in any case, don't drink and drive.

Between meals, Spaniards don't skimp on the **snacks.** For pastry or a slice of cake with tea or coffee, they go to a *pastelería* or *confitería.* Or to a *churrería* for sugared fritters. *Churros* are usually dunked into very thick hot chocolate. (If you *don't* dunk your *churros,* everyone will stare.) On another plane, there are bars called *tascas,* featuring *tapas.* These are bite-sized snacks of infinite variety; just point to what you like.

Whatever you ate for lunch, by **dinner** time you're likely to be famished. Spaniards almost never dine until 9 p.m. (though in tourist areas you can be served from about 8 p.m.). Normally menu prices are "all inclusive"—including tax and service charge. But it's still customary to leave a tip. Ten per cent is quite acceptable, 15 per cent is generous.

What to Eat

The olive, black or green, is a versatile fruit. You can eat it marinated or cooked, or press it for the oil, which is used for salad dressing and cooking. The ancient Romans, who introduced the olive to Spain, used the oil generously for both internal and external use. Most Spanish cooking inevitably involves olive oil. If you're unaccustomed to this taste, as typically Mediterranean as sunshine, you'll get the hang of it soon enough. Incidentally, the Romans are also responsible for the Spaniard's breathless devotion to garlic.

The next colonial cooks were the Moors, who brought rice, and saffron to embellish it, delicious citrus fruits and dates. Something else inherited from the Moors: the Spanish sweet tooth.

Thanks to Columbus and Company, western hemisphere exotica like the potato, tomato and pimento came to round out the Spanish staples. Of course, the really essential ingredients—fresh fish

The harbour of Ciudadela, Minorca: Everything tastes better by the seaside.

and seafood—have been here all along. The regional differences in Spanish food are as vivid as the variations in accent and culture. The local specialities usually involve what's most readily available. But it's also a matter of temperament and climate. The Andalusians originated *gazpacho* ("liquid salad") to keep cool in summer; to warm up in winter the Castilians stumbled on *sopa castellana*, a sort of baked garlic soup with chunks of ham and an egg poaching in it.

One cold-weather dish is all but universal: an extremely rich hotpot called (depending what part of the country you're in) *cocido* or *la olla* or *el pote*. The meal starts with a nutritious broth, perhaps with noodles. The next course presents a portion of the ingredients that were cooked to make the broth in the first place: cabbage, carrots, chickpeas, onions, potatoes, turnips and perhaps more. All of which is to whet your appetite for the climax: chunks of beef, ham, sausage, chicken, pork or whatever, which had been cooked in the same pot. Take the rest of the day off.

Regional Tastes

Every province and almost every town in Spain seems to brag about its culinary achievements—at least a different sort of sausage or a home-made cheese. Here's a suggestion of what's cooking around the country, roughly from north to south.

Galicia. *Caldo gallego*, a hearty vegetable soup, may also contain bits of ham or sausage. In Santiago de Compostela try *vieira*, scallops, associated with St. James; they're cooked in butter here, then baked on the half-shell under chunks of ham and sautéed onions. A Galician standby is the *empanada,* a flaky pastry rather like a Cornish pasty, containing anything from meat to seafood, served hot or cold.

Asturias. Big white beans and sausage give backbone to the delicious hotpot called *fabada asturiana*. *Merluza a la sidra* (hake in cider sauce) makes the most of the local apples and fish in an unusual, winning combination. Asturias produces a pungent cheese, *queso de Cabrales*, which is more piquant and more expensive than imported blue cheese.

Basque Country. Here in the gastronomic capital of all the Spains they do wonders with fish and seafood. For instance, *bacalao al pil pil* (fried cod in a carefully prepared hot garlic sauce) and *angulas a la bilbaína* (eels in a hot olive-oil and garlic sauce, always eaten with a wooden fork). The sublime sauces of the Basques ennoble many a casserole; on menus anywhere look for the suffixes *a la vizcaína, a la donostiarra* and *a la guipuzcoana.*

Navarre. *Trucha a la navarra*, grilled trout with a surprise slice of ham hidden inside, is offered in many parts of the country but, of course, it's best at the source. So is the local asparagus.

The Pyrenees. Typical here are meaty dishes in *chilindrón* sauce (an intriguing alliance of tomatoes and peppers, onion, garlic, chopped ham, and wine). Game and trout also figure in the mountain cuisine.

Catalonia. Start with *esqueixada,* a stimulating salad of cod, beans, pickled onions and tomato. The hot-pot here, *escudella,* is a broth containing beans, pasta, a bit of sausage and maybe even a slice of meatloaf. The showpiece of Catalan cuisine is the *zarzuela de mariscos* ("seafood operetta"), a stupendous stew of every kind of shellfish in the house.

Castile. *Cochinillo asado*, tender Castilian sucking pig, is roasted to a golden crispness. *Cordero asado*, roast lamb, is tender and fragrant, often a gargantuan helping. The favourite condiment here is garlic.

The Levante. The east coast is the land of rice. *Paella* (pronounced pie-ALE-ya) comes from Valencia; it's saffron rice topped by squid and shrimp, mussels, chicken or rabbit, sausage, peppers, onions, peas and beans, tomatoes, garlic, and so on. Many other inspired rice dishes enliven menus up and down this coast. (Spaniards eat paella only at lunchtime and always cooked to order.)

La Mancha. In Quixote country, attention is on the game. There's a favourite rabbit stew called *tojunto*, an abbreviation for "all together". Nationally renowned is *pisto manchego*, an extravagant vegetable stew emphasizing aubergines, tomatoes and courgettes. Spain's most honoured cheese, *queso manchego*, comes from La Mancha.

Estremadura. Far from the sea in isolated Estremadura, country-style pork is the main attraction; the sausages come in countless styles including the spicy *chorizo*. The *caldereta*, lamb stew, is a variation on the old shepherds' recipe.

Andalusia. *Gazpacho* (pronounced gath-PAT-cho) in its native state is a creamy, chilled tomato and cucumber soup to which are added diced fresh vegetables, chopped egg, croutons or whatever. The closer you get to the sea the more authentic is the *pescaito frito*, quick-fried fish.

Sweet-tooth Specials

When it comes to sweet desserts—tongue-tyingly sweet—the Spaniards outdo almost everybody but the Arabs, who taught them many honeyed tricks. Pastries overflowing with whipped cream are easy to find, hard to resist. Many towns have their own recipes for *yema,* a monumentally sweet egg-yolk and sugar confection. Marzipan, made of almonds, egg whites and sugar, comes in various guises with regional variations. *Turrón* (nougat), too, varies in colour, consistency and sweetness depending on the source. And there is a big repertory of cakes, tarts and pastries, flaky or weighty, always sweet but rarely overpowering.

For light relief, you can turn to *flan,* the ubiquitous Spanish caramel custard. *Crema Catalana*, with an additional ingredient, cinnamon, is cooked to a more solid consistency.

The wonder of the fresh fruit is that it tastes so much better than the delayed version familiar at home. Whatever's in season, savour it on the spot—melon, strawberries, figs, grapes, cherries...

Wines

Spain has more square miles of vineyards than any other European country, producing not only oceans of wine but reefs of controversy. Vintage pundits compare the best Spanish wines with the most respected foreign classics. On the opposite side, critics dismiss much of the crop as plonk. The safest place to be is between the extremes, sipping the *vino de la casa.*

The house wine, served in a carafe, is perfectly potable. When the average Spaniard sits down to a meal, he simply orders *vino,* and it's understood that he means *red* wine. Often served chilled, this unpretentious wine can go with meat or fish or anything. In this kind of atmosphere, "winemanship" and fancy tasting rituals seem superfluous. Matching wits with the wine waiter will leave you high and dry here, but discovering the wines of Spain, ordinary and extraordinary, can be part of the adventure.

In the old days a Spaniard would take an empty jug or bottle to the wine shop for a refill of *vino corriente* from a cask inscribed with the degree of alcohol content and the colour: *tinto* for full-bodied red, *clarete* for light red, and *blanco* for white. (Rosé wine—*rosado*—is less common.) Thanks to the tourist invasion and higher living standards, things have become much more sophisticated, although the cask-to-jug supply system still exists. Whether Spaniards buy their wines in the traditional musty *bodega* or in the supermarket, they are choosier. To meet this demand and compete with its European neighbours for the export trade, Spain is bottling ever better wines.

Most of Spain's regions produce wine of one sort or another. They run from earthy east-coast reds to light, fresh Galician whites. The wine industry is regulated (and promoted) by a national institute controlling the *Denominación de Origen.* To spot a bottle awarded the Denominación de Origen look for a small map on the back label, showing precisely where the wine comes from. It indicates

Among autographed casks of prized old sherry in an Andalusian village inn, four brothers—the landlords—compare notes on taste. To enjoy Spanish wines you don't have to be an expert; wine snobs and supercilious waiters are as rare as a bad bottle of "vino de la casa".

East of La Rioja, Aragon contributes *Cariñena* reds and whites, some of them quite powerful. The best-known wines from central Spain come from La Mancha, the smooth reds of *Valdepeñas*. In the east, Catalonia produces wines as memorable as the fruity *Alella*. And Catalonia is the home of *Cava*, the sparkling wine formerly called *champán*. Mass produced, it bubbles in five degrees of sweetness, from *dulce* (very, very sweet) to *brut* (extra dry).

As for southern Spain, where Phoenicians first planted vines 3,000 years ago, the monumental achievement is sherry from Jerez de la Frontera. It is made by the *solera* method, involving three or four rows of superposed oak casks. The bottom row contains the oldest sherry, which is bottled when needed, whereupon the cask is filled from the one above it, and so on. This makes for uniform quality instead of single-year vintages. As an aperitif, try a dry *fino* or a medium dry *amontillado*. A dark, sweet *oloroso* goes well after dinner.

Lunching on a hot day, it's no social misdemeanour to dilute your table wine if you wish. Adding *gaseosa,* a cheap fizzy lemonade, turns heavy red wine into an imitation of *sangría*. Real *sangría*, a popular summer cooler, is a mixture of red wine, lemon and orange juice, brandy, mineral water, ice and slices of fruit—rather like punch, and probably stronger than you expect.

If you're not in the mood for wine at all, have no qualms about ordering beer (good and cheap and served very cold) or a soft drink or mineral water; nobody will turn up a snobbish nose. In Asturias the standard accompaniment for food is the local cider, refreshingly tart.

After-dinner drinkers consider Spanish brandy sweeter and heavier than French cognac. It's stunningly cheap—at least at the bottom end of the market. And every region has its own liqueur; try, for instance, the herbal concoctions of Galicia or Ibiza and the clearly potent aniseed drinks from Chinchón, near Madrid.

that the vintners follow the strictest rules of their art.

Of all the Denominaciones in the field of table wine, the oldest and most vigorously protected is *Rioja*, along the valley of the Ebro in northern Spain. Some truly distinguished wines (mostly reds) proudly bear the Rioja tag. Since they traditionally contain a high quota of tannin, Riojas tend to last longer in the bottle. A 20-year-old Rioja red wine may be no better than when it was eight, but it's still well worth drinking.

The Right Place
at the Right Price

While hotels and restaurants throughout the world tend more and more to uniformity, Spanish accommodation and cuisine can still provide a welcome change. Special mention must be made of government-run *paradores*, (nearly 100 exist). Usually located in attractive surroundings, they offer a high standard of comfort and excellent cuisine.

To help you choose a hotel or restaurant we have made a selection based on the criteria of price, attraction and location, **listed alphabetically by town.** We do not list beach restaurants, fast food outlets and pizzerias where prices will be lower. Many of the restaurants chosen are indeed well known and have received distinctions for their quality.

Restaurants and hotels in cities and fashionable resorts are, of course, often considerably more expensive than those in small towns and villages.

KEY

🛏 Hotel   ⇌ Restaurant

Hotels *(for a double room with bath in pesetas)*

▯▯▯ Higher-priced: above 10,000
▯▯   Medium-priced: 6,000–10,000
▯   Lower-priced: below 6,000

Restaurants *(for a three-course gourmet meal in pesetas)*

▯▯▯ Higher-priced: above 4,000
▯▯   Medium-priced: 2,500–4,000
▯   Lower-priced: below 2,500

Parador   🛏⇌▯▯▯
Costa Brava
17255 Aiguablava
(Gerona 46 km.)
Tel. (72) 62 21 62
87 rooms. Situated on a cliff. Outdoor swimming pool, beach.

Al-Mar   🛏⇌▯▯
Avenida de la Marina, 2 y 3
11201 Algeciras
Tel. (956) 65 46 61; tlx. 78181
192 rooms. View of the harbour. Central location.

Marea Baja   ⇌▯▯
Trafalgar, 2
11201 Algeciras
Tel. (956) 66 36 54
Seafood. Closed Sun.

Reina Cristina   🛏⇌▯▯▯
Paseo de la Conferencia
11207 Algeciras
Tel. (956) 60 26 22; tlx. 78057
135 rooms. Picturesque location in a park. Outdoor and indoor swimming pools, terrace, sauna, tennis.

Adoc   🛏▯
Finca Adoc, Bloque 17-18
03016 Alicante
Tel. (96) 526 59 00
93 rooms. Picturesque location. View, garden, outdoor and indoor swimming pools, tennis. Cafeteria.

Dársena   ⇌▯
Muelle del Puerto
03001 Alicante
Tel. (96) 520 73 99
Good cuisine. Overlooking the port. Closed Sun. evening and Mon.

Gran Sol   🛏▯▯▯
Avenida Méndez Núñez, 3
03002 Alicante
Tel. (96) 520 30 00

150 rooms. Panoramic view. Central location. Cafeteria.

Quo Vadis   ⇌▯
Plaza Santísama Faz, 3
03002 Alicante
Tel. (96) 521 66 60
Rustic decor. Pleasant terrace.

Parador de Almagro 🛏⇌▯▯
Ronda de San Francisco
13270 Almagro
(Ciudad Real 22 km.)
Tel. (926) 86 01 00
55 rooms. Attractive hotel in a 16th-century convent. Swimming pool.

Club de Mar   ⇌▯
Muelle, 1
04002 Almería
Tel. (951) 23 50 48
Overlooking the sea. Terrace.

Costasol   🛏▯▯
Paseo de Almería, 58
04001 Almería
Tel. (951) 23 40 11
55 rooms. Central location. Terrace. Cafeteria.

Nixar   🛏▯
Antonio Vico, 14
04003 Almería
Tel. (951) 23 72 55
38 rooms. Picturesque, central location.

Casa Pablo   ⇌▯▯
Almíbar, 20
28300 Aranjuez
Tel. (91) 891 14 51
Good cuisine. Castilian specialities and decor. Closed Aug.

Parador Casa   🛏⇌▯▯
del Corregidor
Plaza de España, s/n
11630 Arcos de la Frontera

248

Tel. (956) 70 05 00
24 rooms. Picturesque, central location. Splendid view. Terrace.

Mesón Curro el Cojo 〓⚏
11630 Arcos de la Frontera
Tel. (956) 70 10 03
View.

Mesón La Magdalena 〓⚏
Castrillo de los Polvazares
24700 Astorga
Tel. (987) 61 85 39
Attractive restaurant. Simple, tasty food.

La Peseta ⚏〓⚏
Plaza San Bartolomé, 3
24700 Astorga
Tel. (987) 61 53 00
22 rooms. Picturesque, central location. Terrace. Restaurant closed Oct. and Sun. evening

Copacabana 〓⚏
San Millán, 9
05001 Ávila
Tel. (918) 21 11 10
Attractive setting. Regional cuisine.

Palacio Valderrábanos ⚏〓⚏⚏
Plaza de la Catedral, 9
05001 Ávila
Tel. (918) 21 10 23; tlx. 22481
73 rooms. Central location. Historic building. Elegant decor.

Piquio 〓⚏
Estrada, 4
05000 Ávila
Tel. (918) 21 14 18
Popular local restaurant with Castilian specialities.

Cervantes ⚏⚏
Tercio, 2
06002 Badajoz
Tel. (924) 22 51 10
25 rooms. Central location. Historic building.

Río ⚏〓⚏
Avenida Adolfo Díaz Ambrona, s/n
06006 Badajoz
Tel. (924) 23 76 00; tlx. 28784
90 rooms. Picturesque location. Swimming pool, garden, terrace, tennis.

El Toja 〓⚏⚏
Avenida de Elvas, 21
06000 Badajoz
Tel. (924) 23 74 77
Pleasant Galician restaurant. Outdoor dining. Closed last two weeks Aug. and Sun. evening.

Aitor 〓⚏⚏
Carbonell, 5
08003 Barcelona
Tel. (93) 319 94 88
Good cuisine. Closed mid-Aug. to mid-Sept. and Sun.

Barcelona ⚏⚏⚏⚏
Casp, 1 al 13
08010 Barcelona
Tel. (93) 302 58 58; tlx. 54990
63 rooms. Central location.

Bonanova Park ⚏⚏⚏
Capità Arenas, 51
08013 Barcelona
Tel. (93) 204 09 00; tlx. 54990
60 rooms. Central location.

Botafumeiro 〓⚏⚏⚏
Major de Grácia, 81
08012 Barcelona
Tel. (93) 217 96 42
Good cuisine. Seafood specialities. Closed Easter week and Aug.

Can Culleretes 〓⚏
Quintana, 5
08002 Barcelona
Tel. (93) 317 64 85
Closed 3 weeks July.

Can Fayos 〓⚏⚏
Loreto, 22
08029 Barcelona
Tel. (93) 239 30 22
Closed Sun.

Cortés ⚏⚏〓⚏
Santa Ana, 25
08002 Barcelona
Tel. (93) 317 92 12; tlx. 98215
46 rooms. Central location.

Covadonga ⚏⚏⚏
Avenida de la Diagonal, 596
08036 Barcelona
Tel. (93) 209 55 11; tlx. 93394
76 rooms. Central location. Cafeteria.

Duques de Bergara ⚏⚏〓⚏⚏⚏
Bergara, 11
08002 Barcelona
Tel. (93) 301 51 51; tlx. 81257
56 rooms. Picturesque, central location. Historic building. Terrace.

Eldorado Petit 〓⚏⚏⚏
Dolors Monserdà, 51
08017 Barcelona
Tel. (93) 204 51 53
Excellent cuisine. Pleasant restaurant. Outdoor dining. Closed 2 weeks Aug. and Sun.

Florian 〓⚏⚏⚏
Bertrand i Serra, 20
08022 Barcelona
Tel. (93) 212 46 27
Good cuisine. Reservation recommended. Closed Sun.

Gaudí ⚏⚏⚏⚏
Carrer. Nou de la Rambla, 12
08001 Barcelona
Tel. (93) 317 90 32; tlx. 98974
71 rooms. Central location.

Gorria 〓⚏⚏
Diputació, 421
08013 Barcelona
Tel. (93) 245 11 64
Good, traditional Navarre cuisine. Closed Aug. and Sun.

Gótico ⚏⚏⚏
Jaime I, 14
08002 Barcelona
Tel. (93) 315 22 11; tlx. 97206
70 rooms. Picturesque, central location.

Gran Hotel Calderón ⚏⚏〓⚏⚏⚏
Rambla de Catalunya, 26
08007 Barcelona
Tel. (93) 301 00 00; tlx. 51549
263 rooms. Central location. Swimming pool, terrace, sauna.

Gran Vía ⚏⚏⚏⚏
Gran Vía de les Corts Catalanes, 642
08007 Barcelona
Tel. (93) 318 19 00
48 rooms. Picturesque, central location. Historic building. Terrace.

Jaume de Provença 〓⚏⚏⚏
Provença, 88
08029 Barcelona
Tel. (93) 230 00 29
Excellent cuisine. Modern decor. Closed. Aug., Sun. evening and Mon.

Lleo ⚏⚏〓⚏
Pelayo, 24
08001 Barcelona
Tel. (93) 318 13 12; tlx. 98338
42 rooms. Central location.

Majestic ⚏⚏〓⚏⚏⚏
Passeig de Grácia, 70
08005 Barcelona
Tel. (93) 215 45 12; tlx. 52211
336 rooms. Picturesque, central location. Swimming pool, terrace.

L'Olivé 〓⚏
Muntaner, 171
08036 Barcelona
Tel. (93) 230 90 27
Outdoor dining.

El Pescador ⊟
Mallorca, 314
08037 Barcelona
Tel. (93) 207 10 24
Seafood specialities. Closed Sun.

Petit Paris ⊟
Paris, 196
08036 Barcelona
Tel. (93) 218 26 78
Good cuisine. Attractive restaurant.

Princesa Sofía ⊠⊟
Plaça Pius XII, 4
08028 Barcelona
Tel. (93) 330 71 11; tlx. 51032
505 rooms. Modern luxury hotel. Central location. View. Panoramic restaurant. Swimming pool, garden, sauna.

Regencia Colón ⊠
Sagristans, 13 al 17
08002 Barcelona
Tel. (93) 318 98 58; tlx. 98175
55 rooms. Picturesque, central location. Historic building.

Reno ⊟
Tuset, 27
08006 Barcelona
Tel. (93) 200 91 29
Good cuisine. Elegant restaurant.

Royal ⊠
Ramblas, 117
08002 Barcelona
Tel. (93) 301 94 00; tlx. 97565
108 rooms. Central location.

San Agustin ⊠⊟
Plaça de Sant Agustí, 3
08001 Barcelona
Tel. (93) 317 28 82; tlx. 98121
71 rooms. Picturesque, central location.

7 Puertas ⊟
Passeig d'Isabel II, 14
08003 Barcelona
Tel. (93) 319 30 33
Piano music.

Viá Veneto ⊟
Ganduxer, 10 y 12
08021 Barcelona
Tel. (93) 200 72 44; 200 70 24
Excellent cuisine. Elegant restaurant with Belle Epoque decor.

Parador Conde ⊠⊟
de Gondomar
Ctra. de Bayona, km 1,6
36300 Bayona
(Pontevedra 55 km.)
Tel. (986) 35 50 00; tlx. 83424

128 rooms. Typical Galician country mansion. View. Swimming pool, garden, tennis.

Agir ⊠
Avenida Mediterraneo, 11
03500 Benidorm
Tel. (96) 585 51 62
68 rooms. Central location. Terrace. Cafeteria.

La Caserola ⊟
Avenida Bruselas, 7
03500 Benidorm
Tel. (96) 585 17 19
Attractive flowered terrace. French cuisine.

Cimbel ⊠⊟
Avenida de Europa, 1
03500 Benidorm
Tel. (96) 585 21 00; tlx. 67556
144 rooms. Central location. View. Swimming pool, garden, terrace. Night club.

Don Luis ⊟
Avenida Dr. Orts Llorca
03500 Benidorm
Tel. (96) 585 46 73
Elegant, modern restaurant with good Italian cuisine. Outdoor dining. Closed Jan.

Tiffany's ⊟
Avenida Mediterraneo, 51
03500 Benidorm
Tel. (96) 585 44 68
Live music. Reservation recommended. Closed Jan. and lunchtime.

Bermeo ⊟
Ercilla, 37
48011 Bilbao
Tel. (94) 443 88 00; tlx. 32449
Good cuisine. Closed Sun. evening.

Goizeko-Kabi ⊟
Particular de Estraunza, 4 y 6
48011 Bilbao
Tel. (94) 441 50 04
Excellent cuisine. Closed Sun.

Villa de Bilbao ⊠⊟
Gran Vía, 87
48011 Bilbao
Tel. (94) 441 60 00; tlx. 32164
142 rooms. Luxury hotel. Central location. Night club.

Zabálbaru ⊠
Pedro Martínez Artola, 8
48012 Bilbao
Tel. (94) 443 71 00
37 rooms. Central location.

Asubio ⊠
Carmen, 6
09001 Burgos
Tel. (947) 20 34 45
30 rooms. Central location.

Casa Ojeda ⊟
Vitoria, 5
09004 Burgos
Tel. (947) 20 90 52
Good cuisine. Castilian decor. Closed Sun. evening.

Condestable ⊠⊟
Vitoria, 8
09004 Burgos
Tel. (947) 26 71 25; tlx. 39572
78 rooms. Central location. Historic building. Terrace.

Landa Palace ⊠⊟
Ctra. N-1 Madrid-Irún, km 236
09000 Burgos
Tel. (947) 20 63 43; tlx. 39534
42 rooms. Pleasant, luxury hotel in historic building. Outdoor and indoor pools. Excellent cuisine.

Mesón del Cid ⊠⊟
Plaza Santa Maria, 8
09003 Burgos
Tel. (947) 20 87 15
29 rooms. Picturesque, central location. View. Outdoor dining.

Extremadura ⊠⊟
Avenida Virgen de Guadalupe, 5
10001 Caceres
Tel. (927) 22 16 04
68 rooms. Central location. Swimming pool, garden, terrace.

Figón de Eustaquio ⊟
Plaza de San Juan, 12
10003 Caceres
Tel. (927) 24 81 94
Regional cuisine. Rustic decor.

Atlántico ⊠⊟
Parque Genovés, 9
11002 Cádiz
Tel. (956) 22 69 05; tlx. 76316
173 rooms. Central location. View. Swimming pool, garden.

El Faro ⊟
San Félix, 15
11002 Cádiz
Tel. (956) 21 10 68
Good cuisine. Seafood.

Regio ⊠
Ana de Viya ,11
11009 Cádiz
Tel. (956) 27 93 31
40 rooms. Terrace.

Parador Duques 🛏️🍴▯▯
de Cardona
08261 Cardona
(Barcelona 97 km.)
Tel. (93) 869 12 75; 869 13 50
60 rooms. In a medieval castle with view of the mountains.

Parador de Chinchón 🛏️🍴▯▯
Avenida Generalísimo, 1
28370 Chinchón
(Madrid 47 km.)
Tel. (1) 894 08 36
Picturesque location. Former convent. Swimming pool, garden.

Parador Enrique II 🛏️🍴▯▯
Plaza del Castillo, 1
37500 Ciudad Rodrigo
Tel. (923) 46 01 50
27 rooms. In a 15th-century castle. View. Garden.

Almudaina 🍴▯▯
Campo Santo de los Martires, 1
14004 Córdoba
Tel. (957) 47 43 42
Situated in 15th-century Andalusian building with patio. Outdoor dining. Closed Sun. evening.

Andalucía 🛏️🍴▯
José Zorrilla, 3
14008 Córdoba
Tel. (957) 47 60 00
40 rooms. Picturesque, central location.

Parador de 🛏️🍴▯▯▯
la Arruzafa
Avenida de la Arruzafa, s/n
14012 Córdoba
Tel. (957) 27 59 00
83 rooms. Picturesque location. View. Attractive garden and terrace. Swimming pool, tennis.

Bandolero 🍴▯
Torrijos, 6
14003 Córdoba
Tel. (957) 41 42 45
Regional decor. Outdoor dining.

El Caballo Rojo 🍴▯▯
Cardenal Herrero, 28
14003 Córdoba
Tel. (957) 47 53 75
Good cuisine. Tastefully decorated restaurant.

El Churrasco 🍴▯
Romero, 16
14003 Córdoba
Tel. (957) 29 08 19
Pleasant patio. Outdoor dining. Closed Aug. and Tues.

Ciro's 🍴▯▯
Paseo de la Victoria, 19
14003 Córdoba
Tel. (957) 29 04 64
Centrally situated restaurant.

Meliá Córdoba 🛏️🍴▯▯▯
Jardines de la Victoria
14004 Córdoba
Tel. (957) 29 80 66; tlx. 76591
106 rooms. Picturesque, central location. Pleasant, flowered terrace, swimming pool, garden.

Oscar 🍴▯▯
Plaza de los Chirinos, 6
14001 Córdoba
Tel. (957) 47 75 17
Closed Sun.

Selu 🛏️▯
Eduardo Dato, 7
14003 Córdoba
Tel. (957) 47 65 00; tlx. 76659
118 rooms. Picturesque, central location.

Ciudad de la Coruña 🛏️🍴▯▯
Poligono de Adormideras
15002 La Coruña
Tel. (981) 21 11 00; tlx. 86121
131 rooms. Picturesque location. View. Swimming pool, terrace.

Coral 🍴▯
Estrella, 5
15003 La Coruña
Tel. (981) 22 10 82
Good cuisine. Traditional restaurant. Closed Sun. (except in summer).

Mesón de la Cazuela 🍴▯
Callejon de la Estacada
15000 La Coruña
Tel. (981) 22 24 48
Popular restaurant. Closed Dec., Sun. evening and Mon.

Riazor 🛏️▯▯
Avenida Barrie de la Maza
15004 La Coruña
Tel. (981) 25 34 00; tlx. 86260
176 rooms. Central location. Terrace. Cafeteria.

El Figón de Pedro 🍴▯▯
Cervantes, 13
16004 Cuenca
Tel. (981) 22 68 21
Good cuisine. Castilian decor. Closed Sun. evening.

Posada de San José 🛏️▯
Julián Romero, 4
16001 Cuenca
Tel. (966) 21 13 00

25 rooms. Picturesque, central location. Historic building. View. Garden, terrace.

Torremangana 🛏️🍴▯▯
San Ignacio de Loyola, 9
16002 Cuenca
Tel. (966) 22 33 51; tlx. 23400
116 rooms. Central location. Garden, terrace.

Don Jaime 🛏️▯
Avenida Primo de Rivera, 5
03203 Elche
Tel. (96) 545 38 40
64 rooms. Central location.

El Escondrijo 🍴▯
Ctra. de Elche, km 8
03200 Elche
Tel. (96) 568 08 25
Regional and French cuisine. Closed first 2 weeks Sept. and Sun. evening.

Huerto del Cura 🛏️🍴▯▯
Federico García Sanchíz, 14
03203 Elche
Tel. (96) 545 80 40; tlx. 66814
70 rooms. Picturesque, central location. Pleasant hotel with beautiful garden, pool, tennis, sauna.

Navarra 🍴▯▯
Gustavo de Maeztu, 16
31200 Estella
Tel. (948) 55 10 69
Medieval decor. Outdoor dining.

Antonio 🍴▯
Puerto Deportivo
29680 Estepona
Tel. (952) 80 11 42
Outdoor dining.

Santa Marta 🛏️🍴▯
Ctra. Cádiz-Málaga, km 173
Apartado 2
29680 Estepona
Tel. (952) 78 07 16
37 rooms. Picturesque location. Bungalows in garden. Swimming pool. Open Apr. to Sept.

Le Soufflé 🍴▯▯
Urb. El Pilar, km 167
29680 Estepona
Tel. (952) 78 62 89
Attractive French restaurant. Closed mid-Jan. to mid-Feb. and Tues.

Ampurdán 🛏️🍴▯▯
Ctra. Gral Madrid Francia, km 763
17600 Figueras
Tel. (972) 50 05 62
42 rooms. Central location. Garden, terrace. Good cuisine.

Mas Pau ═♦☜▥
Avinyonet de Puigventós
17742 Figueras
Tel. (972) 54 61 54
Attractive restaurant in old farmhouse.
French-Catalan cuisine. 7 rooms.
Closed mid-Jan. to end Feb.

Angela ☜═▥
Paseo Rey de España
29640 Fuengirola
Tel. (952) 47 52 00; tlx. 77342
260 rooms. Central location. View.
Pool, garden, terrace, tennis, beach.

Don José ═▥
Moncayo, s/n
29640 Fuengirola
Tel. (952) 47 90 52
Outdoor dining. Closed Wed.

Oscar ═▥
29640 Fuengirola
Andalusian-style restaurant. Closed
mid-Jan. to mid-Feb. and Tues.

Sedeño ☜▥
Don Jacinto, 1
29640 Fuengirola
Tel. (952) 47 47 88
30 rooms. Central. Garden, terrace.

Pampinot ☜▥▥
Kale Nagusía, 3
20280 Fuenterrabía
Tel. (943) 64 06 00
8 rooms. Pleasant hotel in 15th-cen-
tury building.

Ramón Roteta ═▥▥
Irún, s/n
20280 Fuenterrabía
Tel. (943) 64 16 93
Good cuisine. Tasteful decor. Outdoor
dining. Closed Sun. and Thurs.
(except evenings in summer).

Bayren I ☜═▥
Paseo de Neptuno
46730 Gandía
Tel. (96) 284 03 00; tlx. 61549
164 rooms. Central location. View of
the beach. Garden, terrace, swimming
pool, tennis.

Costabella ☜▥
Avenida Franca, 61
17007 Gerona
Tel. (972) 20 25 24
47 rooms. Garden, terrace.

Europa ☜▥
Carrer Juli Garreta, 23
17002 Gerona
Tel. (972) 20 27 50
26 rooms. Central location.

La Pequena ═▥
Ctra. del Aeropuerto, s/n
17004 Gerona
Tel. (972) 47 71 32
Pleasant restaurant.

Aguera ☜▥
Hermanos Felgueroso, 28
33200 Gijón
Tel. (985) 14 05 00
35 rooms. Central location.

Casa Víctor ═▥
El Carmen, 11
33200 Gijón
Tel. (985) 35 00 93
Elegant, modern restaurant. Closed
mid-Oct. to mid-Dec., Thurs. and
Sun. evening.

Parador Molino Viejo ☜═▥
Parque de Isabel la Catolica
33204 Gijón
Tel. (985) 37 05 11
40 rooms. Picturesque, central loca-
tion. Historic building. Garden, ter-
race.

Alhambra Palace ☜═▥▥
Peña Partida, 2
18009 Granada
Tel. (958) 22 14 68; tlx. 78400
132 rooms. View of Granada and the
Sierra Nevada. Historic Arab-style
building. Garden, terrace.

América ☜═▥
Real de la Alhambra, 53
18009 Granada
Tel. (958) 22 74 71
13 rooms. Pleasant hotel in historic
building.

Baroca ═▥
Pedro Antonio de Alarcón, 34
18002 Granada
Tel. (958) 26 50 61; tlx. 78535
Elegant restaurant. Closed Aug. and
Sun.

Carlos V ☜═▥
Plaza de los Campos, 4
18009 Granada
Tel. (958) 22 15 87
28 rooms. Central location.

Carmen ☜═▥▥
Acera de Darro, 62
18005 Granada
Tel. (958) 25 83 00; tlx. 78546
205 rooms. Central location.

Carmen de San Miguel ═▥
Plaza de Torres Bermejas, 3
18009 Granada
Tel. (958) 22 67 23; tlx. 78535

Beautifully situated on the Alhambra
hill. Panoramic view. Outdoor dining.
Closed Sun. in winter.

Los Girasoles ☜▥
Cardenal Mendoza
18001 Granada
Tel. (958) 28 07 25
23 rooms. Central location.

Juan Miguel ☜═▥
Acera Del Darro, 24
18005 Granada
Tel. (958) 25 89 12; tlx. 78527
66 rooms. Central location.

Mesón de la Reina ═▥
Laurel de la Reina, 13
18000 Granada
Tel. (958) 59 03 43
Andalusian cuisine. Closed mid-Oct.
to mid-Nov., Sun. evening and Mon.

Rallye ☜═▥
Paseo de Ronda 107
18003 Granada
Tel. (958) 27 28 00
44 rooms. Central location.

Ruta del Veleta ═▥▥
Ctra. Sierra Nevada, km. 5,400
Cenes de la Vega
18190 Granada
Tel. (958) 48 61 34
Good cuisine. Typical decor. Closed
Sun. evening.

Parador ☜═▥▥
San Francisco
Alhambra
18009 Granada
Tel. (958) 22 14 40; tlx. 78792
39 rooms. Pleasant luxury hotel in
15th-century former convent. Garden,
terrace.

Sevilla ═▥
Oficios, 12
18001 Granada
Tel. (958) 22 12 23
Traditional Andalusian restaurant.
Outdoor dining. Closed Sun.
evening.

Hospedaría del ☜═▥
Real Monasterio
Plaza Juan Carlos I
10140 Guadalupe
Tel. (927) 36 70 00
40 rooms. Picturesque, central loca-
tion. Former convent. Terrace.

Parador Zurbarán ☜═▥
Marqués de la Romana, 10
10140 Guadalupe
Tel. (927) 36 70 75; tlx. 367076

40 rooms. Picturesque, central location. Historic building. View. Swimming pool, garden, tennis.

Pedro I de Aragón ◨⬛🟰▯▯
Del Parque, 34
22003 Huesca
Tel. (974) 22 03 00; tlx. 58626
52 rooms. Central location. Garden.

Venta del Sotón 🟰▯▯
Ctra. de Tarragona-San Sebastián, km 227
22000 Huesca
Tel. (974) 27 02 41
Good cuisine. Closed Mon.

La Cocina Aragonesa 🟰▯▯
Cervantes, 5
22700 Jaca
Tel. (974) 36 10 50
Typical decor. Closed Tues.

Gran Hotel ◨⬛🟰▯▯
Paseo del General Franco, 1
22700 Jaca
Tel. (974) 360900; tlx. 57954
166 rooms. Central location. Swimming pool, garden.

Avenida Jerez ◨▯▯
Avenida Alvaro Domecq, 10
11405 Jerez de la Frontera
Tel. (956) 34 74 11; tlx. 75157
95 rooms. Central location. Garden. Cafeteria.

Jerez ◨⬛🟰▯▯▯
Avenida Alvaro Domecq, 35
11405 Jerez de la Frontera
Tel. (956) 30 06 00; tlx. 75059
121 rooms. Central location. Luxury hotel in attractive garden. Swimming pool, terrace, tennis.

Tendido 6 🟰▯
Circo, 10
11405 Jerez de la Frontera
Tel. (956) 34 48 35
Andalusian patio. Closed Sun. in summer, Sun. evening rest of year.

Venta Antonio 🟰▯
Ctra. de Jerez-Sanlúcar, km 5
11405 Jerez de la Frontera
Tel. (956) 33 05 35
Good cuisine. Seafood specialities. Closed Mon. (except in spring and summer).

Adonías 🟰▯
Santa Nonia, 16
24003 León
Tel. (987) 25 26 65
Closed Sun. and last 2 weeks July.

Conde Luna ◨⬛🟰▯▯
Independencia, 7
24003 León
Tel. (987) 20 65 12; tlx. 089888
154 rooms. Central location. Heated swimming pool, sauna.

El Racimo de Oro 🟰▯▯
Caño Vadillo, 2
24006 León
Tel. (987) 25 75 75
17th-century building. Rustic decor. Terrace. Closed Sun. evening and Tues.

Riosol ◨⬛🟰▯
Avenida de Palencia, 3
24001 León
Tel. (987) 22 38 50
141 rooms. Central location.

Parador San Marcos ◨⬛🟰▯▯▯
Plaza San Marcos, 7
24001 León
Tel. (987) 23 73 00; tlx. 89809
201 rooms. Central location. Pleasant luxury hotel in 16th-century former monastery. Garden, terrace.

Forn del Nastasi 🟰▯▯
Salmerón, 10
25004 Lérida
Tel. (973) 23 45 10
Good cuisine. Closed two weeks Aug., Sun. evening and Mon.

Molí de la Nora 🟰▯▯
Ctra. Puigcerdà-Andorra, km 7
25000 Lérida
Tel. (973) 19 00 17
Good cuisine. Outdoor dining. Closed Sun. evening and Mon. from Oct. to Mar.

Pirineos ◨▯▯
Paseo de Ronda, 63
25006 Lérida
Tel. (973) 27 31 99; tlx. 53484
94 rooms. Central location. Cafeteria.

Mercedes ◨⬛🟰▯
Avenida Mistral, 32
17310 Lloret de Mar
Tel. (972) 36 43 12; tlx. 57045
88 rooms. Swimming pool, heated swimming pool.

Santa Marta ◨⬛🟰▯▯▯
Playa de Santa Cristina
17310 Lloret de Mar
Tel. (972) 36 49 04; tlx. 57394
78 rooms. Pleasant hotel in large, beachside park. Swimming pool, ennis.

Taverna del Mar 🟰▯
Pescadors, 5
17310 Lloret de Mar
Tel. (972) 36 40 90
Outdoor dining.

Trull, El 🟰▯
Urb. Platja Canyelles
17310 Lloret de Mar
Tel. (972) 36 49 28

Carlton Rioja ◨▯▯
Gran Vía D. Juan Carlos I, 5
26002 Logroño
Tel. (941) 24 21 00; tlx. 37295
120 rooms. Central location. Cafeteria.

La Merced 🟰▯▯
Marqués de San Nicolás, 109
26001 Logroño
Tel. (941) 22 11 66
Good cuisine. Elegant restaurant in a former Marquess' palace with an que furniture and contemporary paintings. Closed 3 weeks Aug. and Sun.

Murrieta ◨⬛🟰▯
Marqués de Murrieta, 1
26005 Logroño
Tel. (941) 22 41 50
113 rooms. Central location.

Zubillaga 🟰▯
San Agustín, 3
26001 Logroño
Tel. (941) 22 00 76
Basque cuisine. Closed 2 weeks July, last 2 weeks Dec. and Wed.

Gran Hotel Lugo ◨⬛🟰▯▯
Avenida Ramón Ferreiro, 21
27002 Lugo
Tel. (982) 22 41 52; tlx. 86128
168 rooms. Central location. Swimming pool, terrace.

Mesón de Alberto 🟰▯▯
Cruz, 4
27001 Lugo
Tel. (982) 22 83 10
Good Galician cuisine. Bodega Closed Sun. out of season.

La Abuelita 🟰▯
Avenida de Badajos, 25
28027 Madrid
Tel. (91) 405 49 94
Closed Aug. and Sun.

Agumar ◨▯▯
Paseo Reina Cristina, 7
28014 Madrid
Tel. (91) 552 69 00; tlx. 22814
111 rooms. Central location.

Ainhoa ⇒🗏☐☐
Bárbara de Braganza, 12
28004 Madrid
Tel. (91) 410 54 55
Good cuisine. Closed Aug. and Sun.

Aroca ⇒🗏
Plaza de los Carros, 3
28005 Madrid
Tel. (91) 265 26 26
Good cuisine. Closed Aug. and Sun.

Arosa 🛏🗏☐☐
De la Salud, 21
28013 Madrid
Tel. (91) 232 16 00; tlx. 43618
126 rooms. Central. Cafeteria.

Barajas 🛏⇒🗏☐☐
Avenida Logroño, 305
28000 Madrid
Tel. (91) 747 77 00; tlx. 22255
230 rooms. Modern luxury hotel. Central location. Swimming pool, garden, sauna. Night club.

Bogavente ⇒🗏☐☐
Capitán Haya, 20
28020 Madrid
Tel. (91) 456 21 14
Seafood. Closed Sun. evening.

Cabo Mayor ⇒🗏☐☐☐
Juan Ramon Jiménez, 37
28036 Madrid
Tel. (91) 250 87 76; tlx. 49784
Good cuisine. Charming decor. Closed Easter week, 2 weeks Aug. and Sun.

Carlos V 🛏🗏☐☐
Maestro Vitoria, 5
28013 Madrid
Tel. (91) 531 41 00; tlx. 48547
67 rooms. Central. Historic building.

Casa Botín ⇒🗏☐☐
Cuchilleros, 17
28000 Madrid
Tel. (91) 266 42 17
Good, traditional cuisine. Popular restaurant in historic building.

Casa d'a Troya ⇒🗏
Virgen del Portillo, 3
28000 Madrid
Tel. (91) 404 64 53
Good Galician cuisine. Closed last 2 weeks July, Aug. and Sun.

Casa Lucio ⇒🗏☐☐
Cava Baja, 35
28005 Madrid
Tel. (91) 265 32 52
Good cuisine. Reservation essential. Closed Aug. and Sat. lunchtime.

El Cenador del Prado ⇒🗏☐☐☐
Prado, 4
28014 Madrid
Tel. (91) 429 15 61
Good cuisine. Pleasant restaurant. Closed 2 weeks Aug. and Sun.

Colón 🛏⇒🗏☐☐
Doctor Esquerdo, 117 y 119
28000 Madrid
Tel. (91) 273 59 00; tlx. 22984
389 rooms. Central location. Swimming pool, garden, terrace, sauna.

Conde Duque 🛏🗏☐☐
Plaza Conde Valle Suchil, 5
28015 Madrid
Tel. (91) 447 70 00; tlx. 22058
138 rooms. Central location.

Eurobuilding 🛏⇒🗏☐☐
Juan Ramón Jiménez, 8
28036 Madrid
Tel. (91) 457 17 00; tlx. 22548
421 rooms. Luxury hotel. Central location. Swimming pool, garden, terrace, sauna.

Fortuny ⇒🗏☐☐
Fortuny, 34
28010 Madrid
Tel. (91) 410 77 07
Excellent cuisine. Pleasant luxury restaurant in former palace. Attractive garden. Good wine cellar. Closed Sun. and Sat. lunchtime.

Horcher ⇒🗏☐☐☐
Alfonso XII, 6
28014 Madrid
Tel. (91) 522 07 31; 532 35 96
Good cuisine. Attractive, luxurious restaurant. Closed Sun., and Sat. and Sun. in July and Aug.

Jockey ⇒🗏☐☐☐
Amador de los Ríos, 6
28010 Madrid
Tel. (91) 419 10 03
Outstanding cuisine. Elegant restaurant. Closed Aug. and Sun.

Mercator 🛏🗏☐☐
Atocha, 123
28012 Madrid
Tel. (91) 429 05 00; tlx. 46129
90 rooms. Central Cafeteria.

Mesón de Aquilino ⇒🗏☐☐
Josué Lillo, 24
28000 Madrid
Tel. (91) 478 79 43
Good traditional cuisine. Closed Easter week, Aug., Sun. evening and Sat.

Mindanao 🛏⇒🗏☐☐
San Francisco de Sales, 15
28003 Madrid
Tel. (91) 449 55 00; tlx. 22631
289 rooms. Central location. Outdoor and indoor swimming pools, terrace, sauna.

Moderno 🛏🗏
Arenal, 2
28013 Madrid
Tel. (91) 531 09 00
98 rooms. Central location.

Palace 🛏⇒🗏☐☐
Plaza las Cortes, 7
28014 Madrid
Tel. (91) 429 75 51; tlx. 22272
518 rooms. Picturesque, central location. Historic building.

París 🛏⇒🗏
Alcalá, 2
28014 Madrid
Tel. (91) 521 64 96; tlx. 43448
114 rooms. Central location.. Historic building.

El Pescador ⇒🗏☐☐
Ortega y Gasset, 75
28006 Madrid
Tel. (91) 402 12 90
Good cuisine. Seafood specialities. Rustic decor. Closed mid-Aug. to mid-Sept. and Sun.

Príncipe de Viana ⇒🗏☐☐
Manuel de Falla, 5
28036 Madrid
Tel. (91) 259 14 48
Excellent cuisine. Attractive restaurant, popular with the jet set. Outdoor dining. Closed mid-July to end Aug., Sun. and Sat. lunchtime.

Puerta de Toledo 🛏🗏☐☐
Glorieta Puerta de Toledo, 4
28000 Madrid
Tel. (91) 474 71 00; tlx. 22291
152 rooms. Picturesque, central location.

Rugantino ⇒🗏☐☐
Velázquez, 136
28006 Madrid
Tel. (91) 261 02 22
Good Italian cuisine.

Sanvy 🛏🗏☐☐☐
Goya, 3
28001 Madrid
Tel. (91) 276 08 00; tlx. 44994
109 rooms. Central location. Swimming pool, terrace.

Serrano 📧〚〛
Marqués de Villamejor, 8
28006 Madrid
Tel. (91) 435 52 00
34 rooms. Central location.

Zalacaín 〜〚〛〚〛
Alvarez de Baena, 4
28006 Madrid
Tel. (91) 261 48 40
Outstanding cuisine. Elegant restaurant. Closed Aug., Sun. and Sat. lunchtime.

Antonio Martín 〜〚〛
Paseo Marítimo
29016 Málaga
Tel. (952) 22 21 13
Attractive location. Waterside terrace. Closed Tues. in winter.

Café de Paris 〜〚〛〚〛
Vélez Málaga, 8
29016 Málaga
Tel. (952) 22 50 43
Attractive, elegant restaurant. Creative cuisine. Closed end June to end July and Wed.

Don Curro 📧〚〛〚〛
Sancha de Lara, 7
29000 Málaga
Tel. (952) 22 72 00; tlx. 77366
105 rooms. Central l ocation. Cafeteria.

Los Naranjos 📧〚〛〚〛
Paseo Sancha, 35
29016 Málaga
Tel. (952) 22 43 17; tlx. 77030
41 rooms. Picturesque, central location.

La Fonda 〜〚〛〚〛
Plaza del Santo Cristo, 9
29600 Marbella
Tel. (952) 77 25 12
Excellent cuisine. Charming Andalusian patio. Dinner only. Closed Sun.

Las Fuentes 📧〜〚〛
del Rodeo
Ctra. Cádiz-Málaga, km 180
29600 Marbella
Tel. (952) 81 40 17; tlx. 77340
85 rooms. Swimming pool, garden, tennis.

El Fuerte 📧〜〚〛〚〛〚〛
Avenida El Fuerte
29600 Marbella
Tel. (952) 77 15 00; tlx. 77523
262 rooms. Central location. Historic building. View. Swimming pool, terrace, mini-golf, tennis.

La Hacienda 〜〚〛〚〛〚〛
Ctra. Cádiz-Málaga, km 193
29600 Marbella
Tel. (952) 83 12 67
Excellent cuisine. Rustic, elegant decor. Terrace. Exceptional view. Closed mid-Nov. to mid-Dec., lunchtime in Aug. and Mon.

Marbella Club 📧〜〚〛〚〛〚〛
Ctra. Cádiz-Málaga, km. 178, 200
29600 Marbella
Tel. (952) 77 13 00; tlx. 77319
76 rooms. Pleasant hotel in attractive garden. Swimming pool, heated swimming pool, terrace, tennis, sauna. Night club.

Emperatriz 📧〚〛
Plaza de España, 19
06800 Mérida
Tel. (924) 31 31 11
41 rooms. Central location. Historic building. Garden. Night club.

Nicolás 〜〚〛
Félix Valverde Lillo, 11
06800 Mérida
Tel. (924) 31 96 10
Regional cuisine. Closed 3 weeks Sept. and Sun. evening.

Parador Vía de la Plata 📧〚〛〚〛
Plaza de la Constitución, 3
06800 Mérida
Tel. (924) 31 38 00
82 rooms. Central location. Former convent. Garden, terrace.

Conde de Floridablanca 📧〚〛〚〛
Corbalán, 7
30002 Murcia
Tel. (968) 21 46 26; tlx. 67391
60 rooms. Central. Historic building.

El Rincón de Pepe 〜〚〛〚〛
Apóstoles, 34
30001 Murcia
Tel. (968) 21 22 39
Good Murcian cuisine. Closed Sun. evening and all day Sun. in summer.

El Ancladero 〜〚〛
Capistrano Playa
29780 Nerja
Tel. (952) 52 19 55
Terrace, garden and view of sea. Closed Tues. from Nov. to end Feb.

Balcón de Europa 📧〚〛〚〛
Paseo Balcon de Europa 1
29780 Nerja
Tel. (952) 52 08 00; tlx. 77685
105 rooms. Picturesque, central location. View. Garden, terrace, sauna, mini-golf. Night club.

Casa Luque 〜〚〛
Andalucía, 27
29780 Nerja
Tel. (952) 52 00 32
Closed Jan., Feb. and Wed.

Sanmiguel 〜〚〛〚〛
San Miguel, 12–14
32005 Orense
Tel. (988) 22 12 45
Good Galician cuisine. Closed Tues.

Sila 📧〜〚〛
Avenida de la Habana, 61
32003 Orense
Tel. (988) 23 63 11
64 rooms. Picturesque, central location.

Ramiro I 📧〚〛〚〛
Calvo Sotelo, 13
33007 Oviedo
Tel. (985) 23 28 50; tlx. 84042
83 rooms. Central l ocation. Cafeteria.

Regente 📧〚〛〚〛
Jovellanos, 31
33003 Oviedo
Tel. (985) 22 23 43; tlx. 84310
88 rooms. Central location.

Trascorrales 〜〚〛〚〛
Plaza Trascorrales
33009 Oviedo
Tel. (985) 22 24 41
Excellent cuisine. Tasteful decor. Closed 2 weeks Aug. and Sun.

El Delfín 〜〚〛
Avenida 11 de setiembre, 93
17230 Palamós
Tel. (972) 31 64 74
Catalan cuisine. Outdoor dining. Closed mid-Oct. to mid-Mar. and Thurs.

Marina 📧〜〚〛
Avenida 11 de setiembre, 48
17230 Palamós
Tel. (972) 31 42 50
62 rooms. Centra. Garden, terrace.

Ciudad de Pamplona 📧〜〚〛〚〛〚〛
Iturrama, 21
31007 Pamplona
Tel. (948) 26 60 11; tlx. 37913
117 rooms. Central location. Modern hotel. Terrace.

Eslava 📧〚〛
Plaza Virgen de la O, 7
31001 Pamplona
Tel. (948) 22 22 70
28 rooms. Picturesque, central location.

Josetxo =☰▯▯▯
Plaza del Príncipe de Viana, 1
31002 Pamplona
Tel. (948) 22 20 97
Excellent cuisine. Elegant decor. Closed Aug. and Sun.

Shanti =☰▯
Castillo de Maya, 39
31003 Pamplona
Closed July, Sun. and Mon. evening.

Casa Severino =☰▯▯
Urb. Las Atalayas
12598 Peñiscola
Tel. (964) 48 07 03
Closed Nov. and Wed. (except in summer).

Hostería del Mar ☒☰▯▯▯
Ctra. Benic.-Peñiscola, km 6
12598 Peñiscola
Tel. (964) 48 06 00; tlx. 65750
85 rooms. Picturesque, central location. Magnificent view. Swimming pools, garden, bowling, tennis.

Parador ☒☰▯▯
Casa del Barón
Maceda
36002 Pontevedra
Tel. (986) 85 58 00
47 rooms. Attractive, historic building. Garden. Outdoor dining.

Casa Solla =☰▯▯
Carretera de la Toja
36000 Pontevedra
Tel. (986) 85 26 78
Good cuisine. Outdoor dining. Closed Sun. and Thurs. evening.

Don Miguel =☰▯▯
Plaza de España, 3
29400 Ronda
Tel. (952) 87 10 90
Andalusian cuisine. In the heart of the town. Terrace overlooking the river. Closed Sun. in summer.

Pedro Romero =☰▯
Virgen de la Paz, 18
29400 Ronda
Tel. (952) 87 10 61

Polo ☒▯▯
Mariano Soubirón, 8
29400 Ronda
Tel. (952) 87 24 47
33 rooms. Picturesque, central location.

Reina Victoria ☒☰▯▯
Jerez, 25
29400 Ronda
Tel. (952) 87 12 40

89 rooms. Picturesque location. Superb view of the valley. Swimming pool, garden, terrace.

Canyelles Platja ☒☰▯▯
Playa Canyelles
17480 Rosas
Tel. (972) 25 65 00
99 rooms. Picturesque location. Swimming pool, garden, terrace.

Hacienda El Bulli =☰▯▯▯
Cala Montjoi, Apt. 30
17480 Rosas
Tel. (972) 25 76 51
Excellent cuisine. Pleasant, rustic decor. Closed mid-Oct. to mid-Mar., Mon., and Tues. lunchtime (except summer).

Chez Víctor =☰▯▯
Espoz y Mina, 26
37002 Salamanca
Tel. (923) 21 31 23
Good cuisine. Closed Aug., Sun. evening and Mon.

Condal ☒▯
Santa Eulalia, 3–5
37002 Salamanca
Tel. (923) 21 84 00
70 rooms. Central location. Historic building. Cafeteria.

Gran Hotel ☒▯▯▯
Poeta Iglesias, 5
37001 Salamanca
Tel. (923) 21 35 00; tlx. 26809
100 rooms. Central location.

La Posada =☰▯
Aire y Azucena, 1
37001 Salamanca
Tel. (923) 21 72 51
Closed 2 weeks Aug.

Regio ☒☰▯▯
Ctra. Salamanca-Madrid, km 4
37000 Salamanca
Tel. (923) 20 02 50; tlx. 22895
121 rooms. Swimming pool, garden, terrace, tennis.

Parador de Salamanca ☒☰▯▯
Teso de la Feria, 2
37000 Salamanca
Tel. (923) 26 87 00
108 rooms. Picturesque location. Panoramic view of the city. Swimming pool, garden, terrace, tennis.

Arzak =☰▯▯▯
Alto de Miracruz, 21
20015 San Sebastián
Tel. (943) 27 84 65

Outstanding traditional Basque cuisine. Rustic decor. Closed 2 weeks in Jun., Nov. and Sun. evening.

Bretxa =☰▯
General Echgüe, 5
20003 San Sebastián
Tel. (943) 42 05 49
Seafood. Closed Sun. evening.

Casa Nicolasa =☰▯▯▯
Aldamar, 4
20003 San Sebastián
Tel. (943) 42 17 62
Excellent cuisine. Closed Sun. and Mon. evening.

Codina ☒☰▯▯
Avenida Zumalacárregui, 21
20008 San Sebastián
Tel. (943) 21 22 00; tlx. 38187
77 rooms.

Costa Vasca ☒☰ =☰▯▯▯
Avenida Pio Baroja, 15
20008 San Sebastián
Tel. (943) 21 10 11; tlx. 36551
203 rooms. Picturesque location. Swimming pool, garden, tennis.

Monte Igueldo ☒☰▯▯▯
Monte Igueldo
20008 San Sebastián
Tel. (943) 21 02 11; tlx. 38096
125 rooms. Picturesque location. Superb view of the city, bay and sea. Swimming pool, garden, terrace. Night club.

Niza ☒☰▯▯
Zubieta, 56
20017 San Sebastián
Tel. (943) 42 66 63
41 rooms. Picturesque, central location.

Panier Fleuri =☰▯▯
Paseo de Salamanca, 1
20013 San Sebastián
Tel. (943) 42 42 05
Excellent cuisine. Closed first 2 weeks June, Sun. evening and Wed.

Bahía ☒☰▯▯▯
Alfonso XIII, 6
39002 Santander
Tel. (942) 22 17 00; tlx. 35859
181 rooms. Central location.

La Concha =☰▯▯
Avenida Reina Victoria, s/n
39005 Santander
Tel. (942) 27 37 37
Splendid view. Outdoor dining. Piano music at night.

256

El Molino ⇒⬛⬜⬜
Carretera N-611
Puente Arce
39470 Santander
Tel. (942) 57 40 00
Excellent cuisine. Situated in a renovated former mill. Closed Mon.

Compostela ⬛⬜⬜
General Franco, 1
15702 Santiago de Compostela
Tel. (981) 58 57 00; tlx. 82387
99 rooms. Picturesque, central location. Historic building. Cafeteria.

Don Quijote ⇒⬛
Galeras, 20
15705 Santiago de Compostela
Tel. (981) 58 68 59

Gelmírez ⬛⬜
General Franco, 92
15702 Santiago de Compostela
Tel. (981) 56 11 00; tlx. 82387
138 rooms. Central location. Cafeteria.

Peregrino ⬛⇒⬜⬜
Avenida Rosalía de Castro
15706 Santiago de Compostela
Tel. (981) 59 18 50; tlx. 82352
148 rooms. View. Heated swimming pool, garden, terrace. Night club.

Retablo ⇒⬜⬜
Rúa Nova, 13
15705 Santiago de Compostela
Tel. (981) 56 69 50
Attractive decor. Closed Sun. evening and Mon.

Los Reyes Católicos ⬛⇒⬜⬜⬜
Plaza de España, 1
15705 Santiago de Compostela
Tel. (981) 58 22 00; tlx. 86004
157 rooms. Luxury hotel in a magnificent 16th-century building. Central location. Garden. Night club.

Vilas ⇒⬜⬜
Rosalía de Castro, 88
15706 Santiago de Compostela
Tel. (981) 59 10 00
Good Basque cuisine. Closed Sun.

Los Blasones ⇒⬛
Plaza de la Gándara
39330 Santillana del Mar
Tel. (942) 81 80 70
Regional cuisine. Closed Nov. to May.

Gil Blas ⬛⇒⬜⬜⬜
Plaza Ramón Pelayo, 11
39330 Santillana del Mar
Tel. (942) 81 80 00

56 rooms. Picturesque, central location. Attractive, historic house. Garden, terrace.

Los Infantes ⬛⇒⬜⬜
Avenida Le Dorat, 1
39330 Santillana del Mar
Tel. (942) 81 81 00
30 rooms. Central location. Historic building. Terrace. Night club.

José Maria ⇒⬜
Cronista Lecea, 11
40001 Segovia
Tel. (911) 43 44 84
Good traditional Segovian cuisine. Closed Nov.

Los Linajes ⬛⬜⬜
Dr. Velasco, 9
40003 Segovia
Tel. (911) 43 12 01
55 rooms. Picturesque, central location. Historic building. Garden, terrace. Night club.

Mesón de Cándido ⇒⬜⬜
Plaza del Azoguejo, 5
40001 Segovia
Tel. (911) 42 59 11
In tastefully decorated 15th-century building.

La Oficina ⇒⬜
Cronista Lecea, 10
40001 Segovia
Tel. (911) 43 16 43
Closed last 2 weeks Nov.

Puerta de Segovia ⬛⇒⬜⬜
Ctra. Soria-Riaza
40003 Segovia
Tel. (911) 43 71 61; tlx. 22336
114 rooms. Picturesque location. Swimming pool, terrace, tennis.

Parador de Segovia ⬛⬜⬜
Apartado de Correos 106
40003 Segovia
Tel. (911) 43 04 62; tlx. 47913
80 rooms. Superb view of Segovia. Modern decor. Heated swimming pool, garden, terrace.

Las Sirenas ⬛⬜
Juan Bravo, 30
40001 Segovia
Tel. (911) 43 40 11
39 rooms. Central location. Terrace.

La Albahaca ⇒⬛⬜
Plaza de Santa Cruz, 12
41000 Seville
Tel. (954) 22 07 14
Historic mansion. Outdoor dining. Closed Sun.

Alfonso XIII ⬛⇒⬜⬜⬜
San Fernando, 2
41004 Seville
Tel. (954) 22 28 50
149 rooms. Majestic luxury hotel in striking Andalusian building. Central. Swimming pool, garden, terrace.

Becquer ⬛⬜⬜
Reyes Católicos, 4
41001 Seville
Tel. (954) 22 89 00; tlx. 72884
126 rooms. Central location. Modern, efficient.

Doña María ⬛⬜⬜
Don Remondo, 19
41004 Seville
Tel. (954) 22 49 90
96 rooms. Picturesque, central location. View of the cathedral. Elegant decor. Swimming pool, terrace.

La Dorada ⇒⬜⬜⬜
Virgen de Aguas Santas, 6
41001 Seville
Tel. (954) 45 51 00
Good cuisine. Fish specialities. In Los Remedios district. Closed Aug. and Sun. evening.

Figón del Cabildo ⇒⬜⬜
Plaza de Cabildo
41001 Seville
Tel. (954) 22 01 17
Elegant dining. Closed Sun. evening and weekends in summer.

Gran Hotel Lar ⬛⇒⬜⬜⬜
Plaza de Carmen Benítez, 3
41003 Seville
Tel. (954) 41 03 61; tlx. 72816
137 rooms. Just beyond the historic centre of the city. Luxurious.

La Isla ⇒⬜⬜
Arfe, 25
41001 Seville
Tel. (954) 21 26 31
Fish and seafood specialities. Closed Aug.

Meson Castellano ⇒⬜
Jovellanos 6
41004 Seville
Tel. (954) 22 57 21
Hearty Castilian food. Just off Calle Sierpes.

Oriza ⇒⬜⬜
San Fernando, 41
41000 Seville
Tel. (954) 22 72 54
Elegant Basque cuisine. Closed Aug. and Sun.

Ox's　　　　≕🍴
Betis, 61
41010 Seville
Tel. (954) 27 95 85
Good Basque cuisine. Closed Aug.
and Sun. evening.

La Raza　　　　≕🍴
Avenida Isabel la Católica, 2
41013 Seville
Tel. (954) 23 38 30
View. Outdoor dining in the park.

Sevilla　　　　🛏🍴
Daoiz 5
41003 Seville
Tel. (954) 38 41 61
Charming remodelled old building.
Very central yet quiet.

Galeón　　　　🛏🍴
San Francisco, 44 y 46
08870 Sitges
Tel. (93) 894 06 12
Picturesque, central location.
Swimming pool, garden.

Mare Nostrum　　　≕🍴
Paseo de la Ribera, 60
08870 Sitges
Tel. (93) 894 33 93
Seafood. Outdoor dining. Closed
midDec. to mid-Jan. and Wed. in
winter.

Terramar　　　🛏≕🍴
Paseig Maritim, 30
08870 Sitges
Tel. (93) 894 00 50; tlx. 53186
209 rooms. Picturesque
location. Beachside. Swimming pool,
garden, terrace, tennis.
Night club.

Parador Antonio　　🛏≕🍴
Machado
Parque del Castillo
42005 Soria
Tel. (975) 213 44 51
34 rooms.
Picturesque, quiet location. Splendid
view. Garden.

Maroto　　　　≕🍴
Paseo del Espolón, 20
42001 Soria
Tel. (975) 22 40 86
Good cuisine.
Elegant, modern restaurant.

Mesón Leonor　　🛏≕🍴
Paseo del Mirón
42005Soria
Tel. (975) 22 02 50
32 rooms. Picturesque, quiet location.
View. Bowling.

Parador Fernando　　🛏≕🍴
de Aragón
50680 Sos del Rey Católico
Tel. (948) 88 80 11
66 rooms.
Picturesque, central location.
View. Terrace.

Astari　　　　🛏🍴
Vía Augusta, 95
43003 Tarragona
Tel. (977) 23 69 11
83 rooms. View. Swimming pool,
garden, terrace.

Lauría　　　　🛏🍴
Rambla Nova, 20
43004 Tarragona
Tel. (977) 23 67 12
72 rooms. Central location.
Swimming pool, terrace.

Sol Ric　　　　≕🍴
Vía Augusta, 227
43007 Tarragona
Tel. (977) 23 20 32
Good wine cellar. Attractive garden.
Outdoor dining. Closed mid-Dec.
to mid-Jan., Sun. evening and
Mon.

Adolfo　　　　≕🍴
Calle de la Granada, 6
45001 Toledo
Tel. (925) 22 73 21
Near the cathedral. Closed Sun.
evening.

Alfonso VI　　　🛏≕🍴
General Moscardó, 2
45001 Toledo
Tel. (925) 22 26 00
88 rooms. Picturesque, central loca-
tion.

Cardenal　　　🛏≕🍴
Paseo de Recaredo, 24
45004 Toledo
Tel. (925) 22 49 00
27 rooms.
Picturesque, central location.
Attractive, historic building. Garden,
terrace.

Casa Aurelio　　　≕🍴
Plaza Ayuntamiento, 8
45001 Toledo
Tel. (925) 22 77 16
Near the cathedral. Patio.

Los Cigarrales　　🛏≕🍴
Ctra. Circunvalación, 32
45000 Toledo
Tel. (925) 22 00 53
69 rooms. Picturesque location. View.
Terrace.

Parador Conde　　🛏≕🍴
de Orgaz
Cerro del Emperador
45000 Toledo
Tel. (925) 22 18 50; tlx. 47998
77 rooms. Splendid view of the city.
Swimming pool, garden, terrace.

Casa Guaquín　　　≕🍴
Carmen, 37
29620 Torremolinos
Tel. (952) 38 45 30
Good cuisine. Seafood specialities.
View. Outdoor dining. Closed Dec.
and Thurs.

Cervantes　　　🛏≕🍴
Las Mercedes
29620 Torremolinos
Tel. (952) 38 40 33
393 rooms. View. Swimming
pool, garden, terrace, sauna.
Night club.

Don Pedro　　　🛏≕🍴
Avenida del Lido
29620 Torremolinos
Tel. (952) 38 68 44; tlx. 77252
290 rooms. Swimming pool, garden,
terrace, tennis. Night club.

Ancora　　　　🛏≕🍴
Avenida de la Palma, 4
17320 Tossa de Mar
Tel. (972) 34 02 99
58 rooms. Central location. Charming
terrace, garden, mini-golf, tennis.
Open June to mid-Sept.

Es Moli　　　　≕🍴
Tarull, 5
17320 Tossa de Mar
Tel. (972) 34 14 14
Good cuisine. Delightful patio-garden.
Outdoor dining. Open mid-Mar. to
mid-Oct.

Mar Menuda　　　🛏≕🍴
Playa de Mar Menuda
17320 Tossa de Mar
Tel. (972) 34 10 00
40 rooms. Picturesque location.
Swimming pool, garden, charming
terrace, tennis. Open Apr. to Sept.

El Choko　　　　≕🍴
Plaza de los Fueros, 5
31500 Tudela
Tel. (948) 82 10 19
Closed Mon.

Nueva Parrilla　　　🛏🍴
Plaza de Toros
31500 Tudela
Tel. (948) 82 24 00
22 rooms. Terrace.

Parador Condestable 🛏🍴▯
Dávalos
Plaza de Vázquez Molina, 1
23400 Ubeda
Tel. (53) 75 03 45
Pleasant hotel in 16th-century palace.
Central location. Patio.

Comodoro 🍴▯
Trànsits, 3
46002 Valencia
Tel. (96) 351 38 15
Closed Easter week, Aug. and Sun.

Eladio 🍴▯
Chiva, 40
46018 Valencia
Tel. (96) 326 22 44
Good cuisine. Closed Aug. and Sun.

La Hacienda 🍴▯
Navarro Reverter, 12
46004 Valencia
Tel. (96) 373 18 59
Tasteful Andalusian decor. Closed
Easter week, Sat. lunchtime and Sun.

Llar 🛏▯
Colón, 46
46004 Valencia
Tel. (96) 352 84 60
50 rooms. Central location.

La Marcelina 🍴▯
Avenida Neptuno, 8
46011 Valencia
Tel. (96) 371 20 25
Close to the beach. Terrace with music
Sat. in summer. Closed Jan. and Sun.
and evenings in winter.

Meliá Valencia 🛏🍴▯
Rey Don Jaime
Avenida Baleares, 2
46023 Valencia
Tel. (96) 360 73 00; tlx. 064252
314 rooms. Swimming pool.

Oltra 🛏▯
Plaza Ayuntamiento, 4
46002 Valencia
Tel. (96) 352 06 12
93 rooms. Central. Historic building.

Plaza 🍴▯
Basilia, 1
4600 Valencia
Tel. (96) 331 59 60
Situated in 18th-century former
palace. View. Closed Sun.

Reina Victoria 🛏🍴▯
Barcas, 4
46002 Valencia
Tel. (96) 352 04 87; tlx. 064755
94 rooms. Central. Historic building.

Enara 🛏▯
Plaza de España, 5
47001 Valladolid
Tel. (983) 30 03 11
26 rooms. Central location.

Mesón La Fragua 🍴▯
Paseo de Zorrilla, 10
47006 Valladolid
Tel. (983) 33 71 02
Good Castilian cuisine. Closed Sun.
evening.

Mesón Panero 🍴▯
Marina Escobar, 1
47001 Valladolid
Tel. (983) 30 16 73
Good cuisine. Castilian decor.
Small restaurant.
Closed Sun. evening.

Olid Meliá 🛏🍴▯
Plaza de San Miguel, 10
47003 Valladolid
Tel. (983) 35 72 00; tlx. 26312
226 rooms. Central location.

Can Pamplona 🛏▯
Ctra. Nal. 152 Vich-Puigcerdá
08500 Vich
Tel. (93) 885 36 12
34 rooms. Central location. Terrace.

La Taula 🍴▯
Miquel Clariana, 4
08500 Vich
Tel. (93) 886 32 29
Close to the cathedral. Ancient
building. Closed Feb., Sun. evening
and Mon.

Parador de Vich 🛏🍴▯
08500 Vich
Tel. (93) 888 72 11
36 rooms. Picturesque, quiet location.
Swimming pool, garden,
tennis.

Bahía de Vigo 🛏🍴▯
Avenida Cánovas del Castillo, 5
36202 Vigo
Tel. (986) 22 67 00; tlx. 83014
110 rooms. Central location. View.
Terrace. Night club.

Ensenada 🛏▯
Alfonso XII, 7
36201 Vigo
Tel. (986) 22 61 00; tlx. 83561
109 rooms. Central location.

Sibaris 🍴▯
García Barbón, 168
36201 Vigo
Tel. (986) 22 15 26
Excellent cuisine. Closed Sun.

Dos Hermanas 🍴▯
Madre Vedruna, 10
01008 Vitoria
Tel. (945) 24 36 96
Good, regional cuisine. Closed mid-
Aug. to mid-Sept. and Sun.

General Alava 🛏▯
Avenida de Gasteiz, 53
01009 Vitoria
Tel. (945) 22 22 00; tlx. 35468
111 rooms. Central. Cafeteria.

El Portalón 🍴▯
Correría, 151
01001 Vitoria
Tel. (945) 22 49 89
Good, traditional cuisine. Attractive
restaurant in 15th-century posada.
Closed Aug. and Sun.

Parador Condes de 🛏🍴▯
Alba y Aliste
Plaza Cánovas, 1
49014 Zamora
Tel. (988) 51 44 97
27 rooms. Central location. Pleasant
hotel in elegant former palace.
Swimming pool, terrace.

Dos Infantas 🛏▯
Cortinas de San Miguel, 3
49012 Zamora
Tel. (988) 53 28 75
68 rooms. Central. Cafeteria.

París 🍴▯
Avenida de Portugal, 14
49002 Zamora
Tel. (988) 51 43 25
Popular restaurant.

Conde Blanco 🛏▯
Predicadores, 84
50003 Zaragoza
Tel. (976) 44 14 11
83 rooms. Central. Cafeteria.

Costa Vasca 🍴▯
Tte. Coronel Valenzuela, 13
50004 Zaragoza
Tel. (976) 21 73 39
Good Basque cuisine. Closed Sun.

Goya 🛏🍴▯
Cinco de Marzo, 5
50004 Zaragoza
Tel. (976) 22 93 31; tlx. 58680
148 rooms. Central location.

Gurrea 🍴▯
San Ignacio de Loyola, 14
50008 Zaragoza
Tel. (976) 23 31 61
Good cuisine. Luxurious restaurant.
Closed Aug. and Sun.

259

All the Nuts and Bolts
for a Successful Journey

CONTENTS

Listed after some entries is the appropriate Spanish translation, usually in the singular, plus a number of phrases that may come in handy during your stay in Spain.

ACCOMMODATION (alojamiento)

See also CAMPING

Hotels are classified in star categories, from one-star frugality to five-star luxury. *Hostales* and *pensiones* range from one to three stars. At the one-star level, rooms rarely have bathrooms. At two stars, chances of private facilities are increased and all rooms have telephones. Three-star establishments provide a lobby and a bar, a shower or bath and toilet assigned to every bedroom and a good chance of having a television set in the room. At four stars, you can expect air conditioning in hot regions, a couple of lobbies, and the TV set will probably receive satellite programmes. Five-star luxury covers all the comforts of world-class hotels, from haute cuisine to shopping facilities.

All hotels, *hostales* and *pensiones* must by law have a rates chart at the reception desk and the price of each room posted behind the door. Check that the VAT *(IVA)* government tax is included. This varies from 6 to 12% in the most expensive hotels. Tour groups often obtain substantial reductions. Breakfast is generally included in the price.

When you check into your hotel, you may have to leave your passport at the reception desk. It will be given back in the morning.

Hostales and **Hotel-Residencias.** These are modest hotels, often without a restaurant, although some do offer optional full board.

Pensiones. Small boarding houses, with few amenities. They provide full board.

Fondas. Village inns, with basic facilities.

Paradores. Spain has a network of 86 state-run hotels, many in converted castles, palaces and monasteries. Most are off the beaten tourist track; however, situated as they are in areas of great beauty or or of historical importance, they make a detour worthwhile. *Paradores* are not cheap, but in fact these hotels run at a loss to promote Spanish culture and tourism. As well as excellent accommodation, they often provide information on the area. A complete list can be obtained from Paradores de Turismo:

Velázquez, 18, Apartado de Correos 50043, 28001 Madrid; tel. (91) 435 97 00/4

The official U.S. representative is Marketing Ahead:

433 Fifth Avenue, 10016 New York; tel. (212) 68 69 213

In the U.K., contact Keytel International:

402 Edgeware Rd, London W2; tel. (01) 402 8182

Youth hostel *(albergue de juventud).* There are 137 youth hostels in Spain. Despite the name, there is no age limit, although theoretically people under 26 have priority. Many hostels have provisions for outdoor sports: sailing, canoeing, cycling, etc. There is usually an 11 p.m. curfew.

A few hostels cater only for groups (advance booking necessary) and some provide facilities for the physically handicapped.

Further information and a complete list of hostels can be obtained from the Red Española de Albergues Juveniles:

c/ José Ortega y Gasset, 71, 28006 Madrid; tel. (91) 401 13 00, ext. 319-265

I'd like	Quisiera
a double/single	una habitación
room	doble/sencilla
with/without bath/	con/sin baño/
shower	ducha
What's the price	¿Cuál es el precio
per night?	por noche?

AIRPORTS *(aeropuerto)*

The airport buildings provide the usual amenities—souvenir shops, snack bars, car-hire counters, currency-exchange offices and hotel reservation desks. Porters are normally available to carry bags to the taxi rank and bus stop. They charge an official rate, paid per piece of luggage. There are also duty-free shops for passengers embarking on international flights. Tour operators provide ground transportation for their clients.

Madrid. Barajas airport, 14 km. (9 miles) east of Madrid handles domestic and international flights. Air-conditioned airport buses leave every 15 minutes for the city terminal at Plaza del Descubrimiento. Getting off at stops in between is possible if you are carrying only hand luggage. The trip takes 30 to 45 minutes. Taxis provide alternative transport, but are four to five times as expensive.

Barcelona. The modern international airport, along the sea at El Prat de Llobregat, is only about 15 km. (10 miles) from the centre of the city. Trains, running every 30 minutes, operate a link between the airport and Central-Sants station in Barcelona. The trip takes 15 to 20 minutes.

Charter flights for resorts near Tarragona often use the military airfield at Reus.

Gerona. Flights to Costa Brava resorts use Gerona airport, some 11 km. (7 miles) from the provincial capital. Taxis take about 20 minutes from the airport to Gerona, from where buses leave to all Costa Brava resorts.

Alicante. El Altet, 12 km. (7½ miles) southwest of the city centre, handles domestic and international flights. An airport bus service runs between the airport and the bus station in the city centre, with several pick-up points en route.

Málaga. The Costa del Sol is served by Málaga's Aeropuerto Internacional (or Nacional if you have a connecting flight within Spain). These airports are halfway between Málaga and Torremolinos. There are bus services every 30 minutes to Málaga, Torremolinos and Benalmádena-Costa. Trains stop beside the airports, providing a half-hourly train connection to the coastal resorts between Málaga and Fuengirola. There are no ticket offices on the platforms; pay on the train, with a low-denomination note.

Majorca. Son San Juan airport has two terminals; one handles scheduled flights, the other is reserved for charter planes. Taxis and coaches link the airport with Palma, a 15-minute trip. Official taxi fares are posted by the airport exit doors. The coach service operates to the railway station at Plaça de Espanya every half hour from early morning till around midnight.

Ibiza's modern terminal serves both international and domestic flights. Airline buses link the airport with the centre of Ibiza Town, a 15-minute ride. There is a public bus service every hour.

Canary Islands. All the islands in the archipelago except Gomera now have airports with modern facilities. The biggest and busiest airport is at Gando, Gran Canaria, about half-way between Las Palmas and the south-coast resorts.

Bilbao, Santiago de Compostela, Seville and Valencia also have international airports.

Porter!	**¡Mozo!**
Taxi	**¡Taxi!**
Where's the bus for...?	**¿Dónde está el autobús para...?**

BEGGING

All towns in Spain have their share of beggars, often accompanied by children. They wait in streets and outside museums, cathedrals and other places where people have money in their hand. Most sit sadly and passively; others can be extremely persistent. Some may try to present you with a flower or other object, before demanding payment. Don't be intimidated into giving money if you do not wish to; remain calm and firm and you'll be left alone.

BICYCLE and MOTORCYCLE HIRE
(bicicletas y motocicletas de alquiler)

In some resorts, bicycles or mopeds may be hired by the hour or day.

Motorbikes, powerful enough for two people, can be as expensive to hire as a car. Use of crash helmets is obligatory, whatever the capacity of the engine.

I'd like to hire a bicycle.	**Quisiera alquilar una bicicleta.**
How much is it per day/week?	**¿Cuánto cobran por día/semana?**

CAMPING

For a complete list and a map of approved campsites in Spain, consult the Spanish National Tourist Office in your country or write to Federación Española de Empresarios de Camping y Centros de Vacaciones: *General Oraa, 52, 2ºD, 28006 Madrid; tel. (91) 262 99 94*

There are official campsites throughout the country. Facilities vary, according to the category, but most have electricity and running water. Some have shops, small playgrounds for children, restaurants, swimming pools and even launderettes.

Ask permission before camping on private land.

May we camp here?	**¿Podemos acampar aquí?**

CAR RENTAL *(coches de alquiler)*

See also DRIVING IN SPAIN

International and local car-hire firms have offices all over Spain, at airports and in town centres. Your hotel receptionist, a travel agency or tourist office can help you make arrangements. The law requires that you have an International Driving Permit, but in practice your national licence will probably be sufficient. (A translation in Spanish can prove useful in case of an accident.)

Many agencies set a minimum age for car hire at 21. A deposit, as well as advance payment of the estimated hire charge, is generally required, although holders of major credit cards are usually exempt from this. A tax of 12% (4% in the Canary Islands) is normally added to the total. Third-party insurance is automatically included, but full collision coverage is optional. Different terms of hire may be available, the choice depending on the mileage you intend to do. Ask for any seasonal deals available.

I'd like to rent a car.	Quisiera alquilar un coche.
for tomorrow	para mañana
for one day/a week	por un día/una semana
Please include full insurance coverage.	Haga el favor de incluir el seguro a todo riesgo.

CHILDREN

The family-minded Spaniards take their children anywhere and at any time. (You may have a domestic insurrection when your children discover that their Spanish counterparts stay up three or four hours later than they do. A prolonged siesta compensates for this precocious enjoyment of Spanish nightlife.)

Tourists travelling with children can count on a tolerant and welcoming attitude. To get the most out of a family holiday, vary the cultural programme with a detour to an open-air swimming pool or a trip to the zoo. Several towns have fun fairs or amusement parks; ask at the tourist office for suggestions.

Spain also has dozens of "waterparks", especially along the coast (Aquapark, Marineland, Hidropark, etc.) with multitudes of attractions for all the family.

It's easy to keep children entertained at seaside resorts. But don't let your guard down: never lose sight of them on a crowded beach and keep an eye on the flag announcing dangerous currents or tides.

Very few hotels have resident baby-sitters, but most will engage one for you. Tourists on a package holiday can make arrangements for baby-sitting at their travel agency.

Can you get me a baby-sitter for tonight?	¿Puede conseguirme una persona para cuidar los niños esta noche?

CIGARETTES, CIGARS, TOBACCO (cigarrillos, puros, tabaco)

Most Spanish cigarettes are made of strong, black tobacco with a high nicotine content. Imported foreign brands are up to three times the price of local makes, though foreign brands produced in Spain under licence can be less expensive than when bought at home. Locally made cigars are cheap and reasonably good. Canary Islands cigars are excellent; Cuban cigars are also readily available. Pipe smokers may find the local tobacco somewhat rough.

Tabacalera S.A. is the government tobacco monopoly: they supply their official shops, tabacos, who supply everybody else. Cigarette shops sell postage stamps, too.

A packet of ...	Un paquete de ...
A box of matches, please.	Una caja de cerillas, por favor.
filter-tipped	con filtro
without filter	sin filtro

CLIMATE AND CLOTHING

The Spanish climate is as varied as the people; holiday clothing will range from ski suits to monokinis. In summer, you will be unlucky not to have fine, warm weather, but take sweaters and wraps for the evening. A light raincoat is always a useful standby, especially if travelling in the north. Don't forget comfortable walking shoes; aching, bruised feet can ruin a holiday!

In Spain, where wearing a bikini was once considered daring, topless bathing has become fairly common. For walking to or from the beach, shirts or informal dresses should be worn over bathing costumes; the same applies when in towns.

When visiting churches, women no longer have to cover their heads. As a mark of respect, more sober clothing—no shorts or mini-skirts—should be worn.

263

Average daily temperatures (Fahrenheit/Celsius):

Temperatures		Jan	Feb	Mar	Apr	May	Jun	Jul	Aug	Sep	Oct	Nov	Dec
in degrees Fahrenheit:													
Madrid	max.	47	52	59	65	70	80	87	85	77	65	55	48
	min.	35	36	41	45	50	58	63	63	57	49	42	36
Barcelona	max.	55	57	60	65	71	78	82	82	77	69	62	56
	min.	43	45	48	52	57	65	69	69	66	58	51	46
Seville	max.	59	63	69	74	80	90	98	98	90	78	68	60
	min.	42	44	48	52	56	63	67	67	64	57	50	44
and in degrees Celsius:													
Madrid	max.	9	11	15	18	21	27	31	30	25	19	13	9
	min.	2	2	5	7	10	15	17	17	14	10	5	2
Barcelona	max.	13	14	16	18	21	25	28	28	25	21	16	13
	min.	6	7	9	11	14	18	21	21	19	15	11	8
Seville	max.	15	17	20	24	27	32	36	36	32	26	20	16
	min.	6	7	9	11	13	17	20	20	18	14	10	7

*Minimum temperatures are measured just before sunrise, maximum temperatures in the afternoon.

COMMUNICATIONS

Post Office *(Correo)*: Main post offices provide facilities for sending telexes and telefaxes as well as a 24-hour telegram service. They also have facilities for sending money orders. You cannot usually telephone from post offices.

Hours vary slightly, but post offices are generally open from 9 a.m. to 1 or 2 p.m. and from 4 or 5 to 6 or 7 p.m. Mondays to Fridays and on Saturday mornings.

Stamps are also on sale from tobacconists *(tabacos)*, identified by a letter T outlined on a stylized tobacco leaf on the exterior of the shop. Postboxes *(buzón)* are yellow, except red ones for express mail.

Telegrams *(telegrama)*. You can send telegrams from post offices, or phone them (the number varies from town to town).

Poste restante/general delivery. If you don't know beforehand where you'll be staying, you can have your mail sent to you *lista de correos*. Take your passport to the post office as identification and be prepared to pay a small fee for each letter received.

Telephone *(teléfono)*. You can make international calls from public telephones. These booths are equipped with instructions in English. If calling long distance, go armed with a pile of 5, 25 and 50 peseta coins. Insert coins before dialling, adding more to prolong the call. Large towns have telephone exchanges, open all day.

In resort areas, there are operator-assisted long-distance telephone installations on or near busy beaches. In addition, private shops operate telephone offices where you can dial directly and pay the owner the sum shown on the meter after the call.

Telephone calls abroad are cheaper between 10 p.m. and 8 a.m. There is no weekend cheap rate.

To make a reverse-charge (collect) call, ask for *cobro revertido*. For a personal (person-to-person) call, specify *persona a persona*. Dial 003 for enquiries.

Area codes for some towns: Alicante 96, Barcelona 93, Benidorm 96, Granada 958, Ibiza and Palma de Mallorca 971, Las Palmas 928, Madrid 91, Málaga, Fuengirola and Torremolinos 952, Santiago de Compostela 981 Sevilla 954.

To make a direct international call from Spain, dial 07 and wait for a high-pitched dialling tone. Dial the country code, followed by the area code, omitting the initial 0, then the telephone number.

Some country codes:

Australia	(07) 61
Canada	(07) 1
Eire	(07) 353
New Zealand	(07) 64
U.K.	(07) 44
U.S.A.	(07) 1

When telephoning Spain from Britain, dial 010 34, then the number, omitting the initial

9 of the area code. To call from the U.S., dial 011 34 then the local number without the initial 9.

Can you get me this number in ...	**Puede comunicarme con este número en ...**
A stamp for this letter/postcard, please.	**Por favor, un sello para esta carta/ tarjeta postal.**
express	**urgente**
airmail	**vía aérea**
registered	**certificado**
I would like to send a telegram to...	**Quisiera mandar un telegrama a ...**
Have you received any mail for ...?	**¿Ha recibido correo para ...?**

COMPLAINTS

Tourism is Spain's leading industry and the government takes complaints from tourists very seriously.

Hotels and restaurants. The majority of disputes are due to misunderstandings and linguistic difficulties and should not be exaggerated. As your host wants to keep both his reputation and his licence, you'll usually find him amenable to reason. In the event of a serious problem, you can demand a complaint form *(Hoja Oficial de Reclamación)*, which all hotels and restaurants are required by law to have available. The original of this triplicate document should be sent to the regional office of the Ministry of Tourism; one copy stays with the establishment against which the complaint is registered and you keep the third.

Recent legislation greatly strengthens the consumer's hand. Many towns now maintain a consumer office: OMIC *(Oficina Municipal de Información al Consumidor)*. Police and *Guardia Civil* stations have forms in English for complaints. The tourist office should normally be able to direct you to the appropriate quarter.

CONTRACEPTION

With the growing problem of AIDS *(SIDA)* in the country, strong Roman Catholic opposition has been overcome and contraceptives are easily available from pharmacies, public toilets and other, less likely, places. The word for a condom is *preservativo*.

CRIME AND THEFT

As in most European countries, crime in Spain appears to be escalating. Don't carry valuables ostentatiously; keep purses and wallets zipped away, carry any large banknotes, traveller's cheques and documents in a money belt. Do not take objects of value to the beach. Lock cars and never leave bags, cameras, etc., visible. Try not to keep all your eggs in one basket—if a purse is stolen, it's a relief to have spare cash sewn away elsewhere.

Many hotels provide safe deposit facilities. At campsites too, it's worth enquiring whether you can leave valuables in a safe.

Should you suffer a theft or break-in, report it to the *Guardia Civil*. If your passport has been stolen, they will issue you with a document enabling you to leave the country. You will need a signed police form to claim for insured items.

I want to report a theft.	**Quiero denunciar un robo.**
My ... has been stolen.	**Me han robado el/la ...**
handbag	**bolso**
money	**dinero**
passport	**pasaporte**
ticket	**billete**
wallet	**cartera**

CUSTOMS, ENTRY AND EXIT REGULATIONS

Nationals of Great Britain, Eire, the U.S., Canada, Australia and New Zealand need only a valid passport to visit Spain, and even this requirement is waived for the British, who may enter on a visitor's passport. A national identity card is sufficient for citizens of Western European countries.

Though visitors to Spain are not currently subject to any health requirements, it is always wise to check with a travel agent before departure in case inoculation certificates are needed.

Currency restrictions: There are no restrictions on the amount of local and foreign currency brought into the country. Non-residents must declare sums exceeding 100,000 pesetas in local currency or 500,000 pesetas in foreign currency on entry to avoid possible problems on departure.

A maximum of 100,000 pesetas may be exported in local currency. Permission must be obtained from the monetary authorities for larger sums. The amount of money taken out of the country must not be greater than that declared on arrival.

Reimbursement of sales tax. Foreign visitors from outside the European Community can have the VAT/sales tax (IVA) refunded on larger purchases in the major stores. Complete a form at the shop, have it stamped and signed and present it at the customs on departure, along with the goods. The rebate will be forwarded to you at home.

DRIVING IN SPAIN

See also CUSTOMS, ENTRY AND EXIT REGULATIONS GETTING TO SPAIN.

To bring your car into Spain you will require:

- an International Driving Permit (not obligatory for citizens of most Western European countries—ask your automobile association—but recommended in case of difficulties with the police as it carries a Spanish translation) or a legalized and certified translation of your home licence
- car registration papers
- Green Card—an extension to your regular insurance policy, making it valid in foreign countries. (Advised, but not obligatory.)

With your certificate of insurance, you are strongly recommended to carry a bail bond. If you injure someone in an accident in Spain, you can be imprisoned while the accident is being investigated. This bond will bail you out. Apply to your home automobile association or insurance company.

A nationality sticker must be displayed prominently on the back of your car. If your car is right hand drive, you must adjust the headlights or have anti-dazzle strips on them. Spanish law requires you to carry a complete set of spare bulbs.

Drivers and front seat passengers must wear seat belts when driving outside towns. (Spot fines can be imposed.) Motorcycle riders and their passengers are required to wear crash helmets.

No person under 18 years of age may drive or ride a vehicle over 75cc.

Travellers driving through France should note that a red warning triangle must be carried.

Driving regulations. Drive on the right (drivers from the U.K. and Eire should pay special attention when starting off first thing in the morning or after a stop); overtake (pass) on the left. Spanish drivers often use their horn when passing other vehicles. Truck and lorry drivers will often wave you on (by hand signals or by flashing their right indicator) when it is clear ahead to overtake. Try not to be impatient; a large percentage of accidents in Spain occur when passing.

As in France, the car coming from the right has priority. This rule is waived in the case of minor roads which join main roads. If in doubt, slow right down.

Motorways *(autopista/autovía).* Spain's motorways are mainly concentrated in the north and along the east coast. On *autopistas*, a toll is charged. *Autovías* are toll free.

On some *autopistas*, you collect a ticket on entering and pay the sum due when you leave the motorway. Others have a flat fee for each segment, paid at each toll *(peaje)* along the way. Change is given. Note that on motorways in Catalonia, the word for "exit" is *sortida*, while in the rest of Spain, it is *salida*.

Speed limits. 120 kph (75 mph) on motorways, 100 kph (62 mph) or 90 kph (56 mph) on other roads, 60 kph (36 mph) in towns and built-up areas. Cars towing caravans

The customs table below shows what you can carry into Spain duty free.

	Cigarettes		Cigars		Tobacco	Spirits	Wine	Perfume		Toilet water
1)	400	or	100	or	500 g.	1 l.	2 l.	50 g.		1 l.
2)	300	or	75	or	400 g.	1½ l. and	5 l.	75 g.	and	⅜ l.
3)	200		50		250 g.	1 l.	2 l.	50 g.		¼ l.

1) Visitors arriving from countries outside Europe.
2) Visitors arriving from EEC countries with non-duty-free items (tax paid).
3) Visitors from EEC countries with duty-free items, or from other European countries.

Fluid measures

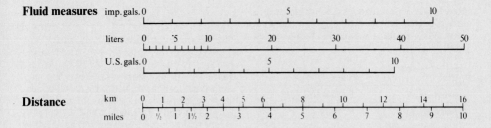

Distance

(trailers) are restricted to 80 kph (50 mph) on the open road.

Traffic lights. Red means stop before the line. Red and amber together also mean stop. Amber alone means stop unless you have crossed the line and cannot go back. Green means go.

Headlights: Should be used in all poor weather conditions and, of course, in tunnels and at night.

Drinking and driving. Don't! The legal limit is 35 mg. of alcohol in 100 ml. of breath, 80 mg. alcohol in 100 ml. of blood. Fines can be severe.

Driving in cities. Nerve-wracking traffic jams are part of the way of life in big cities. (Street vendors may take advantage of the situation to offer you lottery tickets, snacks or assorted bric-a-brac.) To avoid the worst, try to drive in or through cities during the hours of the afternoon siesta break (roughly between 3 and 5 p.m.).

Parking. If driving in cities sometimes resembles a bad dream, parking can be a positive nightmare. Some towns have zones regulating parking during working hours *(horas laborables)*, requiring you to have a parking permit covering the amount of time you need to stay. Under the old system, tickets are sold at tobacconists; newer setups have ticket-vending machines on the streets. You must display your permit inside your front window. These controlled areas, where parking space is at a premium, are carefully patrolled. Don't take the chance on parking in an illegal place; even tourists' cars do not always escape the *grúa* (crane) that hauls away badly parked vehicles.

Supervised car parks are a good solution and underground parking facilities *(aparcamiento subterráneo)* are ever more abundant in cities.

It is forbidden to park the car facing oncoming traffic.

Traffic police. The Traffic Civil Guard *(Guardia Civil de Tráfico)* patrols the highways. Always in pairs, these capable characters are courteous, good mechanics and will stop to help anyone in trouble.

The police are, however, severe on lawbreakers. The most frequent offences include:

● speeding
● travelling too close to the car in front
● overtaking without flashing your indicator
● travelling at night with a burnt-out light

Fines are payable on the spot.

Accidents. In case of accident, dial the police emergency number, 092. Get the driver's name and licence numbers of any other vehicles involved and the names and addresses of any witnesses. Avoid admitting guilt or signing any document that you do not understand.

Fuel and oil: Service stations, once sparsely dotted around the countryside, are now plentiful, particularly in tourist areas, but it's a good idea to keep an eye on the gauge in deserted areas.

Fuel is theoretically available in super (97 octane), normal (92 octane), unleaded (95 octane) and diesel. But not every petrol station carries the full range. It is customary to give the attendant a coin or two as a tip.

Breakdowns. Spare parts are most readily available for Spanish-built cars. For some other brands, spares may be difficult to find. Make sure your car is in top shape before you leave home.

If you have a breakdown on the motorway, use one of the strategically positioned emergency telephones to call for help. Otherwise call the *Guardia Civil*.

Road signs. Most road signs are the standard pictographs used throughout Europe. However, you may encounter these written signs:

¡Alto!	*Stop!*
Apagar luces	*Switch off lights*
Aparcamiento	*Parking*
Autopista (de peaje)	*(Toll)motorway/ expressway*
Calzada deteriorada	*Bad road*
Calzada estrecha	*Narrow road*
Ceda el paso	*Give way (Yield)*
Cruce peligroso	*Dangerous crossroads*
Cuidado	*Caution*
Curva peligrosa	*Dangerous bend*
Desprendimientos	*Landslides*
Despacio	*Slow*
Desviación	*Diversion (Detour)*
Encender luces	*Switch on lights*
Escuela	*School*
Grúa	*Tow-away area*
Peligro	*Danger*
Prohibido adelantar	*No overtaking (passing)*
Prohibido aparcar	*No parking*
Puesto de socorro	*First-aid post*
Salida (de camiones)	*(Lorry/Truck) exit*
(international) driving licence	**carné de conducir (internacional)**
car registration papers	**permiso de circulación**
green card	**carta verde**
Is this the road for...?	**¿Es ésta la carretera hacia...?**
Full tank please. normal super unleaded	**Lleno, por favor. normal super sin plomo**
Can I park here?	**¿Puedo aparcar aquí?**
Please check the oil/tyres/battery.	**Por favor, controle el aceite/los neumáticos/ la batería.**
I've had a breakdown.	**Mi coche se ha estropeado.**
There's been an accident.	**Ha habido un accidente.**

DRUGS

The Spanish attitude to soft drugs has changed several times in the post-Franco years; it is currently an offence to possess them. (In student bars especially, this may seem hard to believe; smoking marijuana is fairly commonplace.) The problem of hard drugs, especially in Madrid and Barcelona, is very real and there is every indication that the Spanish drug squad *(división especial antidroga)* is very harsh on foreigners who deal and indulge in drugs. The obvious advice to travellers is—don't!

ELECTRIC CURRENT
(corriente eléctrica)

Nationwide, 220-volt A.C. is becoming standard, but older installations of 110 and 125 volts can still be found. Check before plugging in. Visitors from North America will need a transformer unless they have dual-voltage travel appliances.

Sockets (outlets) take round, two-pin plugs, so you will probably need an international adaptor plug, on sale at hardware stores or airports.

What is the voltage?	**¿Cuál es el voltaje?**
an adaptor/a battery	**un adaptador/una pila**

EMBASSIES AND CONSULATES
(embajada, consulado)

Contact the embassy or consulate of your home country when in trouble (loss of passport, problems with the police, serious accidents). All embassies are in Madrid. Many countries also maintain consulates in other Spanish cities. Check in the telephone book under "Consulado". Embassies in the capital (prefix 91 if telephoning from outside the city):

Australia. Paseo de la Castellana, 143; tel. 279 85 04

Canada. Núñez de Balboa, 35; tel. 431 43 00

Denmark. Claudio Coello, 91-4°; tel. 431 84 45

Eire. Claudio Coello, 73; tel. 276 35 00/8/9

Finland. Paseo de la Castellana, 15; tel. 419 61 72

India. Avenida Pio XII, 30; tel. 457 02 09

Japan. C. Joaquín Costa, 29; tel. 262 55 46
Netherlands. Paseo de la Castellana, 178; tel. 458 21 00
New Zealand. See under U.K.
Norway. Edificio Pirámide, Paseo de la Castellana, 31; tel. 410 68 63
South Africa. Claudio Coello, 91; tel. 227 31 56
Sweden. Caracas, 25; tel. 419 75 50
U.K. Fernando el Santo, 16; tel. 419 02 08
U.S.A. Serrano, 75; tel. 276 34 00

There are consulates or consular representatives in several towns. Here is a selection—they will be able to help you directly or refer you to a nearer consulate.

U.K.
Madrid. Marquez de la Ensenada, 16; tel. 532 52 17
Barcelona. Avinguda Diagonal, 477-13º; tel. (93) 322 21 51
Málaga. Edificio Duquesa, C. Duquesa de Parcent, 4; tel. (952) 21 75 71
Seville. Plaza Nueva, 8, (dpdo); tel. (954) 22 88 75
Alicante. Plaza Calvo Sotelo, 1/2-1º; tel. (96) 21 61 90/21 60 22
Las Palmas. Edificio Catalunya, C. Luis Morote, 6-3º; tel. (928) 26 25 08
Palma de Mallorca. Plaça Major, 3d, tel. (971) 71 24 45/71 20 85

U.S.A.
The Madrid consulate is at the same address as the embassy. There are consular representatives in several cities, but the only other full-scale consulate is in Barcelona at:
Via Laietana, 33, Box 5; tel. (93) 319 95 50

Canada
Barcelona. Via Augusta, 125-3º; tel. (93) 209 06 34
Málaga. Plaza de la Malagueta, 3; tel. (952) 22 33 46
Seville. Avenida de la Constitución, 30, local 4; tel. (954) 22 94 13

Eire
Barcelona. Torre Oeste, Gran Via Carles III, 94, 10º2a; tel. (93) 330 96 52
Fuengirola (near Málaga). Avenida los Boliches, S/N, Los Boliches; tel. (952) 47 51 08

Consular officers are there to help nationals of their countries in trouble. Their powers are, however, limited. The following is an indication of what they can and cannot do.

A Consul can:
• issue emergency passports
• contact relatives and friends and ask them to help you with money or tickets
• advise on how to transfer funds
• usually (in an emergency) advance money against a small cheque supported by a banker's card
• provide a list of local lawyers, interpreters and doctors
• arrange for next of kin to be informed of an accident or a death and advise on procedures
• contact nationals who are arrested or in prison and, in certain cases, arrange for messages to be sent to relatives or friends
• give some guidance on organizations experienced in tracing missing persons

A Consul cannot:
• pay your hotel, medical or any other bills
• pay for travel tickets, except in very special circumstances
• undertake work more properly done by travel representatives, airlines, banks or motoring organizations
• get better treatment for you in hospital (or prison) than is provided for nationals
• give legal advice, instigate court proceedings on your behalf or interfere in local judicial procedures to get you out of prison
• investigate a crime
• formally assist dual nationals in the country of their second nationality
• obtain work or a work permit for you

EMERGENCIES

If you have a real crisis, dial the emergency number **006** (in the Basque country, **088**)
Depending on the nature of the emergency, refer to the separate entries in this section such as EMBASSIES AND CONSULATES, HEALTH AND MEDICAL CARE, POLICE. The following are some useful (with luck unnecessary) words, which you might like to learn.

Careful	**Cuidado**
Fire	**Fuego**
Help	**Socorro**
Police	**Policía**
Stop	**Deténgase**
Stop thief	**Al ladrón**

FESTIVALS OF MUSIC, DRAMA AND DANCE

Spaniards love flamboyant festivities, but there are also more "serious" festivals of a highly professional nature. These are the main such events:

Festival of Music and Dance in Granada. June–July (concerts, comic and serious opera, classical and contemporary dance and, of course, flamenco).

International Festival of Music in Barcelona. September–October (orchestras, choirs and soloists).

International Festival of Santander. Last fortnight of July and first two weeks of August (exclusively Greek, Latin and Mediterranean classical theatre).

National Festival of Classical Theatre in Almagro. Three weeks in September (National and international classical theatre).

International Festival of Music and Dance in Seville. Two weeks in September (every two years).

Madrid Autumn Festival. Mid-September to early October (concerts, opera, theatre, classical and modern dance).

International Film Festival in San Sebastián. September (short and long films).

International Film Week in Valladolid. October (official programme and selection of other films).

See also pp. 238–239.

GETTING TO SPAIN

See also CUSTOMS, ENTRY AND EXIT REGULATIONS and DRIVING IN SPAIN.

See a reliable travel agent or the Spanish tourist office in your home country well before departure for help with timetables, budget and personal requirements.

By Air

Madrid and Barcelona are Spain's principal international airports, but a vast selection of direct flights link Britain's main airports with those in Spain. Non-stop flights to Madrid leave from several points in the U.S. and Canada. Other long-haul flights are routed via another European gateway city, offering the possibility of a stopover.

The least expensive formula for transatlantic tourists travelling on their own is usually the Advance Booking Charter (ABC) flight or the APEX ticket, payable two to six weeks in advance (depending on the destination). One-Stop Inclusive-Tour Charter (OTC) packages combine air travel with hotel and other ground arrangements at bargain prices. Apart from package tours, available from airlines and travel agencies, you can find interesting alternatives organized by private companies or church groups.

Good deals may involve travelling mid-week or booking a certain number of weeks in advance. If possible, shop around; no single travel agent can know of all the options on offer.

The same applies for package holidays; there is such an enormous choice available, that you should be able to find almost exactly what you want.

Even if you are not travelling with a "package holiday", it is worth asking for any spare seats—often sold off cheaply—on planes carrying tour groups.

Approximate flying times: London–Madrid/Barcelona 2 hours, London–Canary Islands 4 hours, New York–Madrid 6½ hours, Montreal–Madrid 7½ hours.

By Road

Toll motorways (expressways) run across France, skirting Paris, to the Spanish border near Biarritz. There are 17 border points between France and Spain and another two if you travel through Andorra. The Hendaye-Irún border is the best for those travelling to the north or west of Spain. Travellers going to Catalonia and the east coast may choose to stay on the French motorway to Toulouse and, from there, either take the A61 motorway to Narbonne, then the A9 to the border, crossing at La Junquera, or the RN20, crossing at Puigcerdà.

Visitors travelling from Britain and Eire during the summer should be sure to have a cross-Channel reservation.

For British travellers visiting the north of Spain, a ferry links Plymouth to Santander. Otherwise plan on a drive through France. The principal ferry routes link Dover and Folkestone with Dunkirk; Newhaven with Dieppe; Portsmouth with Roscoff; Rosslare, Ireland with Le Havre and Cherbourg; Cork, Ireland with Le Havre and Roscoff.

The hovercraft from Dover to Calais or Boulogne takes about 35 minutes and costs a little more than the ferry.

By Rail

For full information about the range of special tickets available, contact the Spanish national railways:

RENFE, General Agency for Europe, 1–3 Av. Marceau, 75115 Paris

Any serious complaints, that cannot be resolved otherwise, should be addressed to this office.

Rail passes, worthwhile for those planning to travel extensively by train, (in Spain and elsewhere in Europe) are: *Eurailpass:* Those resident outside Europe and North Africa can purchase this flat-rate, unlimited-mileage pass, valid for first-class rail travel in 16 European countries including Spain. It also covers some private railways, buses and many ferries and steamers. You must sign up before you leave home. The *Eurail Saverpass* is a special 1st-class ticket for three or more people travelling together (two or more between October 1 and March 31), while the *Eurail Flexipass*, for North Americans, Mexicans, Australians and New Zealanders (also for 1st class), offers more flexibility for nine days' travel within a 21-day period. The *Eurail Youthpass*, for travellers under 26 years of age, allows one- or two-months' unlimited 2nd-class rail journeys, but surcharges must be paid for travel on fast trains like EuroCity (EC), InterCity (IC), TGV, Rapide, etc. and for certain ferry-crossings during high season. The *Inter-Rail card* permits 30 days of unlimited rail travel in participating European countries and Morocco to people under 26. The *Rail Europ S* ticket entitles senior citizens to purchase train tickets at reduced prices.

Visitors from abroad can buy the *RENFE Tourist Card* for a reasonable price, valid for unlimited rail travel within the country for periods of 8, 15 or 22 days. The *Chequetrén*, valid for 15% extra travel, can be used by individuals and groups.

Rail tickets for trips between Britain and Spain can be obtained from:

European Rail Travel Centre, P.O. Box 303, Victoria, London SW1 1JY; tel. (01) 834 2345

There is no Spanish Railways Office in Britain; couchette and sleeper reservations through France can be made with French Railways in Piccadilly, London W1. Spanish rail timetables are available from:

BAS Overseas Publications, 50a, Sheen Lane, London SW14; tel. (01) 876 2131

All change! Passengers generally have to change trains at the Spanish frontier, as the Spanish tracks are of a wider gauge than the French (the exceptions are the Talgo and the Trans-Europ-Express, which have adjustable axles). Seat and sleeper reservations are compulsory in Spain on longer train journeys.

By coach

Regular coach services operate from major European cities to Spain.

Companies operating from Britain:

Euroways Express Coaches Ltd., 52 Grosvenor Gdns, Victoria, London SW1; tel. (01) 730 8235

SSS International, 138 Eversholt St., London NW1 1BL; tel. (01) 388 1732

GUIDES AND INTERPRETERS
(guía; intérprete)

Local tourist offices, hotels and travel agencies will refer you to qualified guides and interpreters should you wish a personally directed tour or help with business negotiations.

In Madrid, the Asociación Profesional de Informadores Turísticos can provide officially accredited guides and interpreters for business meetings or tours. The address is:

Calle Ferraz, 82, bajo drcha, 28008 Madrid; tel. 242 12 14

HAGGLING

The days of haggling are long past. Prices are marked; PVP means *precio de venta al público*, or retail price, and merchants stick to them. However, street vendors, such as in the Madrid flea market (Rastro), may be open to negotiation.

HAIRDRESSERS AND BARBERS
(peluquería; barbería)

Many hotels have their own salons and the standard is generally good. You may see much lower prices displayed in the windows of independent salons. Prices vary widely according to the class of establishment.

Not too much off (here).	No corte mucho (aquí).	Where is the nearest (all-night) pharmacy?	¿Dónde está la farmacia (de guardia) más cercana?
A little more off (here).	Un poco más (aquí).	I need a doctor/ dentist.	Necesito un médico/ dentista.
haircut	corte	an ambulance	una ambulancia
shampoo and set	lavado y marcado	hospital	hospital
blow-dry	modelado	I've a pain here.	Me duele aquí.
permanent wave	permanente		
a colour rinse/dye	champú colorante/tinte		
a colour chart	un muestrario de tintes		

HEALTH AND MEDICAL CARE

If you already have a health-insurance policy, make sure that it covers you while abroad. Otherwise, take out a policy at your insurance company, automobile association or travel agency before leaving home. The Spanish tourist insurance, ASTES, covers doctor's fees and hospital treatment in the event of accident or illness.

Usually an insurance package includes medical treatment, repatriation, compensation for permanent consequences of accident or illness, as well as theft and loss of valuables. If planning to do "high-risk" sports, such as skiing or mountain climbing, check that these are covered; they usually require an additional premium.

Visitors from EEC countries with corresponding health-insurance facilities are entitled to medical and hospital treatment under the Spanish social security system. Before leaving home, ensure that you are eligible and have the appropriate forms. In Britain, details can be obtained from your local Health Authority Office or from:

Labour Attaché of the Spanish Embassy, 20 Peel St., London W8; tel. (01) 221 0098

For minor ailments, visit the local first-aid post (ambulatorio or permanencia).

Pharmacies (farmacia). After hours, one shop in each area is always on duty for emergencies. Its address is posted daily in all other pharmacy windows and published in the newspapers.

It is a sensible precaution to go equipped with a basic kit of adhesive plaster, antiseptic cream, aspirin, etc. Take an adequate supply of any prescribed medicines.

HITCH-HIKING (autostop)

Hitch-hiking is permitted everywhere in Spain except on motorways and is, on the whole, safe. Women stand a better chance than men of a lift, but are strongly advised to hitch-hike in pairs.

Can you give me/us a lift to ...?	¿Puede llevarme/ llevarnos a ...?

HOURS OF OPENING

See also under COMMUNICATIONS and MONEY MATTERS

Spain traditionally takes a siesta in the afternoon, which accounts for the extended lunch break, still respected by shops and most offices. Unfortunately this relaxed and relaxing Mediterranean custom is gradually becoming an anachronism for modern Spanish business people, whose hours are tending to concord with their European counterparts.

Restaurants start serving lunch about 1 p.m. Dinner begins between 8 and 10 p.m.

While there are regional and seasonal variations, here are some general guidelines to working hours in Spain:

Offices. Generally from 9 a.m. to 2 p.m. and 4.30 to 7 p.m., Monday to Friday in winter; from 8.30 a.m. to 3 p.m. in summer.

Shops. 9.30 a.m. to 1.30 p.m. and 4 or 5 to 8 p.m. Monday to Friday, 9.30 a.m. to 2 p.m. on Saturdays; department stores generally open from 10 a.m. to 8 p.m. without a break, Monday to Saturday.

Tourist information offices. 10 a.m. to 1 p.m. and 4 to 7 p.m., Monday to Friday, and 10 a.m. to 1 p.m. on Saturdays.

Main museums: Prado Museum (Madrid) 9 a.m. to 7 p.m., 9 a.m. to 2 p.m. Sunday (closed Monday); National Archaeological Museum (Madrid) 9.15 a.m. to 1.45 p.m. (closed Monday); National Museum of Contemporary Art (Madrid) 10 a.m. to 6 p.m. (closed Sunday and Monday); Catalonian Art Museum (Barcelona) 9 a.m. to 2 p.m. (closed Monday); Picasso Museum (Barcelona) 10 a.m. to 7 p.m. (closed Sunday p.m. and Monday); National Sculpture Museum (Valladolid) 10 a.m. to 1.30 p.m., 4 to 7 p.m. (closed Sunday p.m.); Museum and Home of El Greco (Toledo) 10 a.m. to 2 p.m., 4 to 6 p.m. (closed Sunday p.m. and Monday). Most museums are closed on public holidays.

LANGUAGE

After Chinese and English, the most widely spoken language in the world is Spanish—at home from Pamplona to Patagonia. Since the end of the Franco era, Spain's regional languages have enjoyed a renaissance. They range from the mysterious Basque to Galician, a sort of half-way between Spanish and Portuguese. With the exception of fierce nationalists, particularly in Catalonia, virtually everyone in Spain will cheerfully speak Spanish. There is wide variety of regional accents.

In tourist resorts, the problem may be to find someone who will speak Spanish—hotel and restaurant staff are proud to display their knowledge of English, German or French. It may not be extensive though, and menu translations can be somewhat peculiar.

The Berlitz phrase book **Spanish for Travellers** covers just about all situations you are likely to encounter in your travels in Spain. The Berlitz Spanish-English/English-Spanish pocket dictionary contains a 12,500 word glossary of each language, plus a menu-reader supplement.

Do you speak English?	**¿Habla usted inglés?**
I don't speak Spanish.	**No hablo español.**

LOST PROPERTY

Check first at your hotel or campsite reception desk. Also ask in any likely shops, cafés or restaurants, where left articles may be kept for a few days before being handed in to the police. If you're not sure where the loss occurred, report it to the nearest police station. You will have to complete a form; as in the case of stolen property, it is necessary to produce an official police form when making an insurance claim.

In Madrid, the lost property office is at:

Plaza de Legazpi, 7

Details of objects left on trains should be reported to the station master at the station of destination. Articles found on trains or in stations should be handed in to the station master, who will issue a receipt for it.

I've lost my wallet/ handbag/passport.	**He perdido mi cartera/ bolso/pasaporte.**
I lost it in ...	**Lo perdí en ...**
this morning *yesterday*	**esta mañana** **ayer**

MAPS AND STREET NAMES

The local tourist office is the best place to get (usually free) maps of the town. Road maps are on sale at most service stations and book shops. The most detailed cartographic information is contained in the official atlas of Spain issued by the Ministry of Public Works. Walking maps may be obtained from the Servicio de Publicaciones del Instituto Geográfico y Nacional:

General Ibañez de Ibero, 3, 28003 Madrid

In Madrid a variety of city maps are sold at newsstands. The municipal bus service issues a chart of all its routes. A city map with metro lines superimposed is posted outside every underground (subway) station, and a pocket-size map of the metro is available free on request at the ticket office in any station. During the Franco era, many streets and squares were renamed to honour heros of his movement. Since his death many have been changed back. Madrid's central thoroughfare, for example, the Avenida de José Antonio, has officially reverted to its traditional name, Gran Vía. Maps cannot keep up with this evolution, so it's worth enquiring of a local inhabitant if you can't find a certain street.

a street plan of...	**un plano de la ciudad de...**
a road map of this region	**un mapa de carreteras de esta región**

MONEY MATTERS

Currency. The monetary unit of Spain is the peseta (abbreviated pta.).
Coins: 1, 2, 5, 10, 25, 50, 100, 200, 500 pesetas.
Banknotes: 100, 200, 500, 1,000, 2,000, 5,000 and 10,000 pesetas.
A 5-peseta coin is traditionally called a *duro*; if someone should quote a price as *10 duros*, he means 50 pesetas.
The 1970 edition of the 100 peseta note is still valid currency, although it is being phased out in favour of the coin.

Banking hours are generally from 8.30 to 4.45 p.m. but some branches close at 2 p.m. Several banks are open on Saturdays until 1 p.m., others are shut all weekend.
Exchange bureaux have longer opening hours. Travel agencies and hotels usually provide an exchange service, but the rate is less advantageous.

Credit cards. All the internationally recognized cards are widely accepted in Spanish stores and at service stations.

Eurocheques. Most hotels and department stores take Eurocheques.

Traveller's cheques. In tourist areas, some shops and all banks, hotels and travel agencies accept them, though you are likely to get a better exchange rate at a national or regional bank. When cashing traveller's cheques, you have to show your passport.

Paying cash. Although many shops and bars will accept payment in sterling or dollars, you are far better off paying in pesetas. Shops invariably give a poor exchange rate.

Where's the nearest bank/currency exchange office?	**¿Dónde está el banco/ la oficina de cambio más cercana?**
What time does the bank open/close?	**¿A qué hora se abre/ se cierra el banco?**
I want to change some pounds/dollars.	**Quiero cambiar libras/ dólares.**
Do you accept traveller's cheques?	**¿Acepta usted cheques de viaje?**
Can I pay with this credit card?	**¿Puedo pagar con esta tarjeta de crédito?**
How much is this?	**¿Cuánto vale?**
Have you anything cheaper?	**¿Tiene usted algo más barato?**

NATIONAL PARKS
(parque nacional)

The Spanish mainland and islands are dotted with national parks, nature reserves and sanctuaries and other protected areas. They offer unique opportunities for hikers and a rich assortment of (sometimes rare) flora and fauna in their natural ecosystem. Most parks have facilities for accommodation—from spartan lodges to *paradores*—or for camping.

In some parks, you can take a guided tour (the Timanfaya park on Lanzarote can be visited on camelback).

Contact a national or local tourist office for documentation about the individual parks.

NEWSPAPERS AND MAGAZINES
(periódico; revista)

In towns and major tourist resorts you can buy British and continental daily papers on their day of publication. Major U.S. magazines as well as U.S.A. Today and the Paris-based *International Herald Tribune* are also widely available.

Several English-language papers and magazines are printed in Spain. The *Guidepost* for visitors to Madrid, the *Iberian Daily Sun*, *Costa Blanca News*, *Ibiza News*, *Majorca Daily Bulletin*, Canaries' *Island Gazette* are some of the publications which provide information about what's on in the region.

Have you any newspapers or magazines in English?	**¿Tiene periódicos o revistas en inglés?**

NOISE

Many people go on holiday to escape the noise and bustle of their daily life; it must be remembered that the Spanish attitude to noise is very different. Blaring radios, hooting horns, shouting and animated gatherings held far into the night are regarded as part of the Spanish ambience, rather than an impingement on neighbours' peace.

Of course you can always ask for a quiet hotel room, looking onto a courtyard or side road, if you fancy an early, undisturbed night.

PETS *(animal doméstico)*

Visitors wishing to take animals into Spain must present, at the border, an internationally recognized certificate of origin and health, signed by an official veterinary surgeon within the month preceding entry. The certificate must include dates of vaccinations, in particular the anti-rabies inoculation.

Many hotels in Spain accept animals. They are not usually permitted in restaurants or shops. (Exceptions are made for guide dogs.)

Before taking your pet abroad, enquire whether there are any quarantine regulations on its return. No animal (apart from racehorses, etc., with special permission) may be reimported into Britain from abroad without spending six months in quarantine.

POLICE *(policía)*

There are three police forces in Spain: the *Policía Municipal*, attached to the local town hall; the *Cuerpo Nacional de Policía*, a national anti-crime unit, who patrol in clearly marked white and blue Citroëns; and the *Guardia Civil*, the national police force, who patrol highways as well as towns. The famous patent-leather hats, worn by the *Guardia Civil* since 1859, are gradually being phased out in favour of more practical headgear and kept for parades and other special occasions.

If you need police assistance, you can call on any of the three. Spanish police are efficient, strict and particularly courteous to foreign visitors.

Where's the nearest police station?	**¿Dónde está la comisaría más cercana?**

PHOTOGRAPHY

Most popular film brands and sizes are available, but they generally cost more than at home. Local shops often give a fast, sometimes one-hour developing service.

The Spanish films Negra and Valca, in black and white, and Negra-color are of good quality and cheaper than the internationally known brands.

In some churches and museums, photography, or the use of flash, is forbidden.

Luggage X-ray machines at airports are nearly always harmless to film. If you prefer, you can always give your film to the person in charge, who will return it once you have passed through the X-ray control.

I'd like a film for this camera.	**Quisiera un rollo para esta máquina.**
a film for black and white/colour pictures	**un rollo en blanco y negro/en color**
a colour-slide film	**un rollo de diapositivas**
35-mm film	**un rollo de treinta y cinco**
super-eight	**super ocho**
How long will it take to develop this film?	**Cuánto tardará en revelar este rollo?**
This camera doesn't work. Can you repair it?	**Esta maquina está estropeada. ¿Puede usted repararla?**

PRICES

(See also under SHOPPING, pp. 230 to 232.)

Inflation in Spain has brought prices more or less in line with those of the rest of Europe. (The Spanish Tourist Board itself wishes to replace the "cheap and cheerful" image by one more up-market.)

The usual rules of thumb apply: resort prices are normally higher than in non-tourist areas; department stores cheaper than trendy boutiques. Most restaurants post menus outside, so you can compare prices before committing yourself.

To give you an idea of what to expect, here's a list of average prices in Spanish pesetas. They must, however, be regarded as approximate, as the cost of living continues to rise. Prices quoted may be subject to a VAT/sales tax (IVA) of either 6 or 12%.

Baby-sitters. 350–400 ptas. per hour.

Camping. *De luxe:* 400–500 ptas. per day per person, 1,500–2,000 ptas. per tent or caravan (trailer). *3rd category:* 300–400 ptas. per day per person, 550–650 ptas. per tent or caravan. Reductions for children.

Car hire. *Ford Fiesta* 2,750 ptas per day, 22 ptas. per km., 36,000 ptas. per week with unlimited mileage. *Ford Escort* 4,000 ptas. per day, 28 ptas. per km., 45,000 ptas. per week with unlimited mileage. *Ford Sierra* 5,500 ptas. per day, 60 ptas. per km.,

275

60,000 ptas. per week with unlimited mileage.

(Prices vary widely according to region and season. Substantial discounts can be obtained by booking in advance through a travel agent in your home country.)

Cigarettes. Spanish brands 50–150 ptas. per pack of 20, imported brands from 180 ptas.

Hotels (double room with bath per night). ***** 22,250 ptas., **** 15,000 ptas., *** 8,500 ptas., ** 5,000 ptas., * 3,500 ptas.

Restaurants. Continental breakfast 400–800 ptas., *plato del día* from 500 ptas., lunch/dinner in good establishment 2,500 ptas. and up, beer 100–250 ptas., coffee 80–150 ptas., Spanish brandy 125–400 ptas.

PUBLIC (LEGAL) HOLIDAYS

January 1	Año Nuevo	New Year's Day
January 6	Epifanía	Epiphany
March 19	San José	St. Joseph's Day
May 1	Día del Trabajo	Labour Day
July 25	Santiago Apóstol	St. James's Day
August 15	Asunción	Assumption
October 12	Día de la Hispanidad	Discovery of America Day (Columbus Day)
November 1	Todos los Santos	All Saints' Day
December 6	Día de la Constitución Española	Constitution Day
December 25	Navidad	Christmas Day
Movable dates:	Jueves Santo	Maundy Thursday
	Viernes Santo	Good Friday
	Lunes de Pascua	Easter Monday (Catalonia only)
	Corpus Christi	Corpus Christi
	Inmaculada Concepción	Immaculate Conception (normally December 8)

These are the Spanish national holidays. There are various regional holidays and special days for different branches of the economy. Consult the local tourist office for information about celebrations, processions and other special events, as well as shop and bank closures.

Are you open tomorrow?   **¿Está abierto mañana?**

RADIO AND TV *(radio; televisión)*

Travellers with medium-wave receivers will be able to pick up the BBC World Service after dark. During the daytime, both the BBC and the Voice of America can be heard on short-wave radios. *"Buenos Días"* is a Madrid radio programme in English, French and German, broadcast on weekdays from 6 to 8 a.m. on 657 megahertz. News broadcasts and tips for tourists alternate with music.

There are two national television channels plus regional networks. In summer some programmes in English are broadcast; consult the newspaper for details. Many hotels have satellite programmes in English, French, Italian and German. BBC 1 can be received by those with a decoder.

RELIGIOUS SERVICES *(servicio religioso)*

The national religion of Spain is Roman Catholic, but other denominations and faiths are represented. Services in English are held in the following churches in Madrid:

Catholic. North American Catholic Church, Av. Alfonso XIII, 165

Protestant. British Embassy Church (Anglican), Núñez de Balboa, 43
The Community Church (Protestant Interdenominational), Padre Damián, 34
Emmanuel Baptist Church, Hernández de Tejeda, 4

Jewish. The synagogue is at Balmes, 3

Church services are conducted in English in many towns in tourist areas.

RESTAURANTS

See also pp. 241–247.

Restaurants are officially graded by forks. Five forks is the top grade. Ratings are, however, awarded according to the facilities available, not the quality of the food. Nor is it necessarily fair to say that you get what you pay for; superb meals can be had in inexpensive and unpretentious restaurants.

Eating establishments come under var-

276

ious names, universal or local. Some definitions:

Bar or **Tasca.** A bar, often with standing space only, serving a range of drinks and *tapas*.

Café. Serves coffee, drinks and snacks.

Cafetería. Coffee shop; not to be confused with the English word cafeteria. The set menu is often very good.

Hostería. Restaurant; frequently specializing in regional cooking.

Pastelería/Confitería. Pastry shop; some serve coffee, tea and drinks.

Dinner *(la cena)* is served from about 8 p.m. in tourist areas; elsewhere from about 9.

To help you order...

We'd like a table for ... people.	**Buscamos una mesa para ... personas.**
Have you a set menu?	**¿Tiene un menú del día?**
The bill, (check) please.	**La cuenta por favor.**
I'd like...	**Quisiera...**
a beer	**una cerveza**
bread	**pan**
coffee/tea	**un café/un té**
cutlery	**los cubiertos**
dessert	**un postre**
fish	**pescado**
fruit	**fruta**
glass	**un vaso**
ice cream	**un helado**
meat	**carne**
menu	**la carta**
milk	**leche**
mineral water	**agua mineral**
napkin	**una servilleta**
potatoes	**patatas**
rice	**arroz**
salad	**una ensalada**
sandwich	**un bocadillo**
sugar	**azúcar**
(iced) water	**agua (con hielo)**
wine	**vino**

and read the menu

aceitunas	*olives*
albóndigas	*meatballs*
almejas	*baby clams*
atún	*tuna*
bacalao	*cod*
besugo	*sea bream*
boquerones	*fresh anchovies*
calamares	*squid*
callos	*tripe*
cangrejo	*crab*
carne	*meat*
carne de vaca	*beef*
cerdo	*pork*
champiñones	*mushrooms*
chorizo	*spicy pork sausage*
cordero	*lamb*
entremeses	*hors-d'œuvres*
fiambres	*cold meat (cuts)*
gambas	*prawns*
huevos	*eggs*
jamón	*ham*
judías	*beans*
langosta	*spiny lobster*
langostinos	*large prawns*
mariscos	*shellfish*
mejillones	*mussels*
melocotón	*peach*
merluza	*hake*
ostras	*oysters*
pastel	*cake*
pimiento	*red pepper*
pollo	*chicken*
pulpo	*octopus*
queso	*cheese*
salchichón	*salami*
salsa	*sauce*
ternera	*veal*
tortilla	*omelette*
trucha	*trout*
uvas	*grapes*

SPAS *(balneario)*

Spain has nearly 100 spa resorts, many dating back to antiquity. All offer a variety of health cures, sports and recreational facilities and a range of hotels. For information and a map showing spas in Spain, contact the Asociación Nacional de Estaciones Termales:

C. Martín de los Heros, 23, 4 derecha, 28008 Madrid; tel. (91) 542 97 75

SPORTS ORGANIZATIONS

Information about sports in Spain can be obtained from the following sports federations: (Dial (91) for numbers in the capital if phoning from outside Madrid.)

Fishing. Federación Nacional de Pesca, Navas de Tolosa, 3, 28913 Madrid; tel. 232 83 53

Golf. Real Federación Española de Golf, Capitán Haya, 9-8°, 8020 Madrid; tel. 455 26 82

Hunting. Federación Española de Caza, Reina Victoria, 53, 28006 Madrid; tel. 253 34 95

Riding. Federación Hipica Española, Monte Esquinza, 8, 28010 Madrid; tel. 419 02 33

Sailing. Federación Española de Vela, Juan Vigón, 23, 28003 Madrid; tel. 233 53 05

Tennis. Real Federación Española de Tenis, Diagonal 618, 08028 Barcelona; tel (93) 201 08 44

Winter sports. Federación Española de Deportes de Invierno, Claudio Coello, 32, 28001 Madrid; tel. 275 89 43

TIME DIFFERENCES

Spain follows Central European Time (Greenwich Mean Time plus one hour). From the last Sunday of March to the last Sunday of September, clocks are put one hour ahead (GMT + 2).

The Canary Islands are an hour behind the rest of Spain.

Summer Time chart:

Los Angeles	3 a.m.
New York	6 a.m.
London	11 a.m.
Canary Islands	11 a.m.
Madrid	**noon**
Johannesburg	noon
Sydney	8 p.m.
Auckland	10 p.m.

What time is it?	*¿Qué hora es?*

TIPPING *(propina)*

Since a service charge is normally included in hotel and restaurant bills, tipping is not obligatory. However, it's appropriate to tip waiters, bellboys, filling station attendants, bullfight ushers, etc., for their services. The following are suggestions:

Hotel porter per bag	50 ptas.
Hotel maid per week	500–1000 ptas.
Waiter	10%
Taxi driver	10%
Tourist guide	10%
Hairdresser	10%
Lavatory attendant	25–50 ptas.
Keep the change.	**Déjelo para usted.**

TOILETS

There are many expressions for "toilets" in Spanish: *aseos, servicios, W.C.* and *retretes.* The first two are most common. Toilet doors are distinguished by a "C" for *"Caballeros"* (gentlemen) and "S" for *"Señoras"* (Ladies) or by a variety of pictographs.

Public toilets exist in most large Spanish towns, but can be somewhat unappealing. A few cities have installed coin-operated, modern, ultra-hygenic toilets, with soap, water, towels and air-conditioning.

However, just about every bar and restaurant has toilets for both sexes, except those which still believe that women should not go to bars and certainly not admit to calls of nature. You are expected to buy a drink if you use the conveniences.

Where are the toilets?	**¿Dónde están los servicios?**

TOURIST INFORMATION OFFICES
(oficina de turismo)

Spain maintains tourist offices in many countries. These offices will supply you with a wide range of colourful and informative brochures and maps in English on the various towns and regions in Spain. If you visit one, you can consult a copy of the master directory of hotels in Spain, listing all facilities and prices.

Australia. International House, Suite 44, 104 Bathurst St., P.O. Box A-675, 2000 Sydney NSW; tel. (02) 2647966

Canada. 60 Bloor St. West, Suite 201, Toronto Ont. M5W 3BS; tel. (416) 9613131

Denmark. Store Kongensgade 1–3, 1264 Kobenhavn K; tel. (1) 147096

Finland. Mechelinincatu, 12–14, 00100 Helsinki 10; tel. (0) 442014

Japan. Daini Toranomon Denki Bldg. 4F, 1–10, Toranomon 3-chome, Minato-ku, 105 Tokyo; tel. (3) 4326141/4

Netherlands. Laan Van Meerdervoort, 8, 2517 Gravennage; tel. (70) 465900/1

Norway. Ruselokkveien 26/Vika Torvet, 0251 Oslo 2; tel. (2) 414183

Sweden. Grev Turegatan, 7, 1446 Stockholm; tel. (8) 207126

United Kingdom. 57–58 St. James's St., London SW1A 1LD; tel. (01) 4990901

United States. Water Tower Place, Suite 915 East, 845 North Michigan Ave., Chicago IL, 60611; tel. (312) 944-0216/230-9025

The Galleria Bldg., Suite 4800, 5085 Westheimer Rd., Houston, TX 77056; tel. (713) 840-7411-13

8383 Wilshire Blvd., Suite 960, Beverly Hills, CA 90211; tel. (213) 658-7188/93

665 5th Ave., New York, NY 10022; tel. (212) 759-8822

Most Spanish towns have a tourist office, equipped to help travellers. If there does not appear to be one, ask at the town hall *(municipio or ayuntamiento)*.

Madrid's tourist offices are at:
Plaza Mayor, 3; tel. 2665477
Edificio Torre de Madrid; tel: 2412325
Duque de Medinaceli, 2; tel. 4294951
Barajas Airport; tel. 2058656
Chamartín Station, Vestíbulo Puerta 14; tel. 3159976

Some other tourist offices in Spain:

Alicante. Esplanada de España, 2; tel. (965) 212285

Barcelona. Gran Via de les Corts Catalanes, 658; tel. (93) 3017443

Badajoz. Pasaje de San Juan, 1: tel. (924) 222763

Cádiz. Calderón de la Barca, 1; (956) 211313

Córdoba. Torrijos, 10; tel. (957) 471235

Gerona. Ciutadans, 12; tel. (972) 201694

Granada. C. Libreros, 2; tel. (958) 225990

Málaga. Marqués de Larios, 5; tel. (952) 213445

Murcia. Alejandro Seiquer, 4; tel. (968) 213716

Oviedo. Plaza de Alfonso II, El Casto, 6; tel. (985) 213385

Pamplona. Duque de Ahumada, 2; tel. (948) 220748

Pontevedra. C/ General Mola, 2; tel. (986) 850814

Salamanca. Gran Vía, 41; tel. (923) 243730

San Sebastián. Miramar, esquina a Andía; tel. (943) 426282

Santander. Plaza Porticada, 1; tel. (942) 310708

Santiago de Compostela. Rúa del Villar, 43: tel. (981) 584081

Santillana del Mar. Plaza Mayor; tel. (942) 818251

Segovia. Plaza Mayor, 10; tel. (911) 430328

Seville. Avda. de la Constitución, 21; tel. (954) 221404

Tarragona. Fortuny, 4; tel. (977) 233415

Toledo. Puerta de Bisagra; tel. (925) 220843

Torremolinos. Bajos de la Nogalera, local 517; tel. (952) 381578

Valencia. Calle de la Paz, 46; tel. (96) 352287

Zaragoza. Torreón de la Zuda, Glorieta Pío XII; tel. (976) 230027

and on the islands:

Balearics

Ibiza Town. Passeig Vara de Rey, 13; tel. (971) 301900

Mahón (Menorca). Plaça de la Constituciò, 13; tel. (971) 363790

Palma de Mallorca. Jaume III, 10; tel. (971) 712216

Canary Islands

Arrecife (Lanzarote). Parque Municipal, s/n; tel. (928) 81 18 60

Las Palmas de Gran Canaria. Parque de Santa Catalina; tel. (928) 26 46 23

Santa Cruz de Tenerife. Calle de la Marina, 57; tel. (922) 28 72 54

Puerto de la Cruz (Tenerife). Plaza de la Iglesia; tel: (922) 38 60 00

Puerto del Rosario (Fuerteventura). General Franco, 33; tel. (928) 85 10 24

TRANSPORT WITHIN SPAIN

(See also GETTING TO SPAIN, DRIVING IN SPAIN and CAR RENTAL for information about advance booking.)

Trains. The Spanish railway network is operated by RENFE *(Red Nacional de los Ferrocarriles Españoles)*. While local trains are slow, stopping apparently in the middle of nowhere, long-distance services, especially the *Talgo* and *TER*, are fast and reasonably punctual. First-class coaches are comfortable; second-class, adequate. Tickets can be purchased at travel agencies as well as at railway stations *(estación de ferrocarril)*. Seat reservations are obligatory on most Spanish trains.

Discounts are available on "blue days" *(días azules)*. These are usually every day except Fridays and Sundays, but check for variations due to off-peak periods and public holidays. Children from 4 to 12 years of age travel half-price.

Stations do not have left-luggage (baggage-check) facilities, but often local bars will store bags and cases for a fee—look for a sign "Se guarda equipaje". Otherwise, up to 20 kg. (44 1b.) of baggage can be forwarded free.

Spain offers two classic train tours: the Al-Andaluz Express, which runs through Málaga, Granada, Córdoba and Seville, and the Transcantábrico, a seven-day trip, visiting towns and small villages of northern Spain, including Santiago de Compostela.

Planes. Internal flights link main Spanish cities and the islands. A regular shuttle service relays Madrid and Barcelona. Ask a travel agent or phone Iberia, the national airline, on (91) 411 10 11 to reserve seats on domestic flights.

In Britain, information and bookings for Spanish flights, domestic and international, may be obtained from Iberia at:

130 Regent St., London W1R 5RG; tel. (01) 437 5622

Ferries. The state navigation company, Trasmediterranea, runs ferry crossings from the Spanish mainland to the Balearics and Canary Islands and to North Africa. Private companies also provide links to and between the islands. The main departure ports are Barcelona, Valencia, Alicante and Cádiz.

Trasmediterranea's headquarters are in:

Calle Pedro Muñoz Seca, 2, 28001 Madrid; tel. (91) 431 07 00

Long-distance Buses. Comfortable coaches link Spanish towns, providing an opportunity to see the countryside in between. Several private companies use the same bus station *(estación de autobuses)*, so check there for the most convenient departure times and best prices. Not all buses have toilets, but there is usually a stop en route at a bar. The sign "No fumar", not, alas, always respected, means "No Smoking".

Municipal Transport
Buses. Madrid's municipal system, EMT, runs 90 bus routes, from about 5.30 a.m. until 1.30 a.m. On blue buses, you generally enter through the rear door and buy a ticket from a conductor seated behind a little desk. On red ones, you enter by the front door and pay the driver. A *Bono Bus*, a pass valid for ten rides, is available at EMT booths or on buses with conductors.

Barcelona has over 50 bus lines. Bus stops have maps showing routes. Pay the driver on entering or buy a *Targeta Metropolitana T-1* card for ten trips, which you validate in the machine by the driver. This *T-1* is also valid on the metro, trams and funicular railway. Buses for towns and resorts on the Costa Brava leave from Passeig de Colom, 3, in the harbour.

All towns and resorts have their own bus system, with transport available to places of touristic interest and to the beaches:

Taxis. Prices are fairly reasonable by European and North American standards. Wherever you're going, in a cab with or without a meter, check the approximate fare before setting off. If you travel outside a town, you'll be charged double the one-way trip.

By law, taxis may only take four passengers per vehicle (although some are willing to risk a fifth if it is a child).

A green light and/or a "Libre" (free) sign indicates that a taxi is available.

Metro. Madrid, Barcelona and Alicante have underground (subway) systems, speedier and cheaper than travelling above ground. Rush-hour metro travel is an ordeal to be avoided; tempers and temperatures reach boiling point.

When's the next bus/ train/boat for...?	¿A qué hora sale el próximo autobús/tren/ barco para...?
A ticket to...	Un billete para...
single (one-way)	ida
return (round-trip)	ida y vuelta
first/second class	primera/segunda clase
Would you tell me when to get off?	¿Podría indicarme cúando tengo que bajar?
Where can I get a taxi?	¿Dónde puedo coger un taxi?

USEFUL EXPRESSIONS

Good morning.	Buenos días.
Good afternoon.	Buenas tardes.
Good evening.	Buenas tardes.
Good night.	Buenas noches.
Good-bye.	Adiós.
See you later	Hasta luego
How do you do? (Pleased to meet you.)	Encantado(a) de conocerle.
yes/no	sí/no
please/thank you	por favor/gracias
excuse me/you're welcome	perdone/de nada
where/when/how/ how long/how far	dónde/cúando/cómo/ cúanto tiempo/a qué distancia
yesterday/today/ tomorrow	ayer/hoy/mañana
day/week/month/year	día/semana/mes/año
left/right	izquierda/derecha
up/down	arriba/abajo

good/bad	bueno/malo
big/small	grande/pequeno
cheap/expensive	barato/caro
hot/cold	caliente/frío
old/new	viejo/nuevo
open/closed	abierto/cerrado
here/there	aquí/allí
free (vacant)/ occupied	libre/ocupado
early/late	temprano/tarde
easy/difficult	fácil/difícil
near/far	cerca/lejos
next/last	próximo/último
Does anyone here speak English?	¿Hay alguien aquí que hable inglés?
What does this mean?	¿Qué quiere decir esto?
I don't understand.	No entiendo.
Please write it down.	Escríbamelo, por favor.
I'd like...	Quisiera...
Where is/are...?	¿Dónde está/están...?
How much is this?	¿Cuánto es?
Have you something less expensive?	¿Tiene algo menos caro?
Just a minute.	Momento.
Can you help me?	¿Puede ayudarme?
Call a doctor quickly!	¡Llamen a un médico rápidamente!
Monday	lunes
Tuesday	martes
Wednesday	miércoles
Thursday	jueves
Friday	viernes
Saturday	sábado
Sunday	domingo
one	uno
two	dos
three	tres
four	cuatro
five	cinco
six	seis
seven	siete

eight	**ocho**
nine	**nueve**
ten	**diez**
eleven	**once**
twelve	**doce**
thirteen	**trece**
fourteen	**catorce**
fifteen	**quince**
sixteen	**dieciséis**
seventeen	**diecisiete**
eighteen	**dieciocho**
nineteen	**diecinueve**
twenty	**veinte**
a hundred	**cien**
a thousand	**mil**

Signs and Notices:

ascensor	*lift*
averiado	*out of order*
caja	*cash desk*
cierre la puerta	*close the door*
completo	*no vacancies*
empujar/tirar	*push/pull*
entrada/salida	*entrance/exit*
no tocar	*do not touch*

peligro	*danger*
pintura fresca	*wet paint*
prohibido entrar	*no entry*
prohibido fumar	*no smoking*
rebajas	*sale*
sala de espera	*waiting room*
se alquila	*to let/for rent*
se vende	*for sale*
toque el timbre, por favor	*please ring*

WATER *(agua)*

In most parts of Spain the water is perfectly safe to drink. Spaniards themselves usually buy bottled water; if you're particularly sensitive to a change in water, you may wish to do the same. Both still (natural) and fizzy (sparkling) water are available.

a bottle of mineral water	**una botella de agua mineral**
fizzy	**con gas**
still	**sin gas**
Is the water safe to drink?	**¿Es potable el agua?**

WEIGHTS AND MEASURES

Spain uses the metric system. For fluid, tyre pressure and distance measures, see DRIVING IN SPAIN.

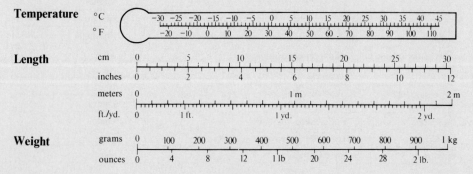

282

Road Atlas

SPANIEN PORTUGAL
ESPAÑA PORTUGAL

ESPAGNE PORTUGAL
SPAIN PORTUGAL

Autobahn mit Anschlussstelle Tankstelle, Restaurant, Motel Autopista con acceso Estacion de servicio, restaurante, motel	Autoroute avec échangeur Station-service, restaurant, motel Motorway with interchange Filling station, restaurant, motel
Autobahn im Bau mit Eröffnungsdatum Autopista en construcción con fecha de apertura	Autoroute en construction avec date de mise en service Motorway under construction with opening date
Autostrasse (international, regional) Autovia (internacional, regional)	Route rapide à chaussées séparées (internationale, régionale) Dual carriageway (international, regional)
Grosse internationale Durchgangsstrasse Carretera de gran circulación internacional	Route de grand transit internationale Major international throughroute
Sonstige internationale Fernverkehrsstrasse Otra carretera de circulación internacional	Autre route de transit internationale Other international throughroute
Überregionale Fernverkehrsstrasse Carretera de circulación interregional	Route de transit interrégionale Interregional throughroute
Regionale Verbindungsstrasse Carretera de comunicación regional	Route de liaison régionale Regional connecting road
Lokale Verbindungsstrasse Carretera de comunicación local	Route de liaison locale Local road
Strassen im Bau Carreteras en construcción	Routes en construction Roads under construction
Entfernungen in km Distancias en km	Distances en km Distances in km
Strassennummern: Europastrasse, Autobahn, Nationalstrasse Numeración de carreteras: carretera europea, autopista, carretera nacional	Numéros des routes: route européenne, autoroute, route nationale Road classification: European road, motorway, national road
Pass, Berg, Ort mit Höhenangabe (m) Puerto, monte, localidad con altitud (m)	Col, sommet, localité avec altitude (m) Pass, summit, locality with altitude (m)
Eisenbahn, Berg-/ Luftseilbahn Ferrocarril, teleférico/funicular	Voie ferrée, téléphérique/Funiculaire Railway, mountain/cable railway
Autoverlad: per Fähre Pasaje para autos: por transbordador	Transport des autos: par bac Car transport: by ferry
Internationaler Flughafen, Flugplatz Aeropuerto internacional, aeródromo	Aéroport international, aérodrome International airport, airfield
Schloss/Burg, Kirche/Kloster, Ruine Castillo, iglesia/monasterio, ruina	Château/fort, église/couvent, ruine Castle, church/monastery, ruin
Höhle, Leuchtturm, Campingplatz Caverna, faro, camping	Grotte, phare, camping Cave, lighthouse, camping site
Bemerkenswerter Ort, Einzelnes Hotel Localidad interesante, Albergue/Posada	Localité intéressante, Hôtel isolé Place of interest, Isolated hotel
Staatsgrenze Frontera de Estado	Frontière d'Etat National boundary

Ⓒ1989 Ⓞ1989
I - VI VII- XII

10
3   3   4   2
5   5
7   2   4   3
10

E7   A9   60

1528
2967   Elm
648.

2 h

1: 1 000 000

0	10	20		40		60		80 km

0		10		20		30		40		50 miles

Cabo Ortegal
Estaca de Bares
Cariño
R. de Sta Marta
Cedeira
Ría de Vivero
Valle
642
Jove
San Ciprián
Ortigueira
23
Vivero
Cervo
C. de Burella
Mera
Bravos
Burella
Foz
Somozas
641
Espiñaredo
Muras
640
Cuadramón
Lorenzana
Ribadeo
E70
Tapia de Cas.
La Caridad
Navia
634
Luarca
C. Busto
Canero
Castropol
Coana
231
Trevias
Capela
Puentes de García Rodr.
640
Cabreiros
Germade
Candamil
Lanzós
Abadin
634
Cruz de Canc
S. Tirso
Folgueiras
Vegadeo
La Roda
644
Villayón
Naraval
La Espina
Bárcena
Tineo
631
Villalba
Moncélos
Villamea
Villaodriz
Paramios
Bobia
Illano
Boal
Embalse de Dorias
26
Aranga
54
Balneario
Guitiriz
Baamonde
641
Moman
Justas
Otero
640
Meira
Sta. Eulalia de Oscos
Neiro
Pradaira
Grandas de S.
Berducedo
Pola
Portiella
Cangas
da Nárcea
Coba de Serpe
Cordal de Ousa
Rábade
Mundriz
Muiña
Fonsagrada
Valles de las Montañas
Las Mestas
Sorrodiles
Rabo Asn
Angeriz
Teijeiro
Pradairo
Paradavella
Valdebueyes
Bimeda
Venta Nueva
Vallad
Pto Son
Sobrado
Friol
Lugo
Castroverde
Baleira
S. Antolin
Cecos
Rengos
631
Pto de Leitariegos
Cerredo
Villag
Tóques
Mellid
Burgo
547
S. Roman
Nadela
Corgo
630
VI
Baralla
Navia de Suarna
San Martín
Miravalles
1970
Degaña
Palacios del Sil
Pto o
Lago
6
aiavilla
Palas de Rey
Guntín
Macéda
Cedron
Trabado
Peña Rubia
Vega de Espinareda
Corbón
Lillo
Páramo del Sil
2118
Villamartín
Monterroso
Puertomarin
546
Gallegos
Triacastela
Becerrea
28
Sra Ancares
2216
Paradaseca
Toreno
631
Rodeiro
Vilela
Currelos
Barbain
Samos
Herreria
Incio
Piedrafita
Pto de Piedrafita
1099
Balboa
Trabadelo
273
el B
Emb. de Bárcena
Bembibre
533
Chantada
Bóveda
Escairón
Veiga
Caurel
Vega de Valcarce
Villafranca
Cacabelos
VI
Columbrianos
Castropodame
Rodeiro
540
Pantón
546
Sober
Folgoso
1616
Pájaro
Corullón
Toral
Priaranza
Ponferrada
San Esteban de Vald.
Raba
Monforte
Quiroga
120
Montouto
1522
Robledo
Rubiana
Cafucedo
Monasterio de Montes
Pombriego
1848
Guiana
Sta Colom
Orense/
Ourense
Meda
Esgos
1320
Leboreiro
Castro Caldelas
A Rua
R. Sil
Bendillo
Puente de Domingo Florez
Riodolas
Montes Aquilianos
Lucillo
Quintanil de Somo
540
Baños de Molgas
Monterramo
Queija
Puebla de Trives
Manzaneda
El Bollo
Santigoso
Emb. de Prada
Casayo
Candeda
La Vega
Peña de Forna
Sierra del Teleño
2188
Teleño
Manzaneda
Allariz
Furriolo
Sandianes
Arnaiz
Junquera
Raigada
1708
Emb. de Rao
533
Viana del Bollo
2024
Peña Trevinca
2051
Moncalvo
Iruela
Torneros
531
Villar de S.
Cortegada
Alberguería
Vilariño de Conso
Pradocaballos
Barjacoba
San Martin de Castañeda
Sierra Cabrera
Castrocont
Juste
Bande
Porquera
Ginzó de Límia
Trasmiras
Campo de B.
163
La Gudiña
El Cañizo
Pias
Ribadelago
L. de Villachica
Calende
525
Espadañedo
Rioconejos
Asturianos
Mombu
Baltar
Cualedro
Laza
Castrelo
Ventas de la B.
Manzalvos
Lubian
32
Requejo
Pedralba
Puebla
de Sañabria
179
Sandin
Verín
Monterrey
525
Fumaces
Manzanedo
Calabor
Peña Mira
Ciona
Sra. de Larouco
1529
Larouco
Gironda
532
Oimbra
Villaderbós
13
Landedo
Parâmio
Coroa
Portéllo
França
Linarejos

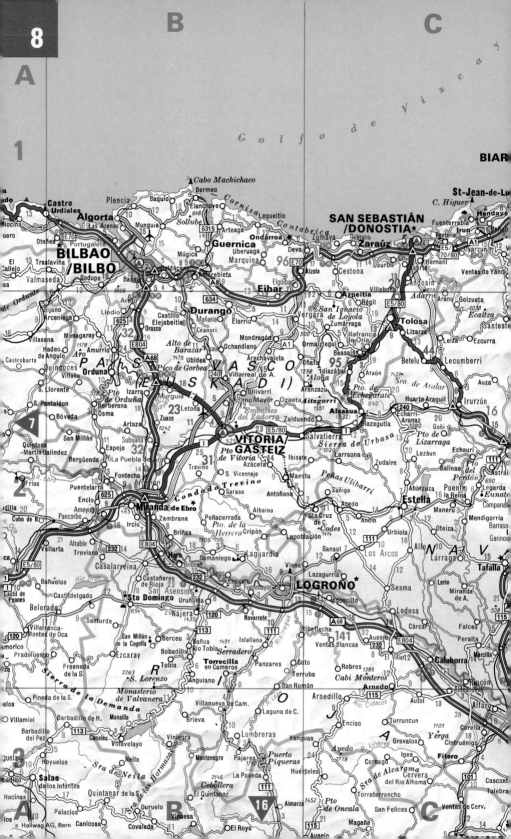

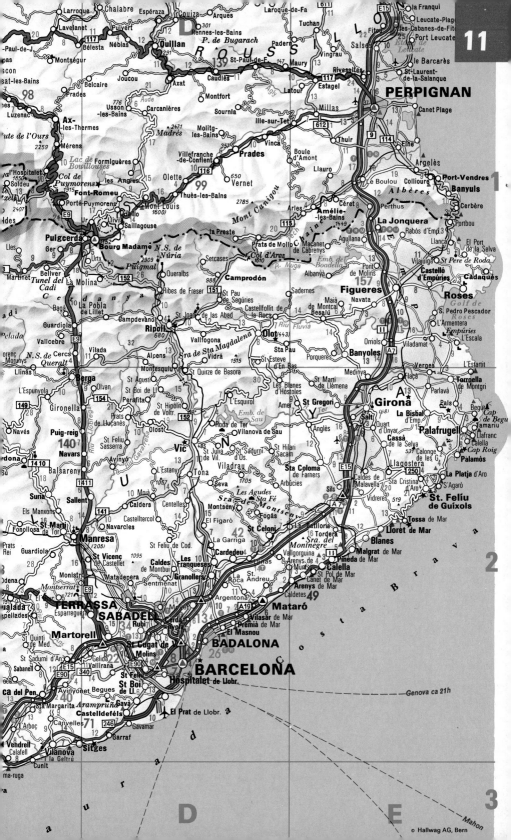

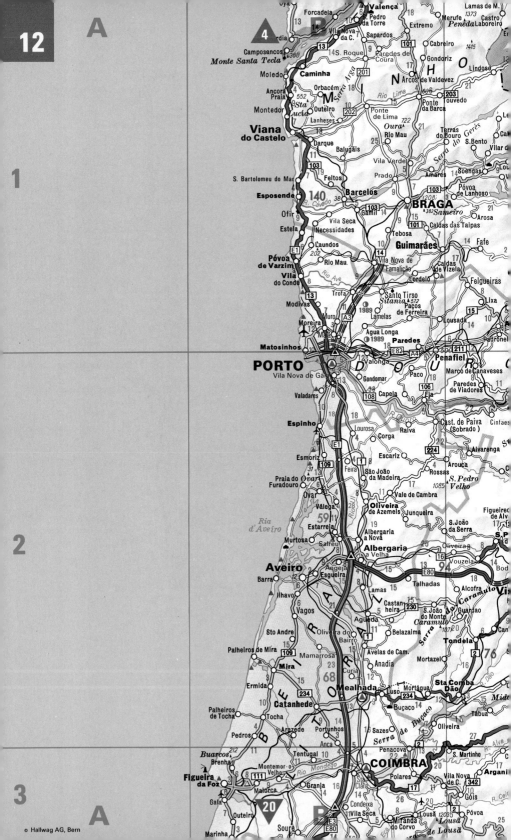

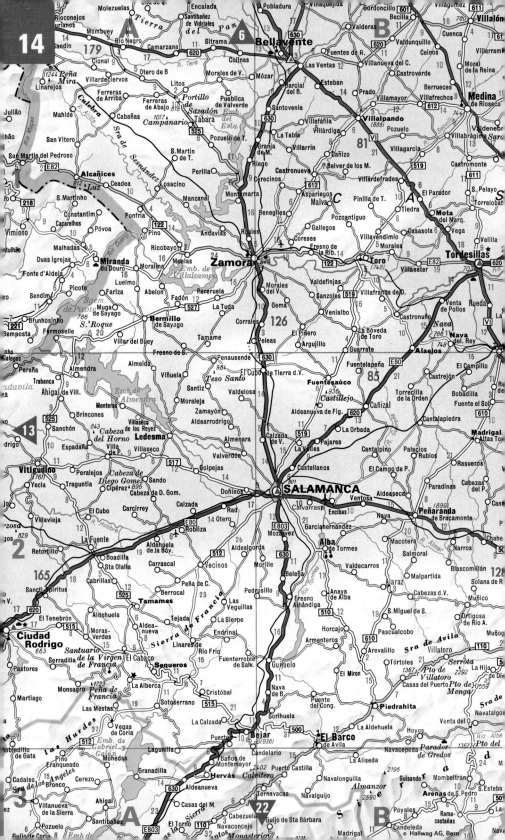

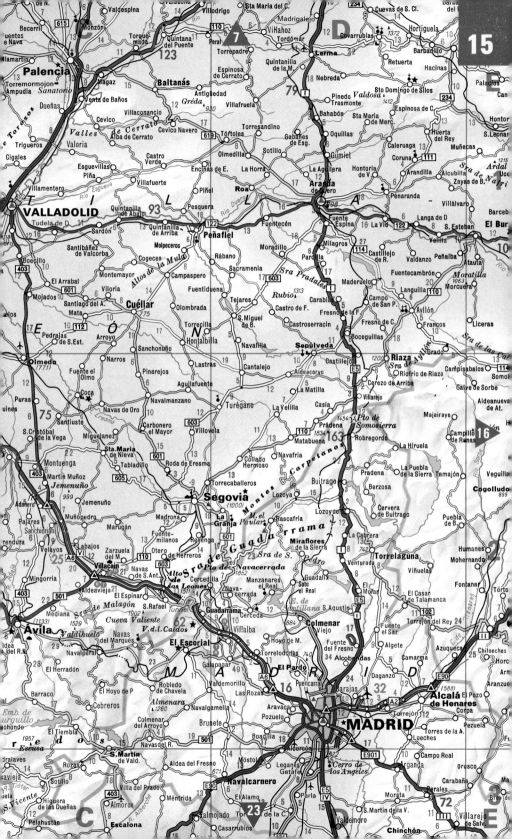

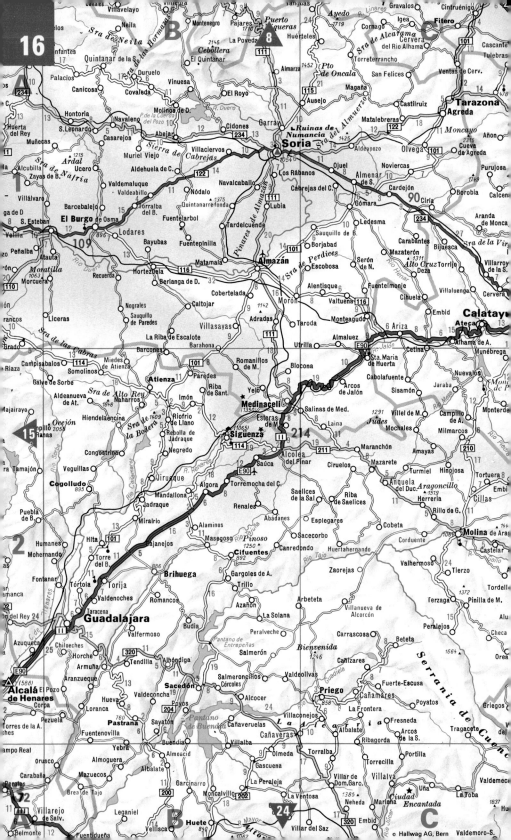

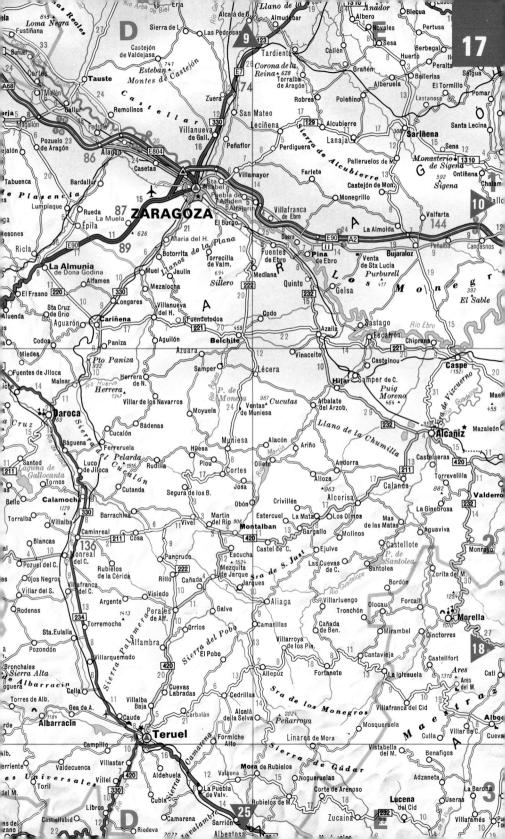

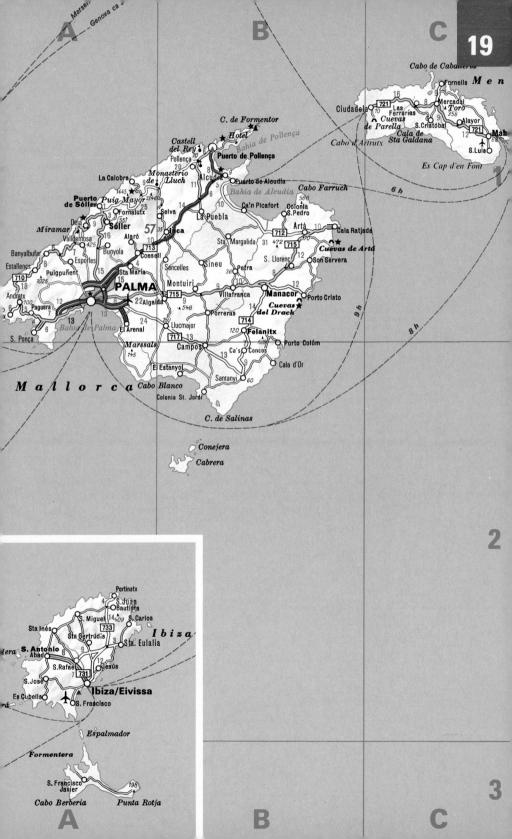

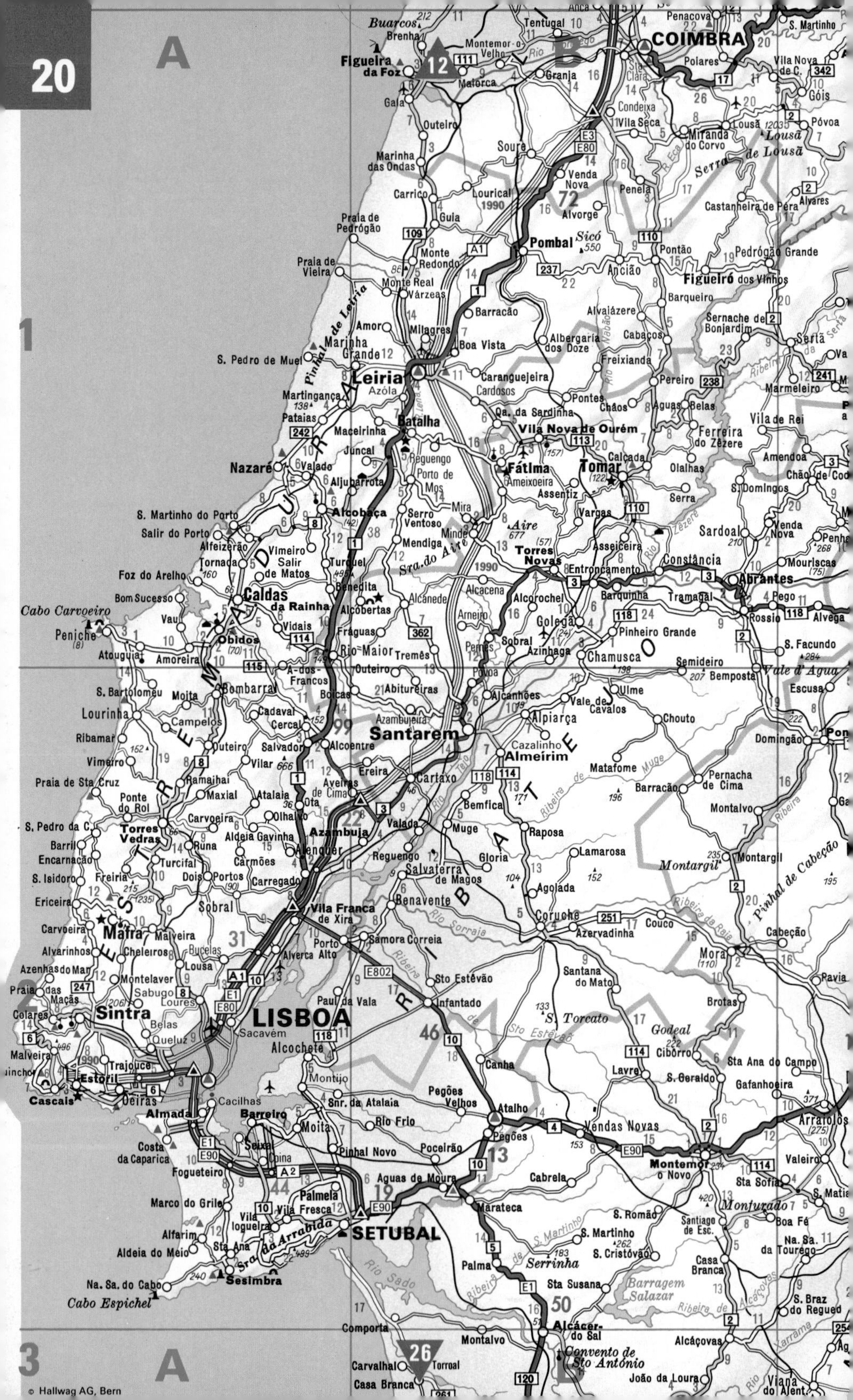

A
B
1
2
3
COIMBRA
Figueira da Foz
Buarcos
Brenha
Montemor-o-Velho
Tentugal
Maiorca
Granja
Penacova
S. Martinho
Polares
Vila Nova de C.
Góis
Condeixa
Vila Seca
Lousã
Miranda do Corvo
Póvoa
Serra de Lousã
Soure
Venda Nova
Penela
Outeiro
Marinha das Ondas
Carriço
Louriçal
Alvorge
Castanheira de Pêra
Alvares
Praia de Pedrógão
Guia
Pombal
Sicó
Pontão
Pedrógão Grande
Monte Redondo
Ancião
Figueiró dos Vinhos
Praia de Vieira
Monte Real
Várzeas
Barreiro
Barracão
Alvaiázere
Sernache de Bonjardim
Amor
Milagres
Boa Vista
Albergaria dos Doze
Cabaços
Sertã
Marinha Grande
Pinhal de Leiria
S. Pedro de Muel
Leiria
Azóia
Caranguejeira
Cardosos
Freixianda
Pereiro
Marmeleiro
Martingança
Pataias
Maceirinha
Batalha
Pontes
Qa. da Sardinha
Chãos
Aguas Belas
Ferreira do Zêzere
Vila de Rei
Vila Nova de Ourém
Juncal
Reguengo
Nazaré
Valado
Aljubarrota
Porto de Mos
Fátima
Ameixoeira
Tomar
Calçada
Olalhas
Amendoa
Chão de Codes
S. Martinho do Porto
Alcobaça
Serro Ventoso
Mira
Minde
Assentiz
S. Domingos
Serra
Salir do Porto
Alfeizerão
Vimeiro
Salir de Matos
Mendiga
Aire
Vargas
Sardoal
Venda Nova
Tornada
Turquel
Sra. do Aire
Torres Novas
Asseiceira
Entroncamento
Constância
Mouriscas
Foz do Arelho
Caldas da Rainha
Benedita
Alcobertas
Alcanede
Alcacena
Alcorochel
Barquinha
Tramagal
Abrantes
Pego
Rossio
Alvega
Bom Sucesso
Cabo Carvoeiro
Peniche
Vau
Obidos
Vidais
Fráguas
Arneiro
Golegã
Pinheiro Grande
Atouguia
Amoreira
Rio Maior
Tremês
Pernes
Sobral
Azinhaga
Chamusca
S. Facundo
Vale d'Agua
A-dos-Francos
Bombarral
Outeiro
Abitureiras
Póvoa
Semideiro
Bemposta
S. Bartolomeu
Moita
Cadaval
Boiças
Alcanhões
Vale de Cavalos
Ulme
Escusa
Lourinha
Campelos
Cercal
Azambujeira
Santarem
Alpiarça
Chouto
Ribamar
Outeiro
Salvador
Alcoentre
Cazalinho
Almeirim
Domingão
Vimeiro
Vilar
Praia de Sta Cruz
Ramalhal
Ereira
Cartaxo
Matafome
Pernacha de Cima
Ponte do Rol
Maxial
Atalaia
Aveiras de Cima
Barracão
Montalvo
Ota
Bemfica
S. Pedro da C.
Torres Vedras
Carvoeira
Olhalvo
Valada
Raposa
Barril
Aldeia Gavinha
Azambuja
Muge
Encarnação
Runa
Alenquer
Reguengo
Lamarosa
Montargil
S. Isidoro
Freiria
Turcifal
Dois Portos
Carmões
Gloria
Salvaterra de Magos
Agolada
Pinhal de Cabeção
Ericeira
Carregado
Sobral
Benavente
Vila Franca de Xira
Coruche
Azervadinha
Couco
Carvoeira
Mafra
Malveira
Samora Correia
Cabeção
Alvarinhos
Cheleiros
Bucelas
Porto Alto
Alverca
Mora
Azenhas do Mar
Lousa
Santana do Mato
Pavia
Praia das Maçãs
Montelavar
Sto Estêvão
Sabugo
Loures
Paul da Vala
Infantado
Brotas
Colares
Sintra
LISBOA
Sacavém
Belas
S. Torcato
Godeal
Malveira
Queluz
Alcochete
Ciborro
Sta Ana do Campo
Trajouce
Canha
Lavre
S. Geraldo
Gafanhoeira
Estoril
Cascais
Oeiras
Montijo
Pegões Velhos
Cacilhas
Almada
Barreiro
Snr. da Atalaia
Atalho
Moita
Rio Frio
Vendas Novas
Arraiolos
Pegões
Costa da Caparica
Seixal
Pinhal Novo
Poceirão
Montemor o Novo
Valeiro
Fogueteiro
Aguas de Moura
Cabrela
Sta Sofia
S. Matias
Marco do Grile
Palmela
Vila Fresca
Marateca
Monfurado
Boa Fé
Vila Nogueira
Alfarim
S. Romão
Santiago de Esc.
Aldeia do Meio
Sta Ana
Sra da Arrabida
SETUBAL
S. Martinho
S. Cristóvão
Na. Sa. da Tourega
Sesimbra
Na. Sa. do Cabo
Palma
Serrinha
Casa Branca
Cabo Espichel
Sta Susana
Barragem Salazar
S. Braz do Regued
Rio Sado
Comporta
Alcácer do Sal
Montalvo
Alcáçovas
Carvalhal
Torroal
Convento de Sto António
Casa Branca
João da Loura
Viana do Alentejo
ESTREMADURA
RIBATEJO
E3
E80
E1
E90
E802
A1
A2

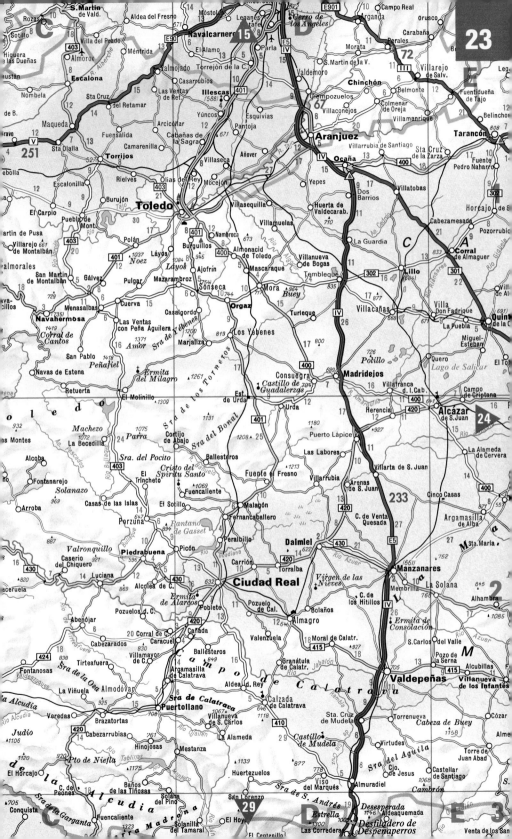

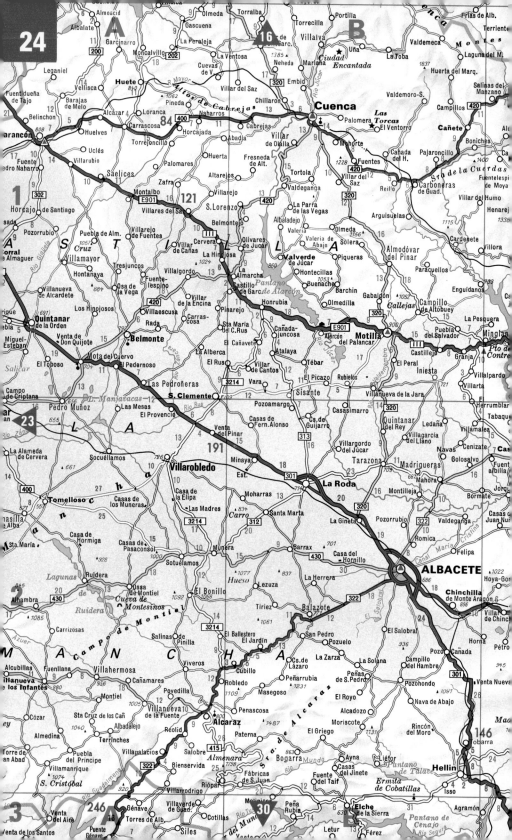

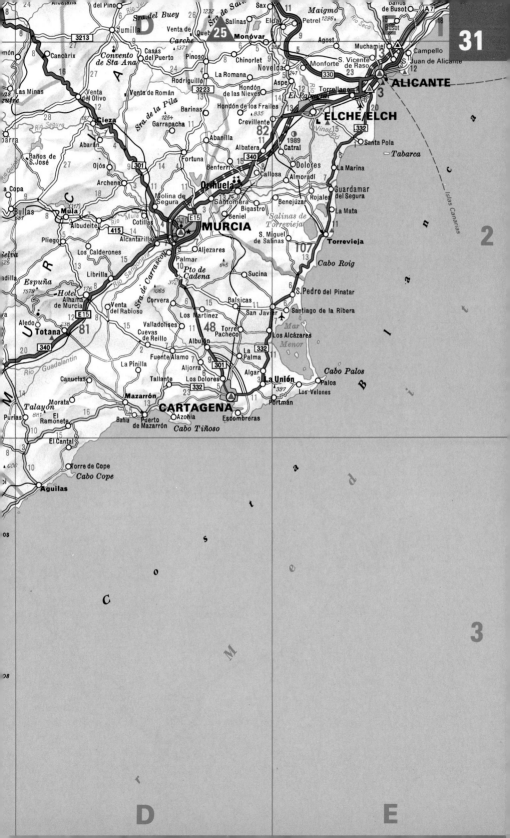

INDEX

Page numbers in **bold face**
refer to the main entry.
Those in *italics* refer to the
hotel and restaurant section.
An asterisk next to a page
number indicates a map.